French society in revolution, 1789–1799

MANCHESTER
UNIVERSITY PRESS

NEW FRONTIERS IN HISTORY

series editors
Mark Greengrass
Department of History, Sheffield University

John Stevenson
Worcester College, Oxford

This important series reflects the substantial expansion that has occurred in the scope of history syllabuses. As new subject areas have emerged and syllabuses have come to focus more upon methods of historical enquiry and knowledge of source materials, a growing need has arisen for correspondingly broad-ranging textbooks.

New Frontiers in History provides up-to-date overviews of key topics in British, European and world history, together with accompanying source material and appendices. Authors focus on subjects where revisionist work is being undertaken, providing a fresh viewpoint, welcomed by students and sixth-formers. The series also explores established topics which have attracted much conflicting analysis and require a synthesis of the state of debate.

Published titles

David Andress French society in revolution, 1789–1799

Jeremy Black The politics of Britain, 1688–1800

Paul Bookbinder The Weimar Republic

Michael Braddick The nerves of state:
taxation and the financing of the English state, 1558–1714

Michael Broers Europe after Napoleon

David Brooks The age of upheaval: Edwardian politics, 1899–1914

Carl Chinn Poverty amidst prosperity: the urban poor in England, 1834–1914

Conan Fischer The rise of the Nazis (2nd edition)

T. A. Jenkins Parliament, party and politics in Victorian Britain

Neville Kirk Change, continuity and class: Labour in British society, 1850–1920

Keith Laybourn The General Strike of 1926

Frank McDonough Neville Chamberlain, appeasement and the
British road to war

Alan Marshall The age of faction

Evan Mawdsley The Stalin years, 1929–1953

Alan O'Day Irish Home Rule 1867–1921

Panikos Panayi Immigration, ethnicity and racism in Britain, 1815–1945

David Taylor The New Police

John Whittam Fascist Italy

French society in revolution, 1789–1799

David Andress

Manchester University Press

Manchester and New York

Distributed exclusively in the USA by Palgrave

Published by Manchester University Press
Oxford Road, Manchester M13 9NR, UK
and Room 400, 175 Fifth Avenue, New York, NY 10010, USA
www.manchesteruniversitypress.co.uk

Distributed exclusively in the USA by
Palgrave, 175 Fifth Avenue, New York,
NY 10010, USA

Distributed exclusively in Canada by
UBC Press, University of British Columbia, 2029 West Mall,
Vancouver, BC, Canada V6T 1Z2

British Library Cataloguing-in-Publication Data
A catalogue record for this book is available from the British Library

Library of Congress Cataloging-in-Publication Data applied for

ISBN   0 7190 5190 8 *hardback*
        0 7190 5191 6 *paperback*

First published 1999

06 05 04 03 02   10 9 8 7 6 5 4 3 2

Printed in Great Britain
by Bell & Bain Ltd, Glasgow

Contents

Acknowledgements

I should first like to thank the editors of the New Frontiers series, and especially Mark Greengrass, for taking on this project, and for help and advice along the way. My thanks also to the various staff at MUP, without whom this book would still be no more than a floppy disk. As usual, one's colleagues are a necessary support in the long-drawn-out business of writing, and I would particularly thank Brad Beaven and Mark Ledbury for their comradeship and a long series of sanity-sustaining conversations. On a more concrete note, Alan Forrest provided helpful commentary on some chapters, and Paul Hanson read and annotated a complete draft, for which I am extremely grateful. Jerry Emery and Emma-Louise Marston also read drafts to give me the viewpoint of the intended readership, and while I hope their education benefited from the experience, I thank them all the same. Finally, like everything else, this book is to Jessica, with love.

Chronology

Events are indicated by the month(s) in which they occurred; particularly notable individual dates are given as numbers in the text. For simplicity, this chronology does not record 'revolutionary' dates as used after October 1793, except to note the names by which certain events were known; wider reference to the new system can be found in the main text.

1786

August
State finances become clearly close to collapse.

1787

February–April
First Assembly of Notables rejects plans for reform.

June–October
Reforms introduced after dismissal of Assembly; *parlements* begin to protest.

November
Convocation of Estates-General agreed for 1792.

1788

January–April
Opposition from *parlements* and public opinion grows.

May
Parlements are abolished by edict (8).

June–July
Widespread protest by privileged groups, supported by local populations in many areas. Publication of views on format for

	Estates-General permitted.
August	Summoning of Estates-General for 1789 conceded as state approaches bankruptcy.
September– October	*Parlement* of Paris loses public favour after taking traditionalist stance on format of Estates-General. Pro-Third-Estate pamphleteering reaches epidemic proportions.
December	After second Assembly of Notables fails to agree a format for Estates-General, Princes of the Blood declare against any concession of the rights of the privileged.

1789

January– February	Elections to Estates-General produce political ferment in general population, while food prices and supplies reach critical levels following several years' difficulties.
May	Estates-General meet at Versailles; stalemate between nobles and Third Estate deputies over forms for meeting. Riots and disturbances continue in many areas; some peasants claim that the Estates-General has already abolished feudal abuses.
June	Third Estate renames itself National Assembly (17), swears to form a constitution (20); the three Estates are ordered to unite (27), but Court begins to plan military action.
July	Parisian mass rising, including capture of the Bastille, prevents use of troops against Assembly (12–14). King concedes existence of new situation (15–17).
July–August	Across France, self-government seized by 'revolutionary' groups in towns, while countryside experiences 'Great Fear' of aristocratic brigands, and continued substantive unrest.
August	National Assembly pronounces abolition of feudalism to calm the countryside (4–11), and produces Declaration of the Rights of

	Man (26) enshrining revolutionary liberal principles.
September–October	Assembly stalemated after king refuses to sign decrees; resolved by march of Parisians, led by women, to Versailles. Royal family and Assembly move to Paris.
October	Tax-payment requirements for voting rights ('active citizenship') are laid down.
November	Church property is nationalised to solve financial crisis.

1790

January–February	Elections to c. 44,000 new municipal councils, and division of France into eighty-three uniform *départements*.
February	Abolition of monasticism. Execution of marquis de Favras for plotting 'rescue' of royal family.
March	Laws ending feudalism reveal that compensation will have to be paid by peasants: widespread rejection of this in countryside.
April–June	Counter-revolutionaries lead risings, especially in south, but are easily defeated.
May	Radical political clubs begin to form, especially in Paris.
June	'Bagarre de Nîmes' leaves several hundred dead in Catholic/Protestant rioting.
July	Catholic Church reorganised under state control, including controversial provisions for election of clergy. 'Festival of Federation' celebrates anniversary of Parisian rising with mass military/religious ceremony (14).
August–January 1791	Judicial system reordered with elected judges.
November	New land tax established in principle.

1791

January	Half of all priests refuse to swear allegiance to new Civil Constitution of the Clergy.

March	Guilds abolished.
March–April	Pope condemns Civil Constitution; clerical opposition becomes increasingly divisive, provoking violence in Paris and elsewhere.
April	Paris crowds prevent royal family leaving the city (18).
June	Workers' organisations or unions are banned. Royal family attempt to flee to eastern frontiers: 'Flight to Varennes' (21).
July	Radical protests at decision to reinstate the king are put down violently: 'Champ de Mars Massacre' (17). Various laws passed against social unrest.
September	King accepts Constitution (13). Elections carried out for new Legislative Assembly.
October–December	Calls from Brissotins in Assembly for military action against *émigré* nobles. Laws passed against *émigrés*, vetoed by king. Measures against non-juror priests, also vetoed by king.

1792

January–March	Growing demands for war, coinciding with widespread protests against food shortages; moderate revolutionaries caught between political radicalism and social conservatism.
April	War declared on Austria (20); initially disastrous, leads to increase in political tensions.
April–June	Republican sentiments grow amongst Parisian and other radicals; demonstrations against the king.
July	Assembly takes emergency powers as war crisis grows (11). Prussia enters war.
August	After weeks of hesitation, Parisian radicals and *fédéré* troops storm the Tuileries palace; royal family are detained (10).
September	Massacres in Paris prisons due to fear of treachery (2–6). New 'National Convention' elected; declares France a republic (22).

	Victory at Valmy (20) sends French armies onto offensive.
October–November	Conflict between Girondins and radicals over blame for September Massacres, and over action to be taken with the king.
December	Trial of king begins (10).

1793

January	King is unanimously convicted, sentenced to death by 387 votes to 334 (14), and publicly executed (21).
February–March	War is declared on Britain, Spain and Holland. Austrians and Prussians counter-attack successfully.
February	300,000 men to be recruited to army (24). Revolt against conscription, aggravated by Catholic-royalist sentiments, in Vendée.
March–April	Series of measures establishing censorship, draconian penalties for rebellion, etc. Rising political conflict between Girondins and radicals in Paris, along with tensions provoked in provinces by commissioners despatched from centre.
April	Defection of Girondin general Dumouriez to enemy (5) compounds internal hostilities.
May	Jacobins and others plan overthrow of Girondins, assisted by mass demonstrations. Anti-Jacobin rising in Lyon (29); anti-Girondin rising in Paris (31).
June	Convention purged of Girondins (2).
June–July	Girondin sympathisers in major cities reject outcome of Parisian purge; branded 'Federalist' rebels; situation moves towards civil war. New 'democratic' Constitution agreed by Convention.
July	All feudal dues abolished definitively, without compensation (17). Plans to divide *émigré* lands amongst the poor (not widely pursued) (21).
July–August	Open conflict with Federalists, especially in

September	south-east, compounds critical war situation. Convention responds to radical demands and votes to declare 'Terror' (5). Suspects will be interned, food prices are controlled ('General Maximum'), new armed forces to monitor supplies.
October– December	Violent repression of Lyon and Toulon, where Federalism has merged with royalist revolt; Vendée rebels put to flight, take up guerrilla campaign.
October	Republican calendar is adopted. Government declared 'revolutionary until peace' (10). Implementation of 1793 Constitution suspended.
November	First organised moves against religion itself; campaign of 'dechristianisation' soon under way amongst extreme radicals.
December	Law of 14 frimaire on revolutionary government tightens central control over government agents (4).
December– February 1794	Protest at direction of Terror begins to emerge from former radicals, led by Danton; others are implicated in plots and corruption scandals. Hébertist radicals demand even tougher measures, and talk of further popular insurrection.

1794

February–March	Measures taken for poor relief; proposal to confiscate suspects' land for redistribution to 'poor patriots' ('Ventôse Decrees').
March–April	Hébertist radicals and Dantonist moderates are successively arrested, tried and executed *en masse*, as terrorist measures tightened further.
April–May	Paris popular movement and local government neutralised as a political force by club closures and arrests.
May	Cult of Supreme Being introduced to replace dechristianisers' Cult of Reason.

June	Law of 22 prairial (10) simplifies still further the mechanisms of trial by Revolutionary Tribunal; executions accelerate. Success in war reduces clear reasons for continued violence of Terror.
July	Various political factions begin to fear Robespierre will purge them. He and his close colleagues increasingly politically isolated. Coup of 9 thermidor outlaws Robespierre, Saint-Just, Couthon (27); Parisian forces fail to rally to them, and they are executed (28).
August–October	Gradual relaxation of terrorist measures; attempts by Jacobins and Paris sections to regain initiative are repressed. Suspects are released, and politics swing sharply rightwards.
November	*Jeunesse dorée* attack Paris Jacobin Club; it is ordered to close. Purge of radicals from Paris sections begins.
December	Trial of Carrier exposes 'horrors' of Terror. Maximum on prices is suppressed (24).
December–February 1795	Bitter winter of '*nonante-cinq*' leads to starvation and widespread deaths.

1795

February–June	'White Terror' of reprisals against radicals, especially in cities of the south-east.
April	Risings of germinal (1–2): Parisian crowds protest to Convention about hardship, calling for 1793 Constitution. Order restored and sympathisers in Convention arrested.
May	Risings of prairial (20–21), with similar demands, leading to further purges of radicals within the Convention, and throughout Paris.
June	'Verona Declaration' by Louis XVIII (24), confirms that restoration would take back Church and *émigré* property, and be fatal to many revolutionary leaders.

August	Constitution of Year III agreed (22), with separation of powers and executive 'Directory'.
October	Vendémiaire rising in Paris (5): royalists attack measures to ensure continuity under new constitution. Bonaparte's troops suppress rising. Elections to new legislative 'Councils' (12). New law reimposes strict penalties on *émigrés* and priests (25).
November	Directory takes office. Radicals in Paris revive organisations.
December	Radical journalist Babeuf forced into hiding from police.

1796

March	Babeuf begins to establish conspiratorial apparatus.
April–May	Bonaparte's Army of Italy wins series of victories.
April	Death penalty imposed for advocating either restoration or 1793 Constitution.
May	Babeuf's conspirators arrested.
June–August	Further victories and capitulations in Italy.
October	'Cispadine Republic' established in northern Italy.
December	Measures against both *émigrés* and radicals are tightened, but priests exempted.

1797

February	Final abandonment of paper currency, return to gold, facilitated by loot from armies. Peace treaty with Papacy.
April	After further victories, peace negotiations with Austria begin from a position of strength: Belgium and parts of Italy formally ceded to France.
April–May	Right-wing victories in elections.
May	Babeuf executed (27).
June	Neo-Jacobin 'constitutional circles' begin to form.

July	Political clubs suppressed.
August	Legislative Councils and Paris sections begin to adopt militantly right-wing posture.
September	Coup of 18 fructidor V (4); Councils forced to pass emergency legislation annulling many elections; Paris occupied by army; Councils purged.
September–December	Directory swings to left and carries out measures against royalist opinion; political clubs allowed to open, military commissions to judge conspirators, new oaths of 'hatred of royalty and anarchy'. Directory gives itself power to purge all officials and elected bodies.

1798

January	Death penalty by military commission for crimes committed by gangs; brigandage an increasing problem.
January–February	Further measures to exclude 'undesirables' from political process.
March	'Managed' elections still return unsatisfactory number of anti-Directory candidates, this time to the left.
May	Leftist elections results annulled, a quarter of legislative and one-third of administrative candidates excluded, 'coup of 22 floréal VI' (11). Bonaparte's army sails for Egypt (19).
September	Conscription introduced in 'Loi Jourdan' (5); 200,000 men called up (24).
December	Kingdom of Naples joins Anglo-Russian alliance against France, after having attacked puppet 'Roman Republic' in November.

1799

January–February	Initial French victories in southern Italy.
March	France declares war on Austria and Tuscany.
April–July	Series of defeats and anti-French risings push French armies almost out of Italy.
April	Additional call-up of conscripts. Elections bring leftist candidates; other anti-Directory

	elements excluded by manipulation.
June	Legislative Councils sit *en permanence*, and at loggerheads with Directory. Two Directors purged under Councils' pressure (18). Further call-up of conscripts (28).
July	New neo-Jacobin club meets. Law making *émigrés'* families hostages passed.
August	Neo-Jacobins closed down by police. Counter-revolutionary insurrection in south-west. Further military defeats.
September	Laws against left-wing and right-wing press. Victory at Zurich; armies re-cross the Rhine.
October	Bonaparte returns to France; plotting begins against Directory. Further royalist risings in west.
November	Coup of 18 brumaire (9–10) brings Bonaparte and collaborators to power in new 'Consulate'.

Biographies

These are brief details on the main figures who make an appearance in this book. A collection of over 600 revolutionary 'lives' in a few lines can be found in C. Jones, *Longman Companion to the French Revolution*, London, 1988, pp. 314–400. Longer biographies on the leading figures can be found in S. Scott and B. Rothaus (eds), *Historical Dictionary of the French Revolution*, 2 vols, Westport, 1984.

Artois, Charles-Philippe, comte d', 1757–1836. Youngest brother of Louis XVI, suspected of involvement in 'aristocratic plot' of July 1789. Emigrated 16–17 July, settled in Turin, moved to Coblentz July 1791. Leading light in *émigré* activity and intrigue with the European powers. Fought in allied armies once war broke out, including leading an unsuccessful expedition to Brittany in 1795. Lived in Britain thereafter, returned to France in 1814. Became King Charles X in 1824, forced to abdicate by July Revolution of 1830, retired to Britain.

Babeuf, François-Noël, 1760–1797. From Picardy, a *feudiste* before 1789, surveying feudal rights for seigneurs. Discovered a radical vocation, and was active pamphleteer and agitator in Somme *département*. Worked for Subsistence Commission 1793–4. After Thermidor, became more prominent as journalist and Jacobin supporter. Arrested late 1794, further club activity in late 1795, by early 1796 was leader of 'Conspiracy of Equals', arrested May 1796, tried and executed at Vendôme.

Bailly, Jean-Sylvain, 1736–1793. Astronomer and historian, topped the poll for Parisian deputies to Estates-General, and was its president for the Tennis Court Oath. Appointed mayor of Paris after 14 July, emphasised social order in his rule, as against popular violence and demands of radical clubs: exemplified by the Champ de Mars Massacre of July 1791. Eventually worn out by the pressures put on him by radical activity. Left office in November 1791, but was arrested and guillotined on the site of the Massacre in November 1793.

Barnave, Antoine-Pierre-Joseph-Marie, 1761–1793. Barrister from Grenoble, leader in 'pre-Revolution' there. Prominent in Estates-General, leading figure by early 1791, forming so-called 'Triumvirate' with Lameth and A. Duport. Feuillant after Flight to Varennes, helped to negotiate king's reinstatement; retired in early 1792, arrested after 10 August 1792.

Barras, Jean-Nicolas-Paul-François, vicomte de, 1755–1829. A dissolute aristocratic officer before 1789, entered the Convention as a radical, went on mission in 1793, led capture of Marseille and Toulon, and subsequent repression. In 1794 a leader of Thermidorian coup, subsequently a Director. Corrupt and devious, organiser of coups, patron of Bonaparte. Would be forced into exile in 1810.

Billaud-Varenne, Jacques-Nicolas, 1756–1819. Schoolmaster, lawyer and aspiring writer, Jacobin and Cordeliers member, served Insurrectionary Commune in 1792, elected to Convention, extreme Montagnard, elected to Committee of Public Safety in September 1793 as '*sans-culotte*' candidate. Threatened by Robespierre, took part in Thermidor. Deported to Guiana for terrorism, later settled in Saint-Domingue as a farmer.

Bo, Jean-Baptiste-Jérôme, 1743–1814. A doctor, elected to Legislative Assembly and Convention from the Aveyron. Worked for poor-relief and educational reforms, and also frequently sent on mission from 1793 to 1795. Worked later as a bureaucrat, went into private practice in 1809.

Bonaparte, Napoléon, 1769–1821. Napoléon I, Emperor of the French, 1804–14, 1815. Son of a Corsican lawyer with noble status, trained at Paris military school, artillery officer from 1785. Associated with Jacobinism from 1791, came to notice for commanding artillery at siege of Toulon. Commanded repression of Vendémiaire rising of 1795, sent to Army of Italy in 1796, led it on a series of brilliant victories and to peace with Austria in 1797. In 1798 commanded expedition to Egypt with dubious success, but evaded British blockade to reach France in October 1799, and brought to power in Brumaire coup the following month. His later career is well-known.

Bouchotte, Jean-Baptiste-Noël, 1754–1840. Career army officer, captain in 1789. Pro-revolution, and came to prominence in the north after Dumouriez's defection. Elected war minister April 1793, introduced *'sans-culotte'* measures to administration. Returned to army April 1794, arrested in June, amnestied in 1795. Some Jacobin activities in later 1790s, but retired on military pension after Brumaire.

Brienne, Etienne-Charles Loménie de, 1727–1794. Allegedly atheist archbishop of Toulouse from 1763. Member of first Assembly of Notables, and appointed to replace Calonne after its failure. Pushed through a similar reform package, but May edicts of 1788 against *parlements* raised opposition to him, resigned August 1788. Went to Italy as a cardinal, returned in 1790 to accept clerical oath. Arrested November 1793, and died under house arrest.

Brissot (or Brissot de Warville), Jacques-Pierre, 1754–1793. Pamphleteer and literary hack before 1789, sometimes reduced to police informing. Formed anti-slavery Société des Amis des Noirs (Society of Friends of the Blacks) in 1788, drawing in many future Girondin contacts. A prominent radical journalist in the early Revolution, entered Legislative Assembly, where he led calls for war, and subsequently Convention, grew increasingly opposed to the Jacobins and the violence of Parisian radicalism, arrested after 31 May – 2 June insurrection.

Cabarrus, Thérèse de, Madame Tallien, 1773–1835. Daughter of Spanish minister, married to member of *parlement* of Paris, allegedly found by Tallien in prison in Bordeaux in 1793. They married, and her salon-keeping abilities made them an influential pair in Thermidorian high society. Moved abroad after the marriage broke up, and married again into Spanish aristocracy.

Calonne, Charles-Alexandre de, 1734–1802. An *intendant* from the 1760s, controller-general from 1783, lost out to noble and *parlementaire* opposition to his proposed reforms in 1787. After dismissal, went to England in disgrace, and from 1789 worked with *émigrés*, especially Artois. He was dropped as an adviser in 1792, and retired to London.

Carrier, Jean-Baptiste, 1756–1794. Lawyer son of a prosperous farmer in the Cantal, elected to the Convention, became a hard-line Montagnard. On mission to Brittany and Nantes from August 1793 to February 1794, where he supervised thousands of executions. After Thermidor, he was sent before the Revolutionary Tribunal, used as a 'show trial' for the excesses of Terror.

Chabot, François, 1756–1794. Capucin priest, accepted clerical oath, elected to Legislative Assembly from Loir-et-Cher. Radical and conspiracy-theorist, denouncing 'Austrian Committee' at Court. Sent on mission by Convention, also served on Committee of General Security. Involved with Austrian bankers through marriage, his suspect private life associated him with 'foreign plotters', arrested November 1793, executed with the Dantonists.

Chalier, Marie-Joseph, 1747–1793. Trained as a monk in Lyon, but left, became travelling salesman around the Mediterranean. Took part in 14 July rising in Paris, returned to Lyon and took prominent role in radical politics. Leader of Jacobin municipality in 1792–3, noted for violent rhetoric, arrested and executed by Federalists after their rising.

Collot d'Herbois, Jean-Marie, 1749–1796. Pre-revolutionary playwright and theatre director, moved to Paris in 1789, joined Jacobins, member of Insurrectionary Commune in 1792, elected to Convention. On mission for much of 1793, then elected to Committee of Public Safety in September 1793 as *'sans-culotte'* candidate. With Fouché, responsible for bloody repression in Lyon. Came under threat from Robespierre in summer 1794, and participated in Thermidor. Left Committee of Public Safety, but prosecuted for terrorism and deported to Guiana.

Corday, Marie-Anne-Charlotte de, 1768–1793. Assassin of Marat. From Caen, an educated woman who sympathised with the Girondins, and whose brothers were *émigrés*. Made her way to Paris alone, and gained admission to Marat's room with a note offering information on Federalists (not asking for help, as in David's painting), then stabbed him. Tried and executed four days later, 17 July 1793. Became a cult figure for counter-revolutionaries, a 'virgin martyr' whose severed head had supposedly blushed when slapped by the executioner.

Couthon, Georges-Auguste, 1755–1794. Lawyer from Clermont-Ferrand, wheelchair-bound by 1789. Elected to Legislative Assembly and Convention, a Jacobin friendly with Robespierre. Sent on mission, including to Lyon, and served on Committee of Public Safety from May 1793. Closely associated with Robespierrist Terror, drafted law of 22 prairial. Executed with Robespierre.

Danton, Georges-Jacques, 1759–1794. A barrister at Paris, took up radical stance from 1789 in Cordeliers district, and later Club, and Jacobins from 1791. Served as municipal prosecutor, involved in 10 August insurrection, minister of justice in Provisional Executive, turned blind eye to September Massacres, but rallied Paris to the war effort. Elected to Convention, Montagnard. Widely suspected of 'sticky fingers', especially when on mission to Belgium in late 1792 to early 1793. Extravagant lifestyle aided suspicions. Supported 'terrorist' institutions, retired due to ill-health in October 1793. Returned to politics later in the autumn, attacking dechristianisation and terrorist excess, became identified as an 'indulgent', and thus suspect, arrested and executed as leader of a counter-revolutionary faction in April 1794.

Desmoulins, Lucie-Camille-Simplice, 1760–1794. Schoolfriend of Robespierre as scholarship boys in Paris. Mediocre barrister at Paris, discovered talent for incendiary journalism in 1789. A Cordelier, and, from 1791, Jacobin, closely linked to Danton, served as his secretary in Ministry of Justice. Elected to Convention, Montagnard. Like Danton, objected to Terror from December 1793, using a new journal, the *Vieux Cordelier* ('Old Cordelier'), to denounce and satirise excesses. Like Danton, executed for this 'indulgent' attitude.

Dumouriez, Charles-François du Périer, 1739–1823. Professional soldier, entered revolutionary local politics in Cherbourg, soon moved to Paris, linked with Mirabeau and Lafayette, and Jacobin Club. Appointed foreign minister March 1792, dismissed with

Girondins in June, returned to army command. Commander at victories of Valmy and Jemappes, responsible for invasion of Low Countries. Girondin in politics; their problems in Paris, simultaneous with defeat in spring 1793, led him to try to lead his army on Paris. Failing, he fled to the enemy. *Emigré* organisations rejected him, settled in England.

Duport, Adrien-Jean-François, 1759–1798. *Parlementaire*, prominent in elite radical politics in 1788–9, the Society of Thirty, and opposition to royal reform. A 'Triumvirate' leader in 1790–1, thus compromised by Varennes. Feuillant thereafter, emigrated as political situation deteriorated. Died in exile in Switzerland.

Fabre d'Eglantine, Philippe-François-Nazaire, 1750–1794. A teacher and, from 1772, playwright. Moved to Paris in 1787, and became linked to Cordeliers from 1789, including Danton and Marat. Radical journalist, elected to Convention, Montagnard. Responsible for elaborating the final version of the Revolutionary Calendar in 1793. Denounced by Robespierre for financial corruption and profiteering, arrested in January 1794, executed with the Dantonists.

Fauchet, François-Claude, 1744–1793. A liberal priest, elected to Paris Commune in 1789, stood for a 'middle way' in municipal politics between Bailly's authoritarianism and Cordeliers direct democracy. Founded Cercle Social in 1790, an elite political club containing many future Girondins, and also a base for Fauchet's popular lectures, notably on Rousseau's philosophy. Elected bishop of Calvados in 1791, and then to Legislative Assembly and Convention. Expelled from Jacobins for excessive moderation in September 1792, arrested in July 1793 accused of links to Charlotte Corday, executed with Girondins in October.

Fouché, Joseph, 1763–1820. Schoolteacher at Nantes, elected to Convention, sent on mission to the west, the centre (where he was an early dechristianiser), and Lyon in November 1793, where he led mass executions. Recalled April 1794, a leader of Thermidor. Protected by Barras from retribution for his terrorism, served as an ambassador in Italy in 1798, then made minister of police in 1799, repressing left-wing and right-wing elements equally. Served Napoleon in this position, and survived the Restoration.

Fréron, Louis-Stanislas, 1765–1802. Son of an Enlightenment literary critic, also a journalist before the Revolution. From 1790 produced the *Orateur du peuple* in imitation of Marat. Cordelier, elected to Commune in 1792. Elected to Convention, on mission to Toulon conducted repression with extravagant violence, recalled January 1794. Thermidorian, then increasingly reactionary in politics, linked to *jeunesse dorée*. Agent of government in the south during White Terror. Became a bureaucrat, died in the Caribbean as sub-prefect of Saint-Domingue.

Gouges, Marie-Olympe de, 1755–1793. A noted female literary figure, took up the largely ignored struggle for women's rights after 1789, producing a 'Declaration of the Rights of Woman' and appealing for its official adoption in 1791. Her mission met with no success. Her public sympathy for Louis XVI after his fall led to her arrest, and execution amongst other 'dangerous women' in November 1793.

Hébert, Jacques-René, 1757–1794. Son of a goldsmith, sought his fortune in Paris, but was scraping a living, for example selling theatre tickets, by 1789. Revolutionary journalism as *Père Duchesne* brought him fame and influence. Cordelier, member of Insurrectionary Commune in August 1792, served as deputy municipal prosecutor. Although attacking *enragés*, was himself a leader of Parisian extreme radical politics, involved in 31 May – 2 June, 5 September 1793, dechristianisation, calls for extensions of Terror (and implicitly overthrow of Committee of Public Safety). By spring 1794 this went beyond Robespierre's tolerance, and 'Hébertists' were condemned and executed.

Hérault de Séchelles, Marie-Jean, 1760–1794. Prosecutor in *parlement* of Paris, aristocratic background, linked to salons. Elected to Legislative Assembly as Feuillant, but became more radical. Elected to Convention, led committee drafting 1793 Constitution, joined Committee of Public Safety, but moderate by terrorist standards, linked to Dantonist 'foreign plot', arrested and executed.

Javogues, Claude, 1759–1796. Lawyer, made a name in local politics near Lyon before election to Convention. Brutally radical while on mission in Lyon region in 1793–4, recalled in spring 1794. Critical of Robespierre, but also imprisoned as terrorist after

Thermidor. Amnestied in 1795, but involved in babouvist plot, and joined an insurrectionary attempt after Babeuf's detention. Executed by military commission.

Lacombe, Claire ('Rose'), 1765–? Actress, arrived in Paris in 1792, involved in 10 August, prominent in Society of Revolutionary Republican Women during 1793. Arrested as Hébertist sympathiser in March 1794, returned to acting, and obscurity, on release.

Lafayette, Marie-Joseph-Paul-Roch-Yves-Gilbert Motier, marquis de, 1757–1834. Aristocratic military hero of American War, liberal, called in 1787 for Estates-General after involvement in Assembly of Notables. Elected to Estates-General, and appointed to command Parisian National Guard after 14 July. Earned hatred of Marie-Antoinette after October Days, but also loathed by Parisian radicals for authoritarian stance, and alleged network of spies in the capital. Led Champ de Mars Massacre, defeated in elections for mayor of Paris in autumn 1791, rejoined army as general. Tried to lead Legislative Assembly in moves against Jacobins after 20 June 1792, and fled to the enemy after 10 August. Held in prison until 1797, returned to France under Napoleon, and would later be instrumental in creation of constitutional monarchy after Revolution of 1830.

Lameth, Alexandre-Théodore-Victor, comte de, 1760–1829. Cavalry colonel, rallied to Third Estate in Estates-General, prominent in Night of 4 August, patriot and 'Triumvirate' leader, rejoined army in late 1791. Fled with Lafayette in August 1792, imprisoned until 1795, served as a prefect under Napoleon.

La Rouerie, Armand-Taffin, marquis de, 1756–1793. Ex-monk, but also military veteran of the American War, and Gardes françaises officer, imprisoned for support for *parlement* of Rennes in 1787. Royalist from 1789, from 1791 agent for *émigré* princes, running a network of secret committees in the west. Went into hiding in late 1792, died the next year, apparently of exhaustion.

Léon, Pauline, 1768–? Parisian chocolate-maker, involved in revolutionary *journées* from 1789, and Cordeliers Club. Co-founder of Society of Revolutionary Republican Women, active with *enragés*, one of whom, Jean Leclerc, she married in late 1794. After brief imprisonment during that year, the couple faded into private life.

Louis XVI, 1754–1793. King of France 1774–1789, King of the French, 1789–1792. Grandson of previous monarch Louis XV, became heir unexpectedly on death of elder brother, thus early education had not fitted him for the role. An amiable, intelligent but indecisive man, lacking the drive to become great or the vices to become notorious. Widely mocked for his failure to consummate his marriage for seven years (1770–7), and seen thereafter as a weak companion to Marie-Antoinette's allegedly libertine personality. Never wholly accepted the agenda imposed on him by events in 1789, as revealed by a manifesto during the Flight to Varennes in June 1791. As constitutional monarch from 1791, did nothing to stop drift towards war, while blocking action against priests and *émigrés*. Conducted himself with dignity during detention, trial and execution.

Marat, Jean-Paul, 1744–1793. A trained doctor, one of the oldest of the revolutionaries. Scientific experimenter and anti-authoritarian writer, nonetheless he held the position of physician to the bodyguard of the comte d'Artois before 1789. Rapidly took up an extreme radical position in journalism. Often forced into hiding in the early Revolution, protected by Cordeliers district and Club, joined Insurrectionary Commune in 1792, allegedly largely responsible for September Massacres, for which Girondins loathed him. Elected to Convention, Girondin attempts to put him on trial were part of conflict leading to 31 May – 2 June. After assassination in July 1793, many others tried to take up his journalistic mantle, and a short-lived 'cult' developed around him.

Marie-Antoinette, Joséphe-Jeanne, 1755–1793. Queen of France, 1774–1792. Youngest daughter of Empress Maria-Theresa of Austria, married to future Louis XVI at fourteen. Widely mocked for her extravagance and reactionary opinions, even before 1789. After calling of Estates-General, blamed for Louis's apparent duplicity in July and September/October, advocated flight, and viewed as centre of reactionary plotting at Court. Maintained contact with Austria after war declared. A blinkered and obstinate woman of little compassion, who would happily have seen the whole Revolution crushed, but not the unnatural monster radical revolutionaries chose to paint her as.

Maupeou, René-Charles-Augustin de, 1714–1792. Appointed chancellor in 1768 by Louis XV, responsible for sweeping attempt to remove *parlementaire* opposition in 1771. In disgrace after Louis XVI's accession, but chancellorship was a lifetime appointment, therefore theoretically chief minister throughout the latter's reign. Lived in retirement until his death.

Mirabeau, Honoré-Gabriel Riquetti, comte de, 1749–1791. Son of a physiocrat author, a dissolute youth included imprisonment via *lettre de cachet*, became outspoken liberal by late 1780s, elected by Third Estate of Provence to Estates-General, which he led through his oratory at crucial moments in spring and summer 1789. Through 1790, tried to set himself up as political broker between the Court and the Revolution, taking payment for his political advice to Louis, which was largely ignored. Died in April 1791 before this had emerged fully, but was rapidly discredited afterwards.

Mounier, Jean-Joseph, 1758–1806. Lawyer from Grenoble, with Barnave led 'pre-Revolution' in Dauphiné. A celebrity when elected to Estates-General, was responsible for proposing the Tennis Court Oath. His proposals for a two-chamber legislature were defeated in September 1789, and he resigned in protest at the October Days. After a small attempt to raise opposition in Grenoble, emigrated to Switzerland in 1790. Returned in 1801, and became a prefect in 1802.

Necker, Jacques, 1732–1804. Banker from Geneva, finance minister of France 1777–81, reappointed after Brienne's dismissal in September 1788. Handled situation ineptly when Estates-General opened, dismissed as part of 'aristocratic plot' on 11 July. On his way to exile when recalled after 14 July, to popular acclaim, but never able to influence events thereafter. Emigrated to Switzerland in September 1790.

Orléans, Louis-Philippe-Joseph, duc d', 1747–1793. Cousin of Louis XVI, a libertine of enormous wealth, became interested in liberal politics in late 1780s, and funded a network of pamphleteers (and allegedly agents). Influential in Assembly of Notables, elected to Estates-General and Convention. Suspicions that he wanted the throne for himself, and was using the Jacobin movement to that end, dogged him, and played a part, for example, in the politics of the post-Varennes period. Renamed himself 'Philippe Égalité' (equality) in late 1792 at the request of his local section. Voted for king's death, but linked to Dumouriez, arrested and executed alongside the Girondins.

Pache, Jean-Nicolas, 1746–1823. Chief steward of the king's household from the early 1780s, a bureaucrat promoted by Roland into the Interior Ministry, later became war minister in October 1792. Moved from Girondin to Montagnard sympathies, and dismissed February 1793. Elected mayor of Paris, helped plan 31 May – 2 June events. Implicated with Hébertists in spring 1794, but survived, though dismissed as mayor. Harassed after Thermidor, stayed in private life.

Pétion, Jérôme, 1756–1793. Lawyer, elected to Estates-General, anti-slavery supporter, close associate of Robespierre, involved in agitation after Varennes. Elected mayor of Paris in November 1791, involved in plans for 10 August. Revulsion at September Massacres pushed his politics towards Girondins after election to Convention. On the run after 31 May – 2 June, committed suicide.

Provence, comte de, 1755–1824. Louis XVIII, King of France, in theory from 1795, in practice 1814/15–1824. Elder of Louis XVI's brothers, involved in pre-revolutionary agitation, but soon swung to criticism of Revolution. Emigrated at time of Flight to Varennes. Joined Artois, declared himself lieutenant-general of the kingdom, and organised an *émigré* army. Declared himself regent in January 1793, and king in 1795. Moved around Europe, based in Russia from 1798, Britain from 1807.

Robespierre, Maximilien-François-Isidore, 1758–1794. Lawyer in Arras, elected to Estates-General, became notorious for extreme democratic views , and 'incorruptible' stance. Influential in Parisian politics during Legislative Assembly, and always prominent in Jacobins. Member of Insurrectionary Commune, elected to Convention, soon in open conflict with Girondins. Spoke out for king's death, and later for Girondins' proscription. Arguably the moral leader of Revolution after election to Committee of Public Safety in July 1793, largely responsible for discrediting Hébertist and Dantonist elements, while simultaneously taking a leading role in many policy areas. Seemed to be planning further purges when Thermidorian coalition rounded on him. Attempted suicide after his outlawing on 9 thermidor, but survived to face the guillotine the next day. Inflexible, dogmatic, ill-equipped to deal with the ambiguities of politics, but an icon for radicals.

Roland de la Platière, Jean-Marie, 1734–1793. Royal factory inspector in Lyon in 1789, lobbyist in Paris for Lyon manufacturers in 1791, became linked to future Girondins socially at this point, brought in as interior minister in March 1792, dismissed June, reinstated after 10 August. Alienated from Montagnards over September Massacres and growing Girondin sympathies, resigned January 1793, fled Paris in June. Committed suicide on news of his wife's execution.

Roland, Marie-Jeanne or Manon Phlipon, Madame, 1754–1793. Parisian by birth, married Roland de la Platière in 1780. Intellectually inclined, aspired to emulate Old Regime salon hostesses' influence, and used her home to co-ordinate Girondin activities. Arrested after 31 May – 2 June, executed in November 1793 during the repression of 'dangerous women'.

Romme, Gilbert, 1750–1796. A tutor before 1789, elected to Legislative Assembly and Convention from Puy-de-Dôme. Captured by Federalist rebels when on mission in Normandy, but released in summer 1793. Educational reformer, important in planning Revolutionary Calendar, and loyal Jacobin even after Thermidor. Implicated in Prairial rising, committed suicide on the way to execution.

Ronsin, Charles-Philippe, 1751–1794. Failed playwright of rural origins, became a club orator after 1789. National Guard officer in Paris, and from 1793 prominent in Bouchotte's War Ministry. Sent to Vendée, highly critical there of generals, recalled and imprisoned December 1793 as extremist, released in February, but began to call for *sans-culotte* insurrection, executed with Hébertists.

Roux, Jacques, 1752–1794. Priest, came to Paris in 1790, elected vicar of Saint-Nicolas-des-Champs, a poverty-stricken area of central Paris. Prominent orator in Cordeliers Club and Gravilliers section, elected to Commune early 1793. Involved in protests of that year, calls for greater economic regulation and Terror. Opposed by Montagnards, and imprisoned as counter-revolutionary on 5 September, when Terror was officially adopted. Committed suicide in prison five months later.

Roux-Fazillac, Pierre, 1746–1833. Army officer, elected to Legislative Assembly and Convention, highly critical of Girondins. Sent on mission, effective Jacobin reformer and regulator in areas less affected by conflict. Served Directory as local official in the Dordogne, then retired.

Saint-Just, Louis-Antoine-Léon, 1767–1794. Officer's son, too young for political involvement in 1789. Emulated Robespierre's austere Rousseauism, elected to Convention, and came to attention with demands for the king's death and attacks on Girondins. Joined Committee of Public Safety in May 1793, frequently on mission to armies in east and north. Attacked Dantonists and Hébertists in 1794, and stood by Robespierre, thus sharing his fate at Thermidor.

Sieyès, Emmanuel-Joseph, abbé, 1748–1836. Church bureaucrat before 1789, wrote highly influential pamphlets condemning privilege in 1788–9. Elected to Estates-General, instrumental in clashes May–July 1789, drafted Tennis Court Oath and worked on Declaration of Rights. Worked on committees concerned with administrative reorganisation. Elected to Convention, but maintained low profile, more active after Thermidor, and also served on Directorial Councils. A central plotter behind Bonaparte's Brumaire coup, like Fouché and Talleyrand one of the Revolution's great survivors.

Talleyrand or Talleyrand-Périgord, Charles-Maurice de, 1754–1838. Dissolute churchman, but effective bureaucrat, given bishopric of Autun in 1788, elected to Estates-General, rapidly joined Third Estate, reformer in education, finance and religion. Performed, with prompting, the Mass at the Festival of the Federation in 1790. Resigned his bishopric, ambassador to Britain in early 1792, stayed in exile after 10 August, to return in 1795. Foreign minister from 1797, rallied to Bonaparte, and would outlast his influence.

Tallien, Jean-Lambert, 1767–1820. A clerk who became a popular society leader and journalist in Paris after 1789, member of Insurrectionary Commune of 1792, involved in 10 August and September Massacres. Elected to Convention, Montagnard, made ferocious attacks on king and Girondins. On mission in autumn to Bordeaux, conducted fierce repression, and met Thérèse de

Cabarrus, whom he later married. Returned to Paris, attacked by Robespierre, Thermidorian who launched attacks on Revolutionary Tribunal and terrorist personnel. Madame Tallien's salon added to his influence, but they parted and his star waned. He later entered diplomatic service.

Target, Guillaume-Jean-Baptiste, 1733–1806. A barrister and *philosophe*, member of Académie française, involved in reform politics by 1788, elected to Estates-General. Did much work on the detail of reform, known as 'Father of the Constitution' (of 1791). Later worked on the new Civil Code under Napoleon.

Théroigne de Méricourt (Anne-Joseph Terwagne), 1762–1817. From Luxembourg, active female participant in Parisian *journées* of 1789, speaker in Cordeliers and Jacobin Clubs, kept salon frequented by leading reformers. Imprisoned by Austrians in Liège in 1791, triumphant welcome on return to Paris, involved again in *journées* of summer 1792. A leading female voice in the Revolution, but of Girondin sympathies by 1793. More radical women attacked and flogged her in public in May, from which she never recovered. Was later confined in an asylum and died insane.

Turgot, Anne-Robert-Jacques, baron de l'Aulne, 1727–1781. Economist and administrator, from 1761 *intendant* of Limoges, where he experimented with rationalisation of local government. Key figure in 'advanced' economic thought in the mid-eighteenth century, and made controller-general of finances by Louis XVI in 1774. Proposed and implemented a series of radical liberalisations, resulting in outcry and the 'Flour War' of 1775. Removed from office in 1776.

Vincent, François-Nicolas, 1767–1794. A jailer's son and clerk, joined Cordeliers Club, involved in planning 10 August, moved into military bureaucracy under Bouchotte. Denounced with Ronsin, like him seemed to preach insurrection in spring 1794, executed with the Hébertists.

Introduction

The French Revolution has generated images and ideas that have become part of the culture of all Europe. The storming of the Parisian fortress of the Bastille on 14 July 1789 stands out, marking the first 'popular revolution' in modern history, and was followed by the drafting of a Declaration of the Rights of Man, overturning a society of 'feudal' aristocratic domination. The Revolution introduced to politics the possibility of making a new start to society, of change as regeneration, and as progress. These features mark out an optimistic version of the French Revolution. This is the period of which the poet Wordsworth could write, 'Bliss was it in that dawn to be alive, but to be young was very heaven!'. Darker images follow, however: descent into intolerance, persecution of religion, aristocrats flung into prison irrespective of age or sex. In the years 1793–4 Revolution becomes Terror, with the erection of that grim symbol, the guillotine, machinery of sudden death, beside which women of the people knit as they cheer on the procession of executions. Out of all this increasing chaos then emerges Napoleon, who in the new century turns France into an empire and seems to sweep away a revolution that has become a slaughterhouse. Such images are at one level mere clichés, but their endurance illustrates the continued significance of the Revolution for our time.

The claim to explain or possess the meaning of the Revolution can be put to many uses. The present-day French state uses all the symbolic paraphernalia of Revolution that suits it: the Tricolour flag, the 14 July holiday, the Declaration of Rights displayed in

1

every public building, the slogan 'Liberty, Equality, Fraternity' carved into façades, the female figure of liberty on stamps and coins. Thus the Revolution is made to stand both for the foundation of one particular modern democracy and for its claim to be a representative of the values of democracy in general. Terror and intolerance are not mentioned. This was, for the French Republic, the predominant message on display in the Bicentennial celebrations of 1989. Yet Margaret Thatcher, as leader of Great Britain, could publicly scorn this. She asserted that the British claim to be founders of democracy went back to Magna Carta in 1215, while the French Revolution, with its commitment to 'dangerous' innovation, had led only to Terror, military dictatorship and war. At the crudest political level, the Revolution remains present in Europe, and subject to incompatible interpretations.

As historians, however, it is our job to try to place all that remains today of the Revolution back in its proper context, to analyse it and contemplate what it may mean for us, and not merely to quarry it for symbols and examples to serve some predetermined agenda. This book is intended to assist this task for those who are approaching the study of the French Revolution in depth for the first time. It attempts to strike the balance between a text in which no previous knowledge is assumed and one which engages with the current state of an ever-expanding mass of writing on the subject. For clarity in this complex task, the text has been framed as a single narrative: the chapters are arranged chronologically and analysis is tied to those points in time when particular features were most prominent. Debts to the work of many historians are acknowledged in the endnotes to each chapter, which also provide some suggestions for further reading, taken up more systematically in the bibliographical essay. The words of the revolutionaries themselves are illustrated in a series of translated documents, which are cross-referenced to the main text. A chronological outline is provided to assist readers in grasping the relations of events over time.

This work aims to do more, however, than merely describe the Revolution. No individual account can aspire to an 'unbiased' presentation of the French Revolution. It was indeed the founding event of modern European society, and as one cannot help having views on one's society, so the debates and deeds of the Revolution demand the taking-up of positions. This has been the story of writing on the Revolution ever since the event itself. Even before Napoleon had installed himself over the remains of revolutionary politics, violently divergent views on the nature of the upheaval had appeared in print. These varied from seeing it as part of the inevitable progress of mankind, the product of Enlightenment and the displacement of religion by philosophy, to seeing it, on exactly the same grounds, as the work of satanic conspirators pledged to the destruction of all that was decent and Christian. Within a generation, views emerged which projected the Revolution as the political consequence of the rise of a middle class; in French terms, a *bourgeoisie*. This group, whose wealth came from trade, industry and professional employment, rather than ancient lands or privileges, was said to have displaced the nobility who had held back more general social progress, and to have opened the way for the industrial century.[1]

Karl Marx was one of the young thinkers influenced by reading such texts, but while they glorified the *bourgeoisie*, he saw the underlying misery provoked by industrial development and the overall social system of capitalism. His theories, developed in the mid-nineteenth century, made revolutions into the key turning-points of history: as in 1789 the *bourgeoisie* had recognised their destiny and led the people to overturn the old order, so one day the people, transformed by economic forces into an industrial proletariat, would rise up for themselves to create not just the superficial legal equalities of a capitalist society, but the real equality of a socialist one.

Marx never wrote at length directly on the Revolution, but it underpinned his thinking, just as Marx underpinned the thinking of the leading historians of the Revolution in the early twentieth century. In 1939 Georges Lefebvre produced one of the most subtle social interpretations of the Revolution, which still has power to provoke thought today. As a Marxist, he saw society as divided into antagonistic socio-economic classes, and he saw every class in France in turmoil in 1789. The aristocracy had paralysed the government, refusing to consent to reforms vital to stave off bankruptcy, because they saw their powers and privileges being eroded by a centralising monarchy. The *bourgeoisie*, called together to elect a consultative body, the Estates-General, overturned the conservative aristocratic agenda and put forward demands for an end to such privileges, along with new restric-

3

tions on royal power and a role for their class in legislation and government. The urban population and the peasantry, each with their own grievances, both rose up separately as the state and the aristocrats seemed to threaten a military response, and the whole structure of the old order was brought down by this complex of demands for social change.[2]

In the years after the Second World War, an interpretation of the Revolution based on the politics of class conflict was relatively unchallenged. However, other strands of thought began to promote alternative views. A diverse group of British and American historians had by the early 1970s put forward much evidence to question the existence of clear-cut class divisions in pre-revolutionary French society. They pointed out that the French nobility contained many men of very liberal political persuasion and enlightened views, while some of France's leading 'industrialists' were also of noble blood. Meanwhile, those rising from below in society aspired to nothing more than joining this elite; there was no long-term emergence of a coherent opposing class interest.[3]

This 'revisionist' position, based on empirical study and standing out against a Marxist interpretation, did not offer any great alternative vision of the Revolution's meaning. It was backed up, however, by a separate strand which considered 1789 more philosophically. François Furet had since the 1960s staked out a position in the French historical profession as the leading critic of the Marxist interpretation, and by the early 1980s had challenged it directly, likening it to the 'catechism' of Church doctrine that children were supposed to learn by heart without questioning. Instead of change in society, what Furet saw as crucial to the Revolution was the emergence of modern forms of politics – ideas of the state, the citizen, individual freedoms and rights. At the same time, he did not hesitate to associate the way in which such ideas emerged early in the Revolution with the descent towards political violence that marked its passage through the 1790s. Marxists, and earlier republican historians, were inclined to excuse the violent period of 1792–4, known generally as the Terror, as the product of external circumstances and necessary self-defence, albeit perhaps that alarms and the response to them were exaggerated beyond what was 'reasonable'. Furet condemned it, and implicitly condemned all the revolutionaries, who had constructed the mental climate in which the Terror was possible.[4]

This was largely the position of historical debate in 1989, when France and the world celebrated the Bicentennial of the events of 1789.[5] It should be immediately apparent that the positions of Marxist and revisionist historians closely parallel socialist and liberal/conservative positions in twentieth-century politics. In many ways, the historians' fight over the meaning of the Revolution was a fight over the survival of a certain kind of socialism as a respectable force in French politics at the end of the 1980s. As in the course of 1989 the countries of eastern Europe broke away from the Soviet bloc, and the control of their communist parties, this seemed to be a geo-political reinforcement of the defeat of Marxist historical interpretation, and of a socialism that had any meaningful link to that position.

It may be the case that the older Marxist version of the French Revolution is now definitively defeated, but that does not necessarily mean that any one other interpretation has triumphed, or that we must draw any particular political conclusion from the defeat. It is one thing to undermine a viewpoint, quite another to erect a new orthodoxy. A vast corpus of historical work was produced in the late 1980s and in the years that followed the Bicentennial, little of which directly challenged the dominance of revisionism, and especially of its rather negative verdict on the value of the Revolution. Nonetheless, new studies extended our knowledge of various elements of the Revolution dramatically, particularly in terms of the details of the culture of the era, the impact of the Revolution on the rural population, and the place of conceptions of gender in the revolutionary 'political culture'.[6] This general broadening of perspectives implicitly questions sweeping views about the political 'meaning' of the Revolution. It is with this work, and the questions it raises, that this book engages most directly.

This book, as its title suggests, aims to bring a perspective on society at large back into the history of the Revolution. Detailed historical research continues to provide us with more evidence to discuss this, but narratives of the Revolution have focused more and more on politics.[7] In refocusing this work on society, some hard decisions have had to be made about content. For example, interesting work has been done recently on the links between religious thought and elite opposition in the eighteenth century, and the role of the press in both Old Regime and Revolution has been extensively discussed.[8] Unfortunately, space could not be found to examine these aspects in any depth. It is only with some difficulty that the immensity of the Revolution has been reduced to the format of this series, and if readers find it either overstuffed, or lacking in aspects that interest them, the author can only apologise and direct them to the bibliographical essay, where a range of other thematic studies are suggested.

The French Revolution emerged out of a society and culture that were highly complex and riddled with conflicts and tensions. Passing into a new political situation, all these problems remained, if sometimes taking new forms, and many were worsened by new conflicts, over politics, property and religion, and then by external and later civil war. The population of France lived through a decade of revolutionary upheaval, growing more and more weary of the turmoil, before sinking into acceptance of dictatorship dressed up as empire. It was not, however, 'the Revolution' which created this turmoil, but the struggle between revolutionaries and their enemies.

The Revolution aspired to change society, and indeed its aspirations grew more radical in the course of the five years after 1789. Not all of those changes are what we at the close of the twentieth century might consider 'progressive', but they were all efforts to rebuild a society on new foundations of liberty and equality. In the process, revolutionaries had to resist continual attempts simply to restore things to their previous, less free, less equal state (attempts which, moreover, would have led to a huge number of deaths). No one can 'excuse' the Terror, nor conceal the fact that many revolutionaries seemed programmed to dismiss any opposition as treachery. Many historians who criticise the violence of the Revolution, however, do not seem to ask themselves how its gains would otherwise have been defended. Indeed, the implicit expectation that political and social change ought to be peaceful seems rather odd, given the history of the last century. The existence of societies in western Europe where violence has (almost) left the political process is an achievement that is extremely confined both in space and time. Many other regions of the world do not share this situation; before 1945 neither did western Europe, and it remains a rather patchy and fragile condition, as the history of Northern Ireland (or the

6

Basque Country, or Sicily) witnesses. Two hundred years ago in France, if the majority of the population wanted change, it had to be fought for. In that fight, some ideals, and many people, were casualties.

This account is therefore a narrative of conflict. It focuses heavily on the lead-up to 1789, and on the processes of change, both constructive and destructive, that marked the Revolution's early years. Rather unusually, perhaps, it does not concentrate on the Terror. By the time the monarchy had fallen in 1792, and war within and against France had become almost general in 1793, patterns of action and response had to a large degree become fixed and polarised. How that came about, however, is a more significant story. It is a story with few heroes, because the modern-day historian can find much to criticise in the actions and attitudes of any eighteenth-century actor. Even in the most 'objective' light, the revolutionaries were often blinkered by social and gender prejudices, and the best of them could scarcely be called open-minded. The society of equal citizens that they fought for remains, however, the basis of all the freedoms that modern Europeans enjoy. The French Revolution, in its time, undoubtedly failed to achieve its political objectives, but it began to change French, and European, society, in ways for which we should all be grateful. In a perfect world, it would have happened differently, but as historians we are all bound to recognise that neither we, nor our subjects, are ever perfect.

Notes

1   The long-term historiography of the French Revolution is summarised incisively by Norman Hampson, 'The French Revolution and its Historians', in G. Best (ed.), *The Permanent Revolution: The French Revolution and its Legacy, 1789–1989*, London, 1988, pp. 211–34. Other chapters in this book, notably by Eugen Weber, Douglas Johnson and Eugene Kamenka, discuss similar themes.

2   G. Lefebvre, *The Coming of the French Revolution*, Princeton, 1947, originally published as *Quatre-Vingt Neuf*, Paris, 1939.

3   A classic account of this historiographical shift is given in W. Doyle, *Origins of the French Revolution*, 2nd edn, Oxford, 1988, Part 1, pp. 7–40.

4   Furet's attack on the Marxist/republican model began in F. Furet and D. Richet, *La Révolution française*, 2 vols, Paris, 1965, and was made

systematic in *Interpreting the French Revolution*, Cambridge, 1981 (first published as *Penser la Révolution française*, Paris, 1978).

5   For a very detailed account and commentary on these events and the controversies that accompanied them, see S. L. Kaplan, *Farewell Revolution*, 2 vols, Ithaca, NY, 1995.

6   Amongst the most significant productions was a four-volume series of essays first given as papers to a series of conferences, and published as *The French Revolution and the Creation of Modern Political Culture*. Furet and his American counterpart Keith M. Baker were amongst the editors. See bibliographical essay for full citations.

7   W. Doyle, *The Oxford History of the French Revolution*, Oxford, 1989, is an example of this. Such trends have not gone unchallenged, as the brief survey by Gwynne Lewis, *The French Revolution: Rethinking the Debate*, London, 1993, indicates. For a selection of views emerging in the last few years, see G. Kates (ed.), *The French Revolution: Recent Debates and New Controversies*, London, 1998.

8   See D. Van Kley, *The Religious Origins of the French Revolution: From Calvin to the Civil Constitution, 1560–1791*, New Haven, 1996. R. Chartier, *The Cultural Origins of the French Revolution*, Durham, NC, 1991; J. Popkin, *Revolutionary News: The Press in France 1789–1799*, Durham, NC, 1990.

1

France before Revolution

Every narrative must begin by setting the scene, in this case the 'state of France' by the mid-1780s. Economic structures are a usual, and necessary, place to start. However, such structures, though significant in the broad picture of France by the 1780s, must be seen as part of the intricate web of social, political and financial relationships that covered the country. There is no simple way of describing the relationship in France between taxation, landowning, political privilege, government debt, 'feudal' rights and social standing – the very complexity of the system is its essence. If we begin with the relatively clear data of economic performance, it is only to lay the foundations for a broader description which gives the whole its significance.

France in the eighteenth century was by far Europe's largest economy, and for half a century after the 1720s appeared to be enjoying boom conditions. Agriculture fed a population that grew by over a third, while some industrial sectors saw growth of several hundred per cent in the reigns of Louis XV and XVI (1715–74 and 1774–92). It is now largely agreed by historians that what was once seen as a unique British 'Industrial Revolution' is now better interpreted as a long period of growth stretching back to 1700 and beyond. On the raw figures over this time, France does well – even as late as 1830, French mills used almost 50 per cent more raw cotton than Britain's. However, by that time Britain was set into a pattern of growth that would see cotton consumption by her mills rise ten-fold in only the next twenty years, whereas France less than doubled her figure in the same time.[1]

This comparison has been grounds for some to claim that the disruption caused by the French Revolution decisively retarded the French economy, but France's mid-century success concealed the fact that her economy was far from being on a 'level playing-field' with Britain's, and indeed contained many of the seeds which led to revolutionary upheaval.[2] Whereas Britain's economic and population structures were increasingly driving workers off the land, most of France's population was pinned into semi-subsistence agriculture. In many senses, France did not have 'an economy', but rather a range of almost unconnected regional economies, unable to link up productively.

Simple facts of geography allied to basic social structures to work against further French development. On the long, narrow island of Britain, ports and trading towns lay close to one another, or were linked by canals and new roads, facilitating migration and transport. The vast hexagon of France, several times larger in surface area, had few navigable waterways to its heartlands, and roads, good though some main routes were, could not make up the difference. Its population rose from some 21 million around 1715, adding some 3–4 million in the next four decades, then moving more swiftly towards 28 million from the 1760s to the revolutionary era, but remaining always primarily agricultural. France's governments were no less keen than the British to promote trade, but at the broadest level they were hindered by the simple fact that they were the losers, and Britain the winners, of the great imperial wars of mid-century. The Seven Years War of 1756–63 stripped France of power in North America and ended a promising venture to gain power and trade in India. Even France's successful, but costly, intervention on the side of the American revolutionaries in the 1770s did not break the new Americans' habit of trading with their mother-country – one of the mainstays of British industrial growth.

The basic patterns of French economic performance were deciphered many years ago by Ernest Labrousse. There was strong growth, indicated by prices and output of basic foodstuffs, from around the 1730s to the 1760s, followed by a period of more hesitant growth in the 1770s, and a decline towards critical conditions in the 1780s. Basic textile production saw boom growth in the 1730s and 1740s, and a less dramatic growth for the next twenty years (contrasting with still-strong rises in food prices). The 1770s saw a split between traditional wool and linen industries, which went into sharp decline, and the modernising cotton manufactures, which continued to rise. Silk production also remained strong throughout the century, with its European reputation and luxury market guaranteed by the social system.[3]

Most French industry, as opposed to luxury production and the wide variety of services required by the social elite, was in fact rural in the eighteenth century, though the urban guilds of tradesmen and artisans exercised a weight on legal and cultural norms in excess of their numbers. The very size of France's population, with its need for basic goods, helped support substantial proto-industrial (or 'cottage-industry') rural regions, such as the cotton-weavers of eastern Normandy and Flanders.[4] Production of goods such as ironware was also healthy – seeing iron production more than treble between 1740 and 1789, well exceeding British figures in total. There remained, however, a fragility to such industries, tied as many of them were to older methods, regional markets and limited resources. For example, the charcoal-dependent iron industry was seriously hit by a Spanish ban on charcoal exports in 1769, and the many small Pyrenean mines and forges most directly reliant on this source were soon running down. The cotton factories that had begun to appear in several regions by the 1770s and 1780s, although they were marvels of their time, and equal to anything Britain could yet boast, lacked the impetus to drag the rest of the massive French economy out of a process of complex decline. Similarly overseas trade, through ports such as Nantes, Bordeaux and Marseille, and especially with colonies, had boomed throughout the century, but the benefits were confined almost exclusively to those towns.

Some of the late eighteenth-century decline can be attributed to a classic 'cyclical' crisis: in the 1770s grain prices stopped rising, as supply, expanded to pursue profit when prices rose, began to exceed demand. The large number of tenant farmers had done well in the preceding decades, with crop prices rising and rents lagging behind. They now saw income fall back just as landlords and their agents caught up and began to turn the screw on their rent. Over time, into the 1780s, this middling sector of the agricultural economy became squeezed between falling prices and rising rents. These farmers were critical to markets for basic goods amongst the bulk of the people, both for their own purchasing power and the wages they gave to a large group of labourers. Thus their relative hardship now rebounded onto all the sectors that produced mass-consumption goods – for example the traditional textile industries, which were also suffering a variety of structural problems of their own. The elite of the country was largely blinded to this issue, at the centre at least, where nobles and ministers contemplated with satisfaction the growing rent-rolls from their estates. Nonetheless, wider structural difficulties in the period after 1770 would soon impinge on this group, and we must now pass to considerations of the socio-political system in all its complexity.

The elite of France in the eighteenth century can be described in a variety of ways, but perhaps the most valid general statement is that they were noble. Not in the sense of all descending in unbroken lines from mediaeval chivalry, but certainly in the sense of belonging to, or emulating while aspiring to join, the formal nobility, and sharing a value system that put a premium on such membership. All those who possessed nobility belonged to the 'Second Estate' of the kingdom, in the mediaeval social categories still sometimes used, and were elevated above the vast majority who remained in the 'Third Estate' (the 'First Estate' was the Catholic clergy, but internally this was a microcosm of the wider society, with senior positions reserved for nobles). Formal nobility, if it had not already been gained by one's ancestors, could be gained in a variety of ways in the eighteenth century. Most traditionally, letters-patent of nobility could be granted directly by the king for significant services. This continued to play a major role, although the services were now more likely to be in state finance or overseas trade than on the battlefield. More normal in the eighteenth century, however, was the purchase of ennobling office.

The idea of 'buying' nobility may seem bizarre, but leaving aside questions of prestige (important though they were), the value of nobility to most who sought it was basically financial. The nobility as a social stratum was essentially distinguished by its exemption from many basic taxes and obligations laid on the bulk of the population, such as the main tax on land and wealth, the *taille*. If, under the pressure of threatened change, nobility would be defined in a variety of other ways in the revolutionary era, this does not alter that basic underlying character.

The monarchy of France had begun selling offices – positions in any number of judicial, administrative and supposedly representative bodies – on a large scale in the strained times of the sixteenth century, as a source of income for the state. The system developed under the rulers of the seventeenth century until this 'venality of office' embraced almost all aspects of public life. Some of these 'offices' were little more than financial expedients – that of *secrétaire du roi* (king's secretary) was by the eighteenth century merely a very expensive way of acquiring noble status that was immediately inheritable. Other offices might have to remain in the family, and their functions be carried out, for one or more generations before the status of the owner was securely, and hereditarily, noble. Most, indeed, were not 'ennobling' offices at all, merely serving to elevate the owner slightly from the common herd and to confer various tax-exemptions – a host of minor judicial, administrative and municipal posts offered such benefits. However, once a man paid the price of a king's secretaryship (up to a quarter-million *livres*), his nobility was assured, and the office itself could later be resold to another aspirant by the owner or, more often, his heirs.

Here lay the paradox of venality – although the crown initially sold the offices, and might try to keep a veto over who later came to own them, each office, with its role, more or less significant, in the workings of the state, was a piece of private property, to be passed on more or less as the owner saw fit. As early as the reign of Henry IV (1589–1610), attempts had been made to extract further value from the system, by making office-holders pay an annual fee (the *paulette*) to secure their right to sell or pass on the office, and in the eighteenth century a growing number of such techniques would be devised, but they did not affect the principle. In France, by the eighteenth century, it was a long-standing feature of the social system that both public office and noble status were commodities, belonging to the social elite at large, and not to the central government.[5]

Naturally the government had long found ways of minimising the inconvenience of this – since the times of Richelieu and later Louis XIV, more directly accountable figures such as the famous *intendants* had been used to counter-balance the power of local elites – but it remained a problem.[6] French government by the 1700s rested on the principle of a corporatist society ruled by an absolute monarch. From the sixteenth century on, the crown had clawed its way from being little more than first amongst its equals in the great aristocratic magnates, to a view of itself as a power ordained of God that held the balance over a complex society of privileged groups and institutions. These were the *corps* (literally 'bodies'), each one of which had a distinct 'corporate' legal identity, be they the ancient nobles of a province, the venal-office-holding judges in a local court, the master-carpenters of a town, or indeed the householders of a rural community. This network of privileged *corps* was more significant to the actual workings of society than the older model of three 'Estates', and would remain so until decisions on the eve of 1789 brought the older pattern back into focus.

The crown guaranteed privileges, which might be tax-exemptions, honorific rights, rights to special judicial treatment, or collective self-government, for example. Its ability to do this was central to its hold on power, and had also served it as a further device for raising revenue. Privilege was sold, sometimes in the creation of new offices, institutions and rights, sometimes in the extortion of funds to reconfirm 'historic' privileges of towns, regions or social groups. In its own way this was an aspect of governance itself – for example the creation of artisan guilds, self-regulating bodies of the 'masters' of a trade in a particular town, allowed regulation of production quality and the 'policing' of labour disputes. It also made tax-gathering easier by delegating this function to the guilds. These could then be held collectively responsible, rather than the state having to pursue individual tradesmen. Privileged municipalities and provinces similarly undertook administrative and fiscal duties for the crown. However, the gradual construction of this system on the basis of a continual creation of new privileged groups, without ever thoroughly undermining older ones, in the end only consolidated opposition to more thoroughgoing change. Every privilege was a right to special treatment, literally a 'private law' not easily challenged in the interests of uniformity.

The pinnacle of the system of privileged corporations was represented by the *parlements*, a network of royal courts of appeal, also known as 'sovereign courts', whose existence was claimed by some to be as old as the monarchy itself. Each *parlement* was composed of a large body of judges, whose positions were ennobling

14

venal offices of the classic type, although unlike for example the *secrétaires du roi*, these *parlementaires* had serious duties to perform. By the beginning of the eighteenth century the *parlementaires* were amongst the wealthiest and most powerful groups in France, providing many of the crown's leading ministers. Historically the older nobility, that of military service (the 'sword' or *noblesse d'épée*), had looked down on the nobility of civilian service (the *noblesse de robe*, from the gowns or robes worn as a mark of office). However, after the reign of Louis XIV the social and political importance of the latter could no longer be disputed, and at the higher levels they were widely intermarried with the former.[7]

The *parlements* participated in the process of law-making, as guardians of the distinct law codes of the various regions of France (which in some cases, with the usual complexity, had different boundaries to those of the courts' actual jurisdictions). Each new law could only take effect officially after its registration by the various *parlements*, but as early as the mid-seventeenth century the *parlementaires* had made more out of this process than a mere formality, thanks to their right of 'remonstrance'. Theoretically a commentary on the legal implications of each act, this had become in extreme circumstances the claim to be able to protest the principle of some proposed legislation, and to refuse to register it.

A central concern of the *parlements* through the eighteenth century was with religious disputes, and with opposition to the royal attempts to suppress the variety of Catholic thought known as Jansenism. According to David Bell, this was 'probably the most divisive political issue of Louis XV's reign', with substantial implications for 'the nature of political sovereignty'.[8] It led to severe political turmoil, for example in the 1730s and mid-1750s, with *parlements*' judges being exiled to small towns in bids to force their obedience, while the judges claimed the right to defend their interpretation of France's relationship with Catholicism, and more broadly, of its constitution. Through struggles like these, the *parlements* gained the reputation of defenders of the nation against royal despotism – indeed, it was *parlementaire* rhetoric that helped to bring concepts like 'the nation' into public discourse. However, by the 1770s the feud between crown and *parlements* had become even more significant.

There is no space here to contemplate the many-faceted impact of the Enlightenment on French life overall, although aspects of it will emerge later.[9] What is worth noting here is that the appeal to 'reason' that underlay enlightened discourse cut across the crown/*parlement* conflict in new and dangerous ways. By the end of the 1760s, ministers were taking office who regarded the *parlements'* opposition as the obstruction of privileged groups, holding up the crown's endeavour to act in the public interest. After years of struggle, the Gordian knot was sliced in 1771 with a 'coup' organised by the chancellor, Maupeou. The *parlements* were abolished, their members sent into rural exile, and a new system of more compliant appeal courts constructed. Some advanced thinkers, such as Voltaire and a group of radical barristers, approved of this assault on an institution that relied on tradition for its legitimacy (and which regularly condemned the works of enlightened authors). Ironically, however, most observers chose to view the coup as royal despotism, and the *parlementaires* as defenders of liberty and free speech.[10] The developing habit of appealing to 'public opinion' was firmly entrenched in public life through this controversy in a blizzard of pamphlets.

Hostility to the coup remained such that the new king, Louis XVI, thought it a wise and conciliatory move to reinstate the *parlements* when he mounted the throne in 1774. However, far from accepting this gesture, the *parlementaires* would prove intransigently opposed to royal policy, when in the 1780s a further wave of reform began to appear necessary. This new sign of royal difficulties would be exploited in a bid to alter the balance of the constitution further in the direction of the views, and arguably the privileged interest groups, that the *parlementaires* represented.

As Louis XVI was restoring the *parlements*, another experiment was under way to reduce privilege and regulation. The new finance minister Turgot, an experienced local *intendant*, was a follower of the branch of economic thought known as physiocracy, an early variant of free-market economics. In a bid to revitalise French agriculture and industry, Turgot abolished the system of guilds that regulated urban production, and freed the trade in grain from the maze of police regulations that governed it. The consequences of this are instructive for an understanding of social thought and social relations at the time.

Guilds and grain regulation were both aspects of the wide scope of 'police' in the eighteenth century. 'Police' meant more than just law and order – it implied a whole system of social administration (for example, the police of Paris had charge of street-sweeping and the regulation of wet-nursing, among many other things). 'Police' rested on the idea that the lower orders were fundamentally in need of management, that for example it was simply not safe to allow anyone who wished to set up in business to do so. When Turgot abolished the guilds some of the first reactions gave reason to believe this – workers were reported as effectively running riot, and social insubordination was supposedly widespread. The police of Paris, on their own initiative, began to obstruct the process of registration of new businesses that Turgot had decreed, demanding that applicants prove themselves moral and solvent before obtaining a licence. Whether workers were actually so riotous is questionable, but the assumption that they were helped to sabotage the reforms. The guilds themselves had appealed vigorously against their dissolution, using the classic 'corporatist' argument that only such collective groups gave individuals a social identity, and preserved stability and order.[11]

The experience of the liberation of the grain trade was even more disastrous. Its main visible consequence was a series of riots and seizures of food by the population of the Parisian region in 1775, extensive enough to earn the title of 'Flour War'. Such disorder arose from the general belief in what was known as the 'Famine Pact' (*pacte de famine*). From common townsfolk and peasants to police authorities, and indeed government ministers, the view was shared that any disruption to the supply of grain and flour was artificial, and destined to profit some interest group at the expense of public hunger. Only police regulation appeased the public mind, and in its absence crowds could substitute *taxation populaire* – seizing grain and offering only what they thought a 'just price' for it. Ironically efforts to alleviate genuine shortage by grain shipments and external purchases could be swept up in this general alarm and used as more evidence of plot. Turgot himself succumbed to this view – if the population was opposing the beneficial results of freeing the grain trade, it had to be because of agitation and bribery by his political rivals. Nonetheless, such was the disorder that the experiment had to stop, as did Turgot's brief ministerial career.[12]

Police of the grain trade was reinstated, as were the guilds, in 1775–6. The latter, however, took on a new form reflecting further social changes underlying the political landscape. Within the guild structure, journeymen – those who had passed an apprenticeship but not progressed to the status of master – had increasingly become a marginalised and wage-dependent group. This decline had both a socio-economic and a legal/cultural aspect. Socio-economically, the volume of work in the guild industries, which included all the traditional wood, metal and leather-working sectors, as well as urban construction, clothing production, goldsmithing, printing and other luxury trades, was increasing faster than guilds were prepared to accommodate by increases in the numbers of masters. Thus, though new apprentices were taken on to cope with demand, the traditional route from apprentice to master via several years as a journeyman was increasingly becoming blocked at the journeyman stage. This had been a long-term process, but the latter decades of the eighteenth century saw further erosion of journeymen's status, as workers began to be taken on in some trades without passing an apprenticeship – these were *alloués*, or 'hired men'. Guilds were increasingly oligarchies who closed ranks against newcomers, either charging extortionate fees for entry to mastership, or reserving available places for relatives of existing masters.[13]

Alongside this went a progressive wearing-down of the legal status of the journeymen. As we have seen, courts such as the *parlements* played a crucial role in politics, and this reflected the pivotal position of legal disputes in eighteenth-century France. As the monarchy had created more and more privileged bodies, they came increasingly into conflict, and as 'privilege' was a legal status, it could be challenged or defended in a court of law. Much of the business and the income of the *parlements* derived from disputes amongst guilds or other privileged bodies about their respective entitlements (this was one reason, it might be argued, that the *parlements* were such ardent defenders of privilege). Journeymen in many guilds had succeeded in previous decades in having courts accept that they had a legal collective identity, derived from their mention in the legally binding statutes of the guilds. Thus they were entitled to sue for 'customary' conditions and payments to be maintained. However, the latter decades of the century saw the erosion of this right, as a stricter notion of employment, and of a 'master–servant' relationship, came to prevail in legal opinions over trade disputes. To add to this, the authorities took the opportunity of the abolition and reinstatement of the guilds in the 1770s to render them more uniform, and to give more emphasis to their social-control aspects. In Paris, for example, forty-four 'new' guilds were reconstituted from over 100 old ones, with statutes all deriving from police decrees, thus losing still more of their 'traditional' status. By the early 1780s, workers were being ordered to register themselves with guilds, and to carry a type of 'pass-book' without which they could not obtain legitimate employment.[14]

The guild industries were one area where the weight of the past might be said to be yielding to the impetus of supposedly progressive, economically liberal thought, despite the workers' chagrin. In the rural environment, however, the reign of Louis XVI seemed to mark a return of the past with a vengeance. A central feature to remember about France's population is the extent to which it was rural and agricultural – only perhaps a million lived in large cities, two million more in other cities and larger towns. This left somewhere over 24 million in the countryside by the 1780s, in villages, or small towns that were themselves embedded in the rural economy.[15] This population was under stress from several directions. The poorer peasantry, who neither owned nor rented enough land to be self-sufficient, had to work for wages to support themselves (either on the land or in proto-industry, and often both). This group may have amounted to over half the rural population, and had seen the price of basic foodstuffs outstrip wages substantially over the previous decades. Tenant farmers, as we have seen, were caught in a 'scissors' of poor crop prices and rising rents. Even those fortunate enough to own their own farms (which might actually be considerably smaller than a prosperous tenant's lands) could not escape the burdens that the wider social system put on the agricultural population.

One such burden was an arbitrary and highly variable taxation system, but what produced even more resentment was the 'feudal' or 'seigneurial' system. Unlike Britain, where capitalist property relations were essentially dominant by the seventeenth century, if not before, France retained many echoes of the mediaeval era of serfdom in its agricultural relations. Peasants were not, except in a few areas, legally bound to the land, but they had to pay a wide variety of 'feudal dues' to whoever was the seigneur – the 'feudal lord' – of their lands. Such dues generally included an element of quit-rent, or *cens* (on top of what rent may have been due to a 'landlord' in the modern sense), as well as a portion of the harvest, in cash or in kind (the *champart*). Many seigneurs had the right of monopoly over milling grain and communal baking-ovens – peasants being obliged to pay for the use of these *banalités*. Various other dues might be collected at certain times, such as on the sale or inheritance of lands (*lods et ventes*). The seigneur might have other rights, such as to plant and harvest trees for wood on common land, or to subdivide and acquire sections of former common land (*triage*).

Many customary rights in the rural economy were more or less reciprocal – such as that of *vaine pâture*, the putting of livestock to graze on commons and fallows, or on fields after the harvest – but seigneurs could abuse such rights in their own favour. They also had a swathe of other rights, notably the exclusive right to breed and hunt game, including rabbits and pigeons, which consumed crops at farmers' expense. To guard their rights, seigneurs also had legal jurisdiction over offences concerning them, thus making the seigneur, or more often his local agent, judge and jury in his own favour.[16] The seigneurial court system is another example of the massive complexity of eighteenth-century French institutions. In Brittany alone in 1769, there were some 3,900 seigneurial tribunals, handling 90 per cent of all litigation. Although the system was in decline, 2,500 of these Breton courts were still operating in 1789. The city of Le Mans in Normandy, with some 2,000 households, fell under the jurisdiction of twenty-nine separate seigneurial tribunals. So intricate was this legal web that even modern estimates of the numbers of courts vary widely – from 20,000 to 80,000.[17]

Looked at as a whole, the seigneurial system reveals its origins in the notion of the 'lord of the manor', who had certain privileges in return for dispensing justice and protection to 'his' peasants. However, by the eighteenth century, this situation was a distant memory. There were many rural nobles who maintained the superficial appearance of being local leaders (in the face of growing resentment), but the royal courts had long taken over most significant judicial powers except over 'feudal' issues. Political power had fled far away, and the seigneurial system was seen by most as essentially a source of revenue. This was all the more so as, like the status of nobility itself, seigneurial rights had become a commodity to be bought and sold. Wealthy absentee aristocrats accumulated these *seigneuries* as secure investments, as too did upwardly mobile bourgeois, who also thus gained the ability to display all the outward signs of noble status, half the battle in actually becoming noble. One who owned a *seigneurie* was able to follow his family name with 'de' and the name of the estate. Such was the social cachet of this label that many, including figures who would be revolutionary heroes, adopted it in the 1770s and 1780s as a piece of social bluff: Maximilien de Robespierre, Georges d'Anton, J.-P. Brissot de Warville.

By the 1780s the system of seigneurial rights was widely perceived by those it weighed upon, however, as rotten to the core. In some areas peasants were already engaged in long-term campaigns of defiance of game laws and resistance to other exactions. In other areas the tendency of seigneurs to abuse their rights over livestock and timber production, producing these valuable commodities at the expense of the peasants' foodstuffs, was becoming an ongoing scandal. In the province of Burgundy, peasants experienced a particularly wide range of burdens. These included for example the obligation to pay for the upkeep of the seigneur's château – dating from when it provided a refuge in troubled times, long past by the late eighteenth century. Institutional changes, such as the growth of royal administration, aided the development of a sense of autonomy at village level, and linked up with a growing army of lawyers eager for fees, to facilitate peasant legal challenges to seigneurial exactions in the later eighteenth century. In practically every case, such challenges failed in the courts, but the fact that they were made in the first place illustrates the changing social climate in the countryside. The failure of seigneurialism to acknowledge this added to the odium in which it was increasingly held.[18]

Peasant resistance to these exactions was echoed, in some cases more strongly, by resistance to royal taxation. Taxes were collected in a bewildering variety of forms across France. A few relatively recent introductions, such as the *capitation* and the *vingtième* (both forms of property tax), were supposedly levied at rates proportional to wealth for all, but other taxes were subject to wide regional variations. The main long-standing direct tax was the *taille*, which in northern France was levied on an ongoing (and often arbitrary) assessment of personal wealth, but in the south was calculated on a register of land values. In some areas these registers had not been updated since the sixteenth century. Moreover, taxes such as the *taille* were generally *solidaire* – calculated on a communal basis. This left the unpleasant task of deciding who would pay what to groups selected from amongst the local householders, who had to pay themselves if some refused. What this communal system also meant was that if some wealthier individuals bought into office or nobility, acquiring the tax-exemption so central to that status, their often substantial share of payments went back into the communal 'pot' to be settled on all the unfortunate remaining commoners.

Further complexities derived from the patchwork constitutional status of the kingdom. Some outlying areas, including substantial provinces such as Brittany, Languedoc and Provence, continued to have the 'Estates' they had possessed in the mediaeval period – representative assemblies, or in some cases small groups, of the privileged, who administered the area with relative autonomy. In such areas, grouped under the general label of *pays d'états*, taxation demands tended to be settled on a province-wide basis, with the local Estates then charged with obtaining the money by whatever means appropriate. In the other parts of France, generally called *pays d'élection*, the agents of central government, *intendants* and their deputies, took their influence down to a much lower level. Sometimes this disparity resulted in a better deal for inhabitants of the outlying *pays d'états* – Brittany, for example, was extremely under-taxed compared with a notional average region, thanks to privileges which dated back to its treaty of union with France in the sixteenth century. Some areas administered by the Estates of Languedoc received a heavier burden than most, however. The state's officials viewed Languedoc as a well-administered province, whose tax burden would be carefully shared out, and could thus justifiably be high. In fact the assessments were based on out-of-date land registers, ignoring substantial shifts in population and economic structure, and thus resulting in widespread complaints of unfairness, and building resentment. Nevertheless, even this burden was little compared to the neighbouring *pays d'élection* of Guyenne, where peasants might pay four times as much tax as in Brittany. Even to view the complications at this level is to introduce massive over-simplifications, however. There was rarely an 'average peasant' whose tax-liability can be extrapolated to cover a whole region, and it might well be claimed that almost every village, certainly every town, in France had some peculiarity about its tax-payments or its privileged status.[19]

It is in this sense that one can agree with William Doyle that 'privilege was universal' in eighteenth-century France, but as we have already seen, the existence of privilege for most might offer a small defence against life's harshness, but it was more usually an addition to an already difficult existence. Privilege, for the relatively unprivileged majority, was a burden to be borne, a possession of others gained not by ancient lineage, valour in battle or religious service, but by wealth alone. As Alexis de Tocqueville remarked some 150 years ago, 'the barrier which separated the nobility from the other classes, though easily surmounted, was always conspicuous, and known by outward and odious marks'. Thus anyone who made the transition 'was separated from his former associates by privileges which were onerous and humiliating for them'.[20]

In this environment, it appears that the widespread impression by the 1780s was that both 'feudalism' and increasingly rapacious tax-gathering were steadily encroaching on the livelihoods of the peasantry. The figures to prove or disprove this empirically are hard to come by, particularly in the matter of taxation. Seigneurial exactions, however, do seem to have been increasing. Although this has been seen by previous generations of historians as part of a 'feudal reaction', an assault by the nobility on rising social groups that helped precipitate the Revolution, it can also be seen as a consequence of the economic situation. Seigneurs' reinforcement of their grazing and wood-planting rights were responses to buoyant livestock and timber prices at a time when other crop prices were stagnant. The revision of the registers of feudal dues (the *terriers*), widely hated by rural communities as an intrusive and exploitative process, was a feature of the accelerated market in *seigneuries*, revisions being required each time one changed hands. A concern to maximise yields from such investments set a whole breed of lawyer, the *feudiste*, loose on the countryside to argue for the increase of existing dues, and indeed the fabrication of new ones.

One of the paradoxes of the idea of the 'feudal', or more broadly 'aristocratic reaction' is that the activity just mentioned is consistent with a more capitalist market in feudal rights as investments. Historians up to the 1970s tended to argue that the 'reaction' was anti-capitalist and anti-bourgeois – indeed that a prime element was the restriction of access to nobility in the dying years of the old order. It was this, supposedly, that helped aggravate social tensions to the point of revolution. However, most evidence, including some only very recently discovered, now points to a healthy ongoing market for feudal rights, and more significantly ennobling office, right up to the mid-1780s at least, and possibly into the 'pre-revolution' of 1787–8.[21] We might suggest as an interim conclusion that there was a 'feudal reaction', as perceived by its peasant victims, which was actually a consequence of the commodification or 'bourgeoisification' of feudalism. Feudal dues were defined as an important element of private property by the 'bourgeois' revolutionaries of 1789, as we shall see.

Meanwhile, as our picture of the state of France in the 1780s develops, we must finally turn to the political system, or more precisely to the convoluted patterns of the administration of France, to see what was going wrong in the reign of Louis XVI.[22] Some aspects have already been touched on above – the long-term creation of ever-more competing layers of jurisdiction, the placing of such jurisdiction in the hands of those whose property it became, and the wide variations in administrative structure, such as the *pays d'états/d'élection* split and the different modes of *taille* assessment. In terms of impact on the population and the economy, it was the systems of customs and taxation that were most onerous, and also most irrational. To take the famous example of the salt tax, the *gabelle*, there were six major possible statuses that regions might have with regard to this tax, from some outlying or salt-producing areas that were effectively exempt or undertaxed, to the *pays de grande gabelle* (most of north-central and northern France) where not only was salt very heavily taxed, but was a state monopoly. Inhabitants were obliged to pay tax on a certain quota of salt annually, regardless of their actual usage. The paramilitary agents who enforced this, the *gabelous*, were so detested that their name lingers in modern French for an intrusive state agent.[23]

The point to be added to this description is that the 'state monopoly' on salt had in fact been leased (or 'farmed out') to agents of major financiers, as had, for example, the *cinq grosses fermes* ('five great farms'), the right to collect a variety of indirect taxes and dues across almost all the northern half of France. Such arrangements in various forms were long-standing – their abuse had formed part of the crisis in French finances in the mid-seventeenth century – but could still foment resentment. Although the state benefited by receiving revenues in advance when it sold the leases, the population suffered as the agents and financiers profited from whatever they could collect over and above the state's expectations.

Many of the financiers (or *fermiers-généraux*) were directly or indirectly connected to the world of the Court and the royal ministers – few others could raise the money or connections to secure such deals – which made the iniquity of profit from the state's needs seem all the greater. A whole series of armed quasi-official forces thus battened on the French population, taxing them when they brought goods into or out of cities, travelled certain roads, purchased certain items, or tried to move goods long distances cross-country. For some of the population, especially in areas which bordered zones of different taxation, this system provided a living through smuggling, but this meant an even more ardent battle with the customs-agents. Such agents burdened the population more indirectly too, as their posts were minor positions in the network of privileged office. They were thus exempted from the taxes they collected, as well as from the *taille*, reducing still further the paying population and raising the individual assessments on the payers.

The essential problem for the state, however, was that even such expedients as this leasing of revenues simply did not bring in enough to fund its expenditure. With the most wealthy and powerful individuals and institutions (notably the Catholic Church) exempt from most taxes, and with more and more of the better-off buying into such privileges, the state had little choice but to burden the poor. These burdens were necessary as France strove to retain its place as both a major continental power and a rival to Britain for world mercantile empire, but were increasingly also insufficient to the contest. Even in years of peace, the long-term rise in expenditure was enormous – almost three-and-a-half times from the 1720s to the 1780s, including a 648 per cent rise in naval expenditure and a 188 per cent increase in overall War Ministry funds. In times of war – 1740–48, 1756–63, 1778–83 – money flowed through the state's hands like water, increasingly provided by borrowing on an enormous scale.

Although the Swiss-born finance minister Jacques Necker thought it wise at the time to fund French intervention in the American War of Independence through loans rather than socially disruptive further taxation, by the mid-1780s the negative consequences of this were becoming clear. Throughout the century repayments on existing debts had run at between a quarter and a third of expenditure in peacetime. By 1775 this had already pushed the crown's accounts into a deficit of some 35 million *livres*. By the later 1780s, tax-receipts for several years ahead had already been signed away to pay back loans, which themselves had been needed to clear old debts. In 1788 the deficit was over 160 million *livres*, and debt repayment alone accounted for 41 per cent of spending – 261 million *livres*. Given that overall income in 1788 was only some 471.6 million *livres*, the size of the public-finance problem becomes evident.

By 1788, of course, the nature of the problem was already evident to anyone who chose to take an interest, as by then the ministers of the crown were locked in battle with the privileged classes over the course to take away from the abyss of bankruptcy. No one can argue that it was not this basic conflict over state finance that precipitated the French Revolution. We have seen, however, the structural problems which underlay and added to these difficulties, and we must now go on to explore the complex ways in which cultural and intellectual developments of the preceding decades had combined by the late 1780s. Out of this situation came the beliefs and actions that ensured that the collapse of state finances would rapidly become the end of an entire social and political structure.

Notes

1 Statistics are given in C. Cook and J. Stevenson (eds), *The Longman Handbook of Modern European History, 1763–1991*, 2nd edn, London, 1992, p. 248. For an incisive introduction to the 'long-term' interpretations of industrial growth, see P. Hudson, *The Industrial*

Revolution, London, 1992.

2 For a recent brief overview, see L. M. Cullen, 'History, Economic Crises, and Revolution: Understanding Eighteenth-Century France', *Economic History Review*, 46, 1993, pp. 635–57. The many works of François Crouzet should be turned to by those interested in pursuing the economic dimension of eighteenth-century French history further.

3 Labrousse's works have never been translated into English: C.-E. Labrousse, *Esquisse du mouvement des prix et des revenus en France au XVIIIe siècle*, 2 vols, Paris, 1933, reprinted 1984, and *La crise de l'économie française à la fin de l'ancien régime et au début de la Révolution*, Paris, 1944, 2nd edn, 1990. See P. M. Jones, *Reform and Revolution in France: The Politics of Transition, 1774–1791*, Cambridge, 1995, chapter 3, on which much of the economic analysis of this chapter draws.

4 On the concept and patterns of proto-industrialisation, see S. C. Ogilvie and M. Cerman (eds), *European Proto-Industrialization*, Cambridge, 1996. Chapter 4 is specific to France.

5 W. Doyle has just produced a major new study of this phenomenon – *Venality: The Sale of Offices in Eighteenth-Century France*, Oxford, 1996. Technically, the king could always revoke any privileges granted, but to do so would have fatally alienated the very elites on which the state depended to run the country.

6 For a definition of the *intendants* – basically high-ranking regional administrators who did not own their offices, and thus were more reliable – see J. B. Collins, *The State in Early Modern France*, Cambridge, 1995, pp. 53–4, and chapters 1 and 3 generally.

7 The classic study on this remains F. L. Ford, *Robe and Sword: The Regrouping of the French Aristocracy after Louis XIV*, Cambridge, MA, 1953.

8 D. A. Bell, *Lawyers and Citizens: The Making of a Political Elite in Old Regime France*, Oxford, 1994, p. 68.

9 An excellent introductory overview is given by D. Outram, *The Enlightenment*, Cambridge, 1995. This is particularly valuable as it focuses on the social and cultural context of Enlightenment, rather than just 'great thinkers'.

10 See Bell, *Lawyers and Citizens*, pp. 138–48.

11 See S. L. Kaplan, 'Social Classification and Representation in the Corporate World of Eighteenth-Century France: Turgot's "Carnival"', in S. L. Kaplan and C. J. Koepp (eds), *Work in France: Representations, Meaning, Organization and Practice*, Ithaca, NY, 1986, pp. 176–228.

12 See S. L. Kaplan, *The Famine Plot Persuasion in Eighteenth-Century France*, Philadelphia, 1982. See also the work of C. A. Bouton, 'Gendered Behaviour in Subsistence Riots: The French Flour War of 1775', *Journal of Social History*, 23, 1990, pp. 735–54.

13 See M. Sonenscher, *Work and Wages: Natural Law, Politics and the Eighteenth-Century French Trades*, Cambridge, 1989.

14 M. Sonenscher, 'Journeymen, the Courts and the French Trades, 1781–1791', *Past and Present*, 114, 1987, pp. 77–109.

15 Jones, *Reform and Revolution*, pp. 50–7, gives a quantitative breakdown of late Old Regime French society, as far as such figures can be estimated.

16 The situation is explored by P. M. Jones, *The Peasantry in the French Revolution*, Cambridge, 1988, pp. 42–59. Note that the names of individual feudal dues varied widely across the country, along with their level of imposition.

17 See S. G. Reinhardt, *Justice in the Sarladais, 1770–1790*, Baton Rouge, 1991, pp. 59ff., for an overview.

18 H. Root, 'Challenging the Seigneurie: Community and Contention on the Eve of the French Revolution', *Journal of Modern History*, 57, 1985, pp. 652–81. The longer-term context of these developments is explored in *Peasants and King in Burgundy: Agrarian Foundations of French Absolutism*, Berkeley, 1987, which takes the story from Louis XIV into the French Revolution.

19 See Jones, *Peasantry*, pp. 34–41.

20 A. de Tocqueville, *The Ancien Régime*, Everyman edn, trans. J. Bonner, London, 1988, p. 71. Doyle's comment is in his *Origins of the French Revolution*, 2nd edn, Oxford, 1988, p. 117.

21 A short piece by M. P. Fitzsimmons, 'New Light on the Aristocratic Reaction in France', *French History*, 10, 1996, pp. 418–31, introduces important new evidence, and discusses the recent historiography of this question.

22 I distinguish administration from 'politics', as it has recently been eloquently argued that the politics of Louis XVI's ministries occurred in a very particular realm where considerations of social structure such as I have been discussing did not intrude to any significant degree – see J. Hardman, *French Politics, 1774–1789*, Harlow, 1995.

23 The map on p. 231 of C. Jones, *The Longman Companion to the French Revolution*, London, 1988, illustrates the regions of the *gabelle*, and various other, inconsistent, customs boundaries. Compare with the maps on pp. 207–9 to see the overlap of numerous jurisdictions to which the French were subject.

2

Reform and politicisation before 1789

By the time that the enormous financial deficit and declining credit-rating of the French state made reform essential in the mid-1780s, it had long been recognised in government circles that reform was in any case desirable. The revolutionaries were to tag all the pre-revolutionary order as the 'Old Regime' (*ancien régime*), but for many years it had not been a solid 'regime', in the sense of a body of doctrine, institutions and practices consistently believed-in by its members. James Collins has recently argued that the Old Regime in this sense was effectively dead from the 1750s onwards.[1] It is certainly the case that from the mid-1760s government persisted in attempting reforms at the highest level. The Maupeou coup of 1771 has already been mentioned, but even before then attempts had been made in the 1760s to alter significant aspects of the socio-political system, for example briefly freeing the grain trade, attacking municipal privileged office-holding, and attempting to stabilise the finances of the state with austerity measures.

Turgot's renewed assault in the new reign on the grain trade and the guilds was part of a broader agenda of radical reform, albeit that 'reform' essentially meant a more efficient use of resources in the interests of the state. One other aspect of this was a bid to end the *corvée*, a system of forced labour for road maintenance that had grown up in the first half of the century. Turgot wished to convert this from a personal obligation placed on the non-privileged to a tax on landowners, including the privileged. This was seen by *parlementaires*, and their sympathisers within

29

the Court and government, as foreshadowing a general end to privilege and the 'ancient constitution' of France, bringing about the rule of 'royal despotism'. Their alarm was reinforced by the knowledge in elite circles that plans to cut back on tax-farms and abolish internal customs (both areas where much of the elite's funds were invested) were also in the making. The strong body of opinion that opposed royal power in the name of ancient rights rallied to defeat Turgot's plans and to remove immediate reform from the agenda of government.

The pressure of financial hardship ensured, however, that it returned again in the late 1770s under Necker, who had ambitious plans to bypass the traditional channels of resistance to innovation by setting up Provincial Assemblies. These would have given the state access to the landowning classes directly through non-venal representative bodies, which could have been manoeuvred into fundamental taxation reforms. Necker, however, demonstrated the tensions and uncertainties within the royal reform agenda in 1781, helping to engineer his own downfall by publishing the royal accounts (in his *compte rendu au roi*). This overstepped the bounds of propriety when government was still essentially conceived of as the 'king's secret'. The appeal to 'public opinion' implicit in such a publication was not yet compatible with serving the king, even if the intention was to give evidence of the sound state of the finances and to promote the government's agenda. Necker's political enemies seized on this imprudence to discredit him. When Necker went, only two pilot Provincial Assemblies had been set up, and though these continued to function up to the Revolution, the impetus behind them was lost.

Recognition of these reform endeavours is nothing new – in the mid-nineteenth century Tocqueville highlighted them as part of his thesis that the Revolution fell into a longer process of state-formation and bureaucratic centralisation. They have been given new prominence in recent writing, however, as historians have debated how French society responded to change from above, and how tensions within society and politics became drawn out into outright conflict.[2]

A key theme is the development of 'public opinion'. This concept became increasingly prominent in French political thinking from mid-century, losing earlier connotations of disorder, dispute

and variability, and acquiring the characteristics – constancy, neu-
trality, rationality – of a 'tribunal' that was competent to judge
government actions and other public affairs. It is a concept, however, which is hard to pin down to real people. In part this is a
reflection of the way it was used by writers and thinkers at the
time. To them, 'public opinion' was amorphous and unlocatable,
and that was its important quality in a society otherwise all too
divided by particularities.[3] Necker's publication of accounts in
1781 may have been aimed at a narrower 'opinion' centred
around the intellectuals and financiers of the capital, but the general usage of the term was already showing a broader aspect. In
this can be seen the emergence of a new kind of 'public sphere',
which would profoundly challenge the old order.

The idea of *bürgerliche öffentlichkeit* (which can be translated as
'bourgeois' or 'civic public sphere') emerged in 1962 from the
German thinker Jürgen Habermas. His work concerned the long-
term construction of 'bourgeois society' in western Europe, on
the basis of a move away from the publicity of display that
marked the aristocratic Court culture (and excluded its 'spectators' from participation). By the eighteenth century, he argued, a
new 'public' existed, based around essentially middle-class
groups. This public derived its judgements from its experience of
private life, engagement with literature and other 'cultural'
media, and the conduct of business; and carried over private values into new political situations. These ideas have attracted considerable attention recently, especially following their forceful
reinterpretation by Joan Landes to record the essential masculinity of the 'public sphere' created through the French Revolution,
and its longer-term consequences for European womankind.[4]

What is quite clear is that many groups within the literate
classes of French society were thinking in new ways by the latter
decades of the eighteenth century. Here we can say with some
certainty that the Enlightenment, in a broad sense, was having an
impact, and indeed had arguably moved France towards Revolution. The first thing to say in qualification of that, however, is that
in no sense was there clearly a 'revolutionary class' or 'revolutionary ideology' emerging in the France of the 1780s. Enlightened
discussion, government propaganda and elite resistances all fed
off each other in complex ways, even as they made many people
aware of political issues. In the end it was this confusion of

messages that precipitated the collapse of the Old Regime's legitimacy, far more than any group's intentions.[5]

This confusion can be seen in the way various elites, both bourgeois and privileged corporations, responded to political conflicts in Lille during this period. In their declarations and disputes there was a clear adoption of new rhetorics – of equality, justice, nationhood – and a modification of an older language of 'rights' which brought it more in line with these others. What is most noticeable, however, is the blind self-interest with which such rhetorics were deployed. With particular regard to rhetorics of equality, groups amongst the administrative and judicial hierarchies were happy to deploy such arguments against their 'superiors', while simultaneously resisting the efforts of their 'inferiors' to use the same arguments against them. Thus their own claims undermined their position, while their refusal to recognise this built up hostility for the future.[6]

While this illustrates the use of new rhetorics within the administrative structure, the rewriting of languages of wider public debate also took place through the legal system, through what have been labelled *causes célèbres*. In these court cases, the privilege of publishing legal briefs without censorship allowed lawyers to appeal to public opinion on behalf of their clients. Individual cases may or may not have involved important personages, but were argued to involve issues of public morality, and sometimes social status, that demanded public attention. Legal *mémoires* that often took the form of lengthy first-person sentimental narratives, echoing the forms of contemporary novels, were printed in runs of up to 10,000, and were widely sought-after and commented on. After the turmoil within the legal profession around the time of the Maupeou coup, lawyers and men of letters were growing increasingly close. Some 10 per cent of practising barristers listed around 1770 were authors on other subjects, lawyers and Enlightenment *philosophes* collaborated on sensational cases, and even legal textbooks recommended sentiment rather than argument as the way to win a case. Moreover, the contradictions shown by the elites of Lille also existed in the practices of the barristers: in disputes amongst them after the Maupeou episode, the tactics of the leadership were 'essentially democratic', but in the pursuit of 'rigid, sectarian and inegalitarian' political goals. At the same time, those who opposed the leadership, and who were coming to oppose many of the Old Regime's institutions, could use all the passion stirred by the *causes célèbres* to publicise their views.[7]

The eighteenth century, and particularly its later decades, saw a growth in official and unofficial sites for the formation of the kind of 'public opinion' envisaged by the rhetorical use of the term. The trend had begun in the late 1600s with the creation of various state-sponsored Academies – learned societies designed to bring together thinkers, with an underlying slant towards a state-centred interpretation of public utility. It was, for example, the essay competitions of the Academy of Dijon in the mid-1750s that gave Jean-Jacques Rousseau his first fame. However, the Academies came over time to seem increasingly conservative, grouping those with high status in the local area, often with the tacit or open supervision of *intendants*, and shying away from the more controversial fringes of enlightened thought. At the opposite end of the organisational spectrum was the *salon*, a gathering of men for discussion in the company of a hostess in her home. This practice had migrated from the Court to Parisian high society since the 1600s, and provided a forum for some of the leading Enlightenment thinkers to air their views to friends and associates. The doings of leading salons were commented on widely, and some were powerhouses of literary and philosophical talent, but they were an institution for those within a cultural elite, rather than a means of widening the circles of publicity.[8]

Potentially more radical, and accused by many over the last 200 years of fomenting the Revolution, were the Masonic lodges. Freemasonry entered Europe from Britain in the 1730s, bringing with it an air of mystery, insisting upon secret oaths and complex ceremonies for the initiation of members, and carrying a commitment to the equality of all Masons at the heart of its doctrine. It spread like a rash through French cultured society, drawing in nobles, judges, clerics (though the Church formally opposed it), military officers, lawyers, merchants, and anyone else who might meet the social standards of existing members. At its head as Grand Master by the eve of the Revolution stood the king's cousin, Philippe, duc d'Orléans. His later dabbling in liberalism and radicalism would confirm for some the thesis of Freemasonry as the conspiratorial origin of social and religious collapse. More serious recent scholarship, however, paints a more limited picture

33

of the lodges' influence.

Masonic gatherings were places of sociability, and doubtless assisted in the enhanced circulation of urban society that was a general feature of the late eighteenth century. They were also, however, deeply hierarchical organisations, and far from immune to social snobbery. In the early 1770s a newly centralised Grand Lodge tried to enforce its authority nationwide, and even those it was trying to discipline agreed that 'bourgeois of the lowest state, to artisans, workers, menial workers, even domestics [servants] had defiled our mysteries'.[9] There is clear evidence of social critique coming from Masonic lodges, but usually expressed as concern for the poor rather than attacks on the social order – in the form for example of campaigns to improve charitable giving. By the late 1780s speculation was taking place on the model that Masonic organisation might offer for a regenerated state, but by that stage such thinking had ceased to be unusual.

One area where the 'enlightened public' might conceivably have produced more radical outcomes is in the *sociétés de pensée* – 'philosophical societies', or more prosaically reading clubs, which also spread far and wide across France before 1789. These were far more spontaneous and autonomous groups than Academies or lodges, and might indeed represent no more than the more literate and leisured members of a small-town elite meeting in a café and subscribing to one or more newspapers.[10] As such, they were a concrete symbol of the explosion of printed matter occurring in the latter half of the century, and of the desire of substantial sections of the educated population to engage with it. Many went further, and might run their own literary competitions and discussions on 'enlightened' topics, possibly touching on reform. Maximilien Robespierre, barrister, future politician and architect of the Terror, was a member of such a group in his home town of Arras, and between legal briefs defending various local underdogs, wrote poetry in honour of the rose they took as their emblem. Socially such groups might embrace minor nobility and officials alongside lawyers and merchants, but they were essentially unofficial. Attempts have been made to draw a relatively simple progression from such groups' opportunity for radicalisation to the fundamental overthrow that occurred in 1789, but these rest on rather dubious generalisations.[11] Nonetheless, quite clearly a new sociability, centred around the discussion of

34

ideas that evidently had social and political implications, was widespread, and indeed general, by the 1780s.[12]

Recent work has also argued that a similar penetration of the 'king's secret' by more popular opinion, at least within Paris, had been taking place through the century.[13] Parisians appear to have persistently pushed at the borders of permissible public expression, claiming the right to comment on state events, from disputes with the *parlement* in the 1730s and 1750s, to the Maupeou coup and Turgot's experiments. Harassed and often detained indefinitely by the police, individuals could be tipped over the edge of insanity by the authorities' near-paranoid pursuit of every disloyal word. The overall effect, however, was a stripping-away of the sacred aura of the monarchy. In the eyes of the great city's public, government was becoming something inherently corrupt, and something about which many demanded their critical say, long before any ideas of revolution made themselves felt. Robert Darnton has documented a cascade of obscene and subversive material about the elite that grew to epic proportions by the last years of the Old Regime, but this only added to a long tradition of both voyeuristic and moralising popular comment on Court life.[14] The higher and more literate sections of the population were finding new ways of coming together and expressing themselves outside the frameworks allowed by official doctrine, but beneath them it appears that the common city-dwellers had got there first.

For the Old Regime as a state, such shifts in rhetoric and sociability went along with, and helped to intensify, growing problems over the status of privileged bodies. While leaning on these *corps* as institutions of social order, the state also increasingly took advantage of their crucial underlying function as long-term creditors. Whenever the crown expanded the membership of a body, selling new offices, this 'sale' was akin to the individuals concerned loaning money to the state. An annual payment, the *gages*, was made in return, effectively representing interest on the investment. The crown also at intervals tapped this source again by demanding *augmentations de gages* – additional payments, forced loans in effect, from all those who wished to retain their offices.

An example is the *bureaux des finances*, which originated as a corps of public auditors in the sixteenth century, and by the eighteenth had effectively lost their functions to the *intendants* or other courts, while keeping their privileges. Their members collectively paid four million *livres* in such an *augmentation* in 1770. This was the fourth such demand that century, and the members of the *bureaux* usually had to contract loans collectively to meet the payments. In this way the crown used privileged groups as sources of credit, effectively demanding that they borrow money on its behalf, since its credit-rating was worse than theirs.

With the declining state of the crown's finances, such expedients came to be of increasing importance, as did the extent to which privileged groups' exemptions from other exactions could be reduced. This latter process was a long-term one, and rendered the very existence of a group such as the *bureaux des finances* problematic – with its functions gone, if its privileges were eroded, what status did it retain? As with other issues we have examined, a critical point was reached in the early 1770s, when financial reforms proposed replacing various payments made to ensure heritability of office with a single 1 per cent annual surcharge on current values of the office. The uniformity of this proposal threatened the particularity of the corporate society, especially as, in the case of the *bureaux*, their membership in various provinces claimed particular and unique privileges. For the rest of the 1770s, and into the mid-1780s, members of the *bureaux* brought together a fragile and fluctuating alliance amongst them to fight the proposals and to attempt a restoration of old functions, privileges and revenues. In banding together in this way, as the *parlements* also did, they were also defying the model of the Old Regime as many particular bodies joined only through the king.

In 1775 Turgot abandoned the surcharge, but planned to abolish many of the offices in the *bureaux* that had been created in earlier reigns solely for financial reasons. With his fall the policy reversed again – the crown needed the revenue that would come from the surcharge, and could not raise the capital necessary to buy back the surplus offices. This threw the market for such offices into turmoil – in 1777 it was reported from Caen that ten of the twenty-five local *bureau* members were trying, and failing, to sell out.[15] In 1786, after tortuous disputation, a one-million-*livre* payment was agreed to buy the *bureaux* out of the surcharge. By this time, however, fifteen years of uncertainty had prompted some amongst the privileged to wonder if there was not a better ordering of things possible. Before 1789 new languages of citizenship would inflect public and private discussion of such offices' purpose and worth.[16]

The extent to which 'national/public' modes of thought had penetrated the political system by the mid-1780s is seen in the memoranda of controller-general (finance minister) Calonne to the king in November 1786. Here, at the very heart of monarchical power, extraordinary arguments were now being used for radical alterations in the administrative system: 'It is as advantageous to the maintenance of royal authority as it is in conformity with the fundamental principles of monarchy that there should exist a national interest which ties subjects to their sovereign'. Calonne added that representative assemblies to allocate taxation would 'excite ... a sort of patriotic effervescence that, if managed wisely, can do much good'. In a later memorandum he noted that 'authority is never stronger than when it ... is supported by reason and the national interest'.[17]

If some of the suggested reforms were little different from those attempted in the 1760s and 1770s, and if beneath them the conception of the essential legitimacy of the monarchical government persisted, such arguments were still separated by a vast gulf from the royal rhetoric of that earlier generation. In 1766 Louis XV had reminded the *parlement* of Paris, '... as if anyone could forget that the sovereign power resides in my person only ... that the plenitude of ... authority ... always remains with me', and that any attempt to challenge that 'would reduce me to the unhappy necessity of using all the power which I have received from God to preserve my peoples from the terrible consequences of such enterprises'.[18] By the 1780s the state was in no condition to issue such threats – after all, when they were carried out, as in 1771, they had failed.

Faced with imminent fiscal collapse and the need to reform the taxation system, Calonne hand-picked an 'Assembly of Notables' to give approval to his schemes in early 1787: 144 leading lights of the kingdom, conceived in traditional terms – all the Princes of the Blood, a selection of high church officials, leaders of the *parlements*, royal councillors, provincial and municipal representatives. All but a handful were noble, all were influential in the present system, but they rejected both the methods of the past and the state's solutions with almost one voice. The minister interpreted this as the continued resistance of 'privilege' to reform, but there is much in the deliberations of the Notables that suggests they too were finding new ways of thinking.[19]

Their objections were frequently couched in solid practical terms, and their emphasis, particularly on the new land-tax proposals, was that of concern for the efficient use of property and adequate security for its returns. They objected, for example, that the proposed ability of the state to define the proportion of revenue to be paid in taxes on land, for an indefinite period, rendered investment in land hazardous. It also breached the political principle that extra taxation should be voted for specific totals, and for specific periods, but it was the economic consequences of this that troubled many amongst the Notables. They also spent much time raising the issue of excessive state expenditure. This in part harked back to the long-obsolete principle that the crown should live from its own revenues in peacetime, and not tax its subjects. It also served, however, as a vehicle for criticism of the Court and its excesses. Here a new avenue of 'public opinion' showed the failure of Calonne's policy of demonstrating confidence by embarking on major public expenditure. We can also note that there were some amongst the Notables, such as the marquis de Lafayette and the duc d'Orléans, who would soon be posing unambiguously as 'liberals' against royal power, and for a new constitutional order.

Calonne's failure to talk the Notables round to his plans, aided by intrigues against him, led to his dismissal in April 1787 and the appointment the following month of one of his major opponents in the Notables, Loménie de Brienne, as effective chief minister. Brienne, however, also failed to convince the Notables of the government's position, despite modifying the proposed reforms. The balance of power was temporarily in the state's favour, nonetheless, and after the Notables were dissolved at the end of May 1787, major reforms were enacted. Provincial Assemblies were to be created for all the *pays d'élections*, the grain trade was again freed, the *corvée* was unilaterally commuted to a tax, the royal household budget was trimmed severely, and changes were introduced into military and fiscal administration. By the standards of previous decades, this was already a revolution.

While this was under way, however, socio-political opposition continued to grow. At the end of July, the *parlement* of Paris presented remonstrances against the reforms. They effectively demanded the calling of an Estates-General, the ancient assembly of the kingdom, and, they claimed, the only body with the public authority to create new taxes. Early August saw state attempts to force new tax-decrees through the *parlement*, its resistance causing it to be sent into exile at Troyes. This political turmoil sparked violent demonstrations in Paris from the clerks of the court and the general population, while other sovereign courts expressed their support for the *parlementaires*' stand. After a period of political negotiation, Brienne withdrew the new taxes in return for the *parlement*'s agreement to two new temporary *vingtièmes* (5 per cent property taxes), and at the end of September the Parisian crowds joyfully greeted the return of the judges from exile.

Thus in the autumn of 1787 the new limits of royal power had apparently been exposed. The Provincial Assemblies decreed earlier in the year met in November, but were unable to offer an alternative centre of power to a 'public opinion' that continued to support the resistance of the privileged institutions against 'royal despotism'. On 19 November this opposition was confirmed. A stormy royal session of the *parlement* of Paris succeeded in extracting the promise from the king of an Estates-General by 1792, but then saw a dramatic clash between the king and the duc d'Orléans. Louis tried to cut the session short and impose decrees to register further loans; Orléans rose to protest, to little avail, but for his pains was sent into internal exile, leading to a string of increasingly vehement protests from the *parlement* through the winter of 1787–8.

The *parlement* increasingly adopted the mantle of an organ of public opinion and guardian of national liberties, the role it had begun to stake out since the 1750s. In April 1788 it issued general condemnations of 'royal despotism', and on 3 May issued a 'Declaration of the Fundamental Laws of the Kingdom'. This opposed most notably the power of arbitrary arrest and exile embodied in *lettres de cachet*, and insisted that only an Estates-General could approve new taxes. The state response the very next day was to seek to arrest two leaders of the *parlement* with just such *lettres de cachet*, only to see its troops defied by the court *en masse*. Two days later the two men surrendered, but this compliance was not enough to protect the *parlement* from a government determined now to clear the path to reform. In a more sweeping repeat of the

Maupeou coup, edicts were issued on 8 May, stripping many powers from the *parlements* in favour of lower courts, abolishing several layers of jurisdiction, and creating a single *Cour plénière* to register all national legislation and taxes. The response to this demonstrated how far the French polity had come in the generation since 1771.

Protest from both general urban populations and elite groups came from across the kingdom. The Assembly of the Clergy, the largest single privileged *corps*, met in June, registered its opposition to the new measures, and halved its annual payment to the crown, instead of doubling it as had been requested. The majority of provincial *parlements* and other sovereign courts joined in a wave of formal protest, matched by assemblies of nobles in several provinces. Rennes saw riots in favour of its *parlement*, and in distant Grenoble the population defied troops sent against their court in the 'Day of Tiles', 7 June, as they pelted the soldiers from, and with, the rooftops. The future revolutionaries Barnave and Mounier convened a meeting of nobles, clergy and Third Estate representatives of Grenoble a week later, backing the *parlements* and calling for an immediate Estates-General, but also asking for the restoration of the provincial Estates of Dauphiné. There was not yet an open call for the reconstruction of society on new lines, appeals concentrating on restoring and defending what was, or had been, threatened by the state. The same demands were echoed by a gathering of representatives for the whole province of Dauphiné at Vizille on 21 July.

While overt political assemblies still stood back from excessive radicalism, it is instructive at this point to see the responses of the *bureaux des finances*, who like the *parlements* were formally dissolved by the May edicts. The impact of uncertainty on their collective position had been clear since 1786, when the member charged with arranging a loan to finance their buying-off of the surcharge wrote that the usual sources of such loans 'laughed up their noses' at him. Suggestions that the best solution was to dissolve the *corps* and reimburse its office-holders had been heard from the membership as long before as 1777. However, the 1788 edicts were another matter entirely. In the first place, reimbursement was not specified, and though it might ultimately be assumed, the prospect of receiving any money from the state in its present circumstances was not bright. In the second, any member of the *bureaux* that had held office for less than twenty years became immediately liable for the *taille*, that most degrading of taxes. Under these conditions, it would have been understandable to have seen an immediate stand being made on conservative principles, but what actually emerged was rather different.

By late 1788, *bureaux des finances* across France were corresponding about, discussing and declaring a new model of their existence, one based on public utility. They expressed a new sense of the need for uniform citizenship, which would mean giving up their tax-privileges in a new order, but also of their right to a relatively privileged place in that order, as 'magistrates' who earned distinction through public service. A certain short-term self-interest lay behind this, as it had been ruled that the *bureaux* would count amongst the Third Estate for the upcoming Estates-General. The view amongst the *bureaux* was that only a renunciation of tax-privileges would give any members wishing to join that body a chance of election by a non-privileged electorate.

There was nonetheless some fundamental rethinking in progress – privilege 'was being redefined as an honourable sign of participation in the state, rather than a means of withdrawal from it'.[20] The needs of the state, conceived in terms of patriotic and national obligations, were coming to be seen as paramount. These were superficially similar terms to those the government now used, though undoubtedly with very different underlying premises. Moreover, in the minds of the *bureaux'* members, privilege and the notion of *corps* could still exist alongside this. The very fact that the separate *bureaux* had been in correspondence for over a decade reflects on new political formations that were becoming possible, but the rather exalted form of civic equality envisaged in their proposals was too delicate to withstand the social and political storm that continued to brew.

During this period the state had continued its own attempts at mobilising popular support, playing on the theme that privileged interests were behind the unrest. Provincial Estates were restored to Dauphiné, and also to the Franche-Comté, with enhanced Third Estate representation, in a bid to sidestep these protests, but there is no evidence of a weakening of the anti-state front. In early July 1788, facing a crisis of short-term credit, the government gave in to demands for an immediate Estates-General. A

41

month later the date would be fixed for 1 May 1789, and the *parlements'* replacement suspended, but in the meantime a further step was taken to the political inclusion of 'public opinion'. Informed persons, *corps* and municipalities were invited to publish freely their thoughts and proposals on the mode of business the Estates-General should follow. The body had not met since 1614, and it was a legitimate question as to how it should be organised in a new era – after all, in 1614 the judges of the *parlements* were counted amongst the Third Estate, which was hardly where they saw themselves at this point. The solicitation of proposals, however, was effectively a licence for open political comment, and caused an explosion in the public discussion of the political situation and its social implications.

The state continued to crumble – in mid-August it could no longer pay the interest on its debts and went through a barely disguised partial bankruptcy. Brienne lost his post to Court intrigues later in the month, and public rejoicing greeted the news that Necker was to be his successor. He immediately reinstated the *parlements'* full powers, believing that he was heading off civil war. The response to this from the *parlementaires* of Paris, however, would begin a new phase of open, and explicitly social, discord.

On 25 September 1788 the *parlement* of Paris decreed that in its formal opinion the Estates-General should follow the forms it had used in 1614. This meant that the numbers of clerical, noble and Third Estate deputies should be equal, and that the three Estates should meet and vote separately (or 'by order', as it was termed). Each Estate would thus be one voice of three, and the first two would always be able to outvote the Third. This raised an issue which until this point had been successfully glossed over in the opposition to the crown – if an ancient institution was to be France's salvation, it would most naturally take an ancient form. This could only revive the sharp divisions in society (especially between the Second and Third Estates, but potentially also between provinces) that had blurred in the general recourse to 'public opinion'.

That opinion now split decisively, as the broad 'public' that had supported resistance to the state now saw the prospect of the privileged orders managing the Estates-General solely in their own interests. By December, some 800 petitions had flowed into

Paris from the provinces as various Third Estate groups protested at the selfishness of the 'privileged orders'. The *parlement* further antagonised non-noble opinion by repeated attempts to censor pro-Third Estate pamphlets through the autumn, such pamphlets having harped on, and encouraged, the themes of the petitions. December saw a partial retreat from their position by the *parlementaires*, as they agreed to the 'doubling' of the Third Estate – that it should have a number of deputies equal to the other two combined. They held out for voting by order, however.

The extent to which the political and social landscape was altering was visible later in December 1788. The *parlement* of Paris, bidding for renewed public support and under pressure from liberals in its own ranks, declared its support for the abolition of tax privileges, arguably the basis of the whole Old Regime, and key to their previous defences of the 'ancient constitution'. This failed completely to regain the initiative. New forces speaking for the Third Estate had by now mapped out an independent political position, while other forces had taken up the banner of reaction. On 12 December, after the fruitless conclusion of a second Assembly of Notables called to deliberate on forms for the Estates, the Princes of the Blood, titular leaders of the nobility, issued what was effectively a manifesto for privilege. They demanded that the king support his loyal nobility against demands for social change, and insisted on the forms of 1614 for the Estates.

This last-minute 'breakaway' may actually reflect a further tension within the Old Regime. Richard Andrews has recently highlighted the continuing distinction maintained in practice between the robe and sword nobilities right into the revolutionary era. The former stood as judges and administrators for the control of civil society, the latter as military officers for the defence of the realm. Soldier-nobles married amongst themselves and bred large families, often seeing them killed or wounded in their monarch's service. Many were relatively poor, and historically many old noble families had died out or lost their status, often bought out or replaced on their lands by bourgeois who subsequently or concurrently entered the robe. The robe or civil nobility also tended to marry amongst themselves, in order to keep their valuable offices 'in the family'; they had fewer children, and bred them up for a life of study and deliberation.

Beyond the formal fact of their nobility, the two groups had very little in common, and the sword looked on the robe as inferior, while resenting its power over law and property and its effectively greater wealth and influence.[21] A significant split was marked in 1781, when the carefully drafted Ségur Ordinance closed admission to the military officer-corps to all those lacking four generations of pure nobility in their background. This was expressly designed to reinforce a divide between careers for the sword nobility and the social climbing feared from the robe. These tensions were to be highlighted even more dramatically in the forthcoming elections to the Estates-General.

At the end of 1788 the state found itself painfully caught between forces previously united. Still needing public support, and an Estates-General, to save it from complete fiscal disaster, it was obliged to compromise. On 27 December the Royal Council decreed that the Third Estate representation would be doubled in number, but voting would be by order, unless the whole Estates-General agreed otherwise when it met. Press freedom was permitted, and election arrangements were laid out that would bring a sudden democracy to every corner of France. Along with electing deputies for the Estates, Frenchmen would also be able to exercise the traditional right of presenting grievances via the new assembly for the king to consider. Thus in early 1789 the country was allowed to debate and decide on every issue that was on its collective mind, and to compose registers (*cahiers de doléances*) carrying these grievances to the heart of government.

Within the *cahiers*, many different viewpoints on the nature of the body politic would be expressed, and it is worth stepping back here, after the details of the 'Pre-revolution', to consider what some of the wider political conceptions in the minds of the French may have been, at least at the level of the educated. There is little doubt that these views were closely related to conceptions of gender, and to the networks of gendered power we might term 'patriarchy'.[22] In some ways, this was an entirely overt practice: the association of the king as father of the people was a commonplace, and the idea that paternal and God-given authority was both natural and absolute, and hence unchallengeable, was a fundamental element of royal absolutism. The metaphor of the father was ever-present in monarchical discourse. Furthermore, the early modern French monarchy had at least partially been erected by granting legal powers to patriarchal elite families over marriage and inheritance, in return for these dynasties' support of the throne. Yet the growing volume of literature produced for the reading public in the eighteenth century raised a challenge to such patriarchalism. The novel, a form based essentially on dramas within the family, accelerated in production from a handful in the early decades to hundreds by the 1780s. In these novels, the general picture of the father-figure changed over time. At first the figure of the stern patriarch represented authority, even if also provoking conflict, but by the 1750s and 1760s fathers were becoming softer, more sentimental, and often ineffectual figures. By the late 1780s, the vogue was for novels with no fathers at all, such as the tale of *Paul and Virginie*, two fatherless children raised on the paradise island of Mauritius, which was the literary sensation of 1788.

All of this is suggestive of how the educated French public was coming to conceptualise the relation between personal and public affairs. It is noticeable that the revolutionaries themselves would continually replay the issues of what it meant to overthrow a father-figure, to the extent that Lynn Hunt has written of the whole Revolution as paralleling later Freudian ideas about conflict in the family and politics. Meanwhile, those same (male) revolutionaries, especially in the Revolution's most radical stages, would act out, in their own bodies and on the bodies of women, further anxieties and convictions about the meaning of masculinity and femininity in their society.[23] Although the late-Enlightenment reading public was clearly composed of both sexes, and the *salon* gathering centred on a female hostess had been a prime agency for the diffusion of Enlightenment, public opinion in the 1780s was resolutely hostile to female political involvement. Much of this took its cue from a revulsion against the life of the royal Court, where sexual favours were seen as both the currency and the goal which generated corruption and the clearly desperate plight of the nation. Few *causes célèbres* were without some sexual element, even if only implicit, and the 'Diamond Necklace Affair' of the mid-1780s, where Queen Marie-Antoinette herself was linked (through no actual fault of her own) with criminal adventurers and prostitutes, was the high-water mark of public interest and revulsion. This was the environment of *Les Liaisons Dangereuses*, the scandalous novel first published in 1782, where sexuality was a tool of predatory intent, and human feelings were rigidly concealed behind a mask of manipulative ambition.[24]

The provincial middle classes who were to be largely responsible for the new goals of the Revolution had by this time a wholly different set of ideals. Epitomised by the more sentimental writings of Rousseau, and a wider aspiration to love and emulate 'nature' and the 'natural', these ideals produced new, and increasingly separate, sets of behaviour for men and women. The 'natural' woman would no longer be the hostess and schemer, but the mother who breast-fed, rejecting the unnatural convenience of foisting her children onto a wet-nurse. She would remain in the household, to support the husband and father, who was now discovering his public duties. From Rousseau, and from a complex relationship with models of ancient Greco-Roman public behaviour, such men were fashioning a self-image which could combine private 'natural' emotions with a rigid public face of stoic virtue. Virtue in the antique sense, as they defined it, meant to put the public good (*la chose publique*, the 'public thing', which in Latin is *res publica*, the Republic) above all else – the individual, family, community or 'party'. Such internalised ideals, generated in an atmosphere without the tempering influence of genuine political choices to make, would underlie even the more pragmatic politics of the Revolution's early years, and be part of the long process of developing conflict that marked the 1790s. Such a model did not encourage the idea that there were options in politics, as opposed to simple right and wrong, or that opposition could be legitimate. If we note that, for very different reasons, the aristocrats who had already repudiated change in 1788 believed much the same thing, we can grasp one more dimension of what was to follow.

Notes

1 See J. B. Collins, *The State in Early Modern France*, Cambridge, 1995, chapter 6, 'Reform, Renewal, Collapse', esp. pp. 216–24.

2 P. M. Jones, *Reform and Revolution in France: The Politics of Transition, 1774–1791*, Cambridge, 1995, is the most direct recent consideration of governmental reform in its wider context.

3 See esp. K. M. Baker, *Inventing the French Revolution*, Cambridge, 1990, chapters 1, 5, 8; and M. Ozouf, '"Public Opinion" at the End of the

Old Regime', in T. C. W. Blanning (ed.), *The Rise and Fall of the French Revolution*, Chicago, 1996, pp. 90–110. This volume gathers many seminal pieces previously published in the *Journal of Modern History*.

4 A brief introduction to Habermas can be found in B. Nathans, 'Habermas's "Public Sphere" in the Era of the French Revolution', *French Historical Studies*, 16, 1990, pp. 620–44. Landes's work is *Women and the Public Sphere in the Age of the French Revolution*, Ithaca, 1988.

5 These themes are dealt with in an exchange between two noted scholars: see W. Sewell, 'Ideologies and Social Revolutions: Reflections on the French Case', in Blanning, *Rise and Fall*, pp. 285–313, and T. Skocpol, 'Cultural Idioms and Political Ideologies in the Revolutionary Reconstruction of State Power: A Rejoinder to Sewell', in Blanning, *Rise and Fall*, pp. 314–24.

6 See G. Bossenga, *The Politics of Privilege: Old Regime and Revolution in Lille*, Cambridge, 1991, esp. pp. 84–8, discussing this in relation to the nobility.

7 See S. C. Maza, *Private Lives and Public Affairs: The Causes Célèbres of Prerevolutionary France*, Berkeley, 1993; and D. A. Bell, *Lawyers and Citizens: The Making of a Political Elite in Old Regime France*, Oxford, 1994, pp. 129ff., 162. The pieces by Bell, D. Gordon, and Maza, which make up 'Forum: The Public Sphere in the Eighteenth Century', *French Historical Studies*, 17, 1992, pp. 882–950, examine both the philosophical roots of this 'judicial' definition of public opinion, and its practical effects within the legal establishment and the wider literate society.

8 For an interesting argument that the nature of Enlightenment sociability shifted dramatically from the mid-1770s, away from private gatherings orchestrated by women, the classic 'salon', to all-male gatherings which advertised commercially and competed for subscribers, see D. Goodman, *The Republic of Letters: A Cultural History of the French Enlightenment*, London, 1994.

9 M. C. Jacob, *Living the Enlightenment: Freemasonry and Politics in Eighteenth-Century Europe*, Oxford, 1991, p. 210. See esp. chapter 9, 'Le Régime Ancien et Maçonnique: The Paris Grand Lodge and the Reform of National Government'.

10 See D. Outram, *The Enlightenment*, Cambridge, 1995, chapter 2, for a general outline of this environment and its intellectual habits.

11 François Furet took up the early twentieth-century work of Augustin Cochin in this respect – see his *Interpreting the French Revolution*, Cambridge, 1981.

12 A general interpretation of the role of literacy, bourgeois sociability and other 'cultural' factors can be found in R. Chartier, *The Cultural Origins of the French Revolution*, London, 1991.

13 See Arlette Farge, *Subversive Words: Public Opinion in Eighteenth-*

Century France, Cambridge, 1994.

14 See R. Darnton, *The Literary Underground of the Old Regime*, Cambridge, MA, 1982.

15 This may seem to contrast with the comments in the previous chapter on the health of the market for office, but reflects more on the relative costs and benefits of different types of office – as a *secrétaire du roi*, one's nobility was a 'done deal'; with an office in the *bureaux des finances*, two generations of royal demands had to be tolerated to secure such a status.

16 This process is described in detail in G. Bossenga, 'From *Corps* to Citizenship: The *Bureaux des Finances* before the French Revolution', *Journal of Modern History*, 58, 1986, pp. 610–42.

17 Cited by V. R. Gruder, 'A Mutation in Elite Political Culture: The French Notables and the Defense of Property and Participation, 1787', in Blanning, *Rise and Fall*, pp. 111–47; p. 111. The language of these exchanges can be followed in a wider selection in J. Hardman, *The French Revolution: The Fall of the Ancien Régime to the Thermidorian Reaction, 1785–1795*, London, 1981, Part I, chapter 2.

18 *Séance de la flagellation*, 3 March 1766, translation from K. M. Baker (ed.), *The Old Regime and the French Revolution*, Chicago, 1987, pp. 49–50.

19 Gruder, 'Mutation'; the classic account of the whole 'pre-revolutionary' political process is J. Egret, *The French Pre-Revolution, 1787–8*, Chicago, 1977. A briefer account can be found in W. Doyle, *Origins of the French Revolution*, 2nd edn, Oxford, 1988, pp. 96–114; see Doyle's following chapters for his view of the contending social and political forces.

20 Bossenga, 'From *Corps* to Citizenship', p. 635.

21 See R. M. Andrews, *Law, Magistracy and Crime in Old Regime Paris, 1735–1789*, vol. 1 *The System of Criminal Justice*, Cambridge, 1994, esp. Part 1, chapter 4, 'A Fourth Estate'. Andrews is not the first to point out the continuing robe–sword tension, but it has not generally been made central to explanations of the events of the 1780s.

22 Research into gender and power represents a massive and ever-growing field. For some pathways into this, see Landes, *Women and the Public Sphere*; the works cited at note 7 above; S. Hanley, 'Engendering the State: Family Formation and State Building in Early Modern France', *French Historical Studies*, 16, 1989, pp. 4–27; L. Hunt, *Politics, Culture and Class in the French Revolution*, Berkeley, 1984, Part I; L. Hunt, *The Family Romance of the French Revolution*, London, 1992, esp. chapters 1–4.

23 For another view of the 'embodiment' of public action, see D. Outram, *The Body and the French Revolution*, New Haven, 1989, an interpretation sometimes at odds with, for example, Hunt's work.

24 This is one of the main themes of Darnton, *Literary Underground*.

3

The great year of
Revolution – 1789

On the nature of the *cahiers de doléances*, it is instructive to read the
impressions of Alexis de Tocqueville, who surveyed them some
150 years ago:

> I have read attentively the cahiers of the Three Estates ... I observe
> that here a law and there a custom is sought to be changed, and I
> note it. Pursuing the immense task to the end, and adding together
> all the separate demands, I discover with terror that nothing less is
> demanded than the simultaneous and systematic repeal of all the
> laws and the abolition of all the customs prevailing in the country;
> and I perceive at once that one of the great revolutions the world
> ever saw is impending.[1]

This or similar dramatic views prevailed until the revisionism of
the 1960s and 1970s, which, in line with its doubts about the 'aristocratic reaction' and the nature of a bourgeoisie, also raised
doubts about the revolutionary nature of the *cahiers*. It was
claimed, on the basis of re-examination of a sample of peasant
demands, that they were monopolised by entirely local concerns,
and that there was no sign of impending social catastrophe in the
views that they were prepared to voice.[2] This view itself is now
subject to revision.

The moment in January 1789 when instructions went out from
the state to elect representatives, or 'deputies', to the Estates-
General marked the coming-together of the complex and evolv-
ing social conditions in France with the new public sphere, and all
its contradictions, outlined in the previous chapter. The results

could not be expected to be simple. At a merely superficial level, the arrangements for the elections were momentous. Some four to five million Frenchmen, all those over twenty-five who paid any kind of tax, were eligible to participate in an electoral process that continued for several months. The central electoral unit was the *bailliage* or *sénéchaussée*, an area representing the jurisdiction of one of the lower royal courts. Some 200 of these hosted electoral assemblies for each of the three Estates. Parish clergy and bishops attended First Estate meetings in person, while monks and nuns sent representatives. The Second Estate admitted only individuals with fully established hereditary nobility, all others were lumped into the Third – a significant decision.

The vast numbers of the Third Estate were managed in a more complex fashion. In the countryside, each parish met to send one or more delegates to the local assembly. In the towns, meetings of trade guilds and other groups sharing status (or privilege) were used to select representatives. Both types of process might go through several levels before reaching a formal *bailliage/ sénéchaussée* assembly. Local clergy and officials were expected to supervise the process, and in many villages it probably resembled nothing so much as the usual meeting of heads of households to debate community matters. Nonetheless, those attending each of these meetings were able to formulate their *cahier* of grievances and send it forward to the electoral assemblies.

At the assemblies, model reform *cahiers* produced by opposition leaders had a wide circulation, the pamphlet war continued to rage, and the political ambitions of the legal classes began to come to the fore. Such groups took control of the Third Estate meetings, drafting composite 'general *cahiers*' that spoke of representation and constitutional government in a fashion alien to the bulk of the population.[3] Inspired by the bitter socio-political disputes of the previous months, many of the general *cahiers* spoke in broad terms of reforms to privilege, even of an end to feudal dues. Few, however, seem to have threatened the complete end to noble and Church power that was soon to be on the cards.

Clearly the formulators of the general *cahiers* had felt able to write off the peasants' demands as localised griping. Though revisionists have essentially followed this pattern, more recent work suggests that the *cahiers* held strong evidence of the conflicts that were to follow. John Markoff has studied the electoral processes and rural disturbances of 1789 in depth, and suggests that 'French villagers engaged in a multifaceted evaluation of their burdens, making at times rather fine judgments about the tolerable and the intolerable'. They were able to discuss the 'utility and fairness' of the various obligations that the state and the seigneurial system placed upon them, condemning the onerous and illogical distribution of indirect taxes such as the *aides* and *gabelle* particularly harshly. Even more significantly, Markoff shows that over a third of his very large sample of parish *cahiers* contained demands for the abolition without compensation of seigneurial rights. In addition to these, over 45 per cent demanded some kind of reform or passed unfavourable comment on the seigneurial system in general, or a specific local grievance, thus adding up to a substantial majority for change on the 'feudal' issue. On taxation, 42 per cent wanted reforms, while almost 24 per cent were prepared to voice the demand for abolition of various taxes. Comparing peasants' demands with the general Third Estate *cahiers*, and those of the nobility, Markoff observes that on the three great socio-economic issues of taxation, seigneurial rights, and payments to the Church, the peasants were 'consistently the most radical' and, unsurprisingly, 'the nobles least' (document 1).[4]

The radicalism of peasant demands should not come as a surprise when we consider their general situation in early 1789. Since the mid-1780s harvests had been consistently poor in France: in 1786 peasants had been forced to sell livestock after a widespread shortage of forage crops, and in 1787 a poor harvest had been worsened by disruption caused by liberation of the grain trade. 1788 was a cold and wet year, and on 13 July a freak hailstorm devastated crops in a swathe of central and northern France. The result was an appallingly bad harvest, upon which followed a fiercely cold winter. A dramatic failure of subsistence thus imposed itself upon a population struggling under the weight of 'feudal reaction'. Nor should it be overlooked that much rural industry had collapsed as a result of the ill-judged 'Eden Treaty' of 1786, which gave favourable terms to imports of English merchandise. In central Picardy, for example, some 80 per cent of rural cloth manufacturing shut down in the later 1780s, unable to compete, and throwing the peasantry back onto the shrinking resources of agriculture for their survival.[5]

Few historians have evoked the consequences of this as well as Georges Lefebvre. The rural population had seen two million extra mouths added to its burden in a generation, even as landlords, seigneurs and tax-agents had battened down upon them. By the end of the 1780s, 'at least one-tenth of the rural population did nothing but beg from one year's end to the other'.[6] Hundreds of thousands were on the move by the eve of the Revolution, the habitual beggars joined by landless labourers with no work, those whose harvests had failed catastrophically, and those urban workers who travelled regularly from one region to another. They merged with the flow of tinkers, pedlars and other wanderers, expanding it to unprecedented size. When the choice was stay and starve, or move, the French population proved remarkably willing to hit the road.

As they did so, they provoked fear. Even the *cahiers* at times reflected this, with denunciations of the wandering sellers, along with carters and waggoners who smashed fences and crops *en route*, and the beggars whose demands at the farm door had to be met, for fear of nocturnal theft, assault, or worst of all, fire. By 1789 beggars were moving in bands, seeking out a natural companionship on the road, but also thus able to intimidate rural communities with their demands. What made the peasants' concerns all the more pressing was the continued state effort to disarm them. Under pressure from the nobility, who saw a gun in the hand of a peasant as a threat to their game, several provinces had seen systematic disarmaments carried out by force in the 1770s and 1780s, and even at the beginning of 1789 nobles could call in the rural police to search villages for weapons.[7]

As rural producers feared for their meagre stocks and the protection of their growing crops, so the urban consumers lived in terror of the disruption of their food supply. Necker had moved swiftly as soon as the state of the 1788 harvest became clear, suspending grain exports and initiating all the usual policies of overseas purchases and import subsidies, but few seem to have believed in this. The Famine Pact was a much more convenient explanation for why shortage persisted, when the roads were full of wagons moving supplies from one point to another, from farm to market, market to store, town to town. Each authority – town, province, *intendant* – was attempting to insure against the looming food crisis, and all these movements only exaggerated fears which already had ample justification. In Paris the price of bread by February 1789 was around 60 per cent above its normal level, approaching the point at which many simply could not afford to eat, and it would soon rise higher.

The consequence was riot, in most of the major population centres of France, particularly in March and April 1789. In the far north alone, where Lefebvre carried out detailed studies, there were nine significant urban outbreaks in those two months, followed by ten more in May and June. The cities of southern Provence – Marseille, Toulon, Aix – experienced severe disorders in this period, usually involving attacks on shops and food stores, but also leading to the forced abolition of some local charges and dues, and showing the signs of future patterns in attacks on prestigious religious establishments and seigneurial châteaux. In April in the Dauphiné, villages were already declaring themselves freed of feudal demands by the convocation of the Estates-General. Before the summer, Flanders, Franche-Comté and the Mâconnais would see widespread rural insurrection. Around Paris, a campaign of assaults on the game-preserves of the elite had begun in 1788, and into the late spring of 1789 the princes de Conti and de Condé, the duc d'Orléans, the Austrian ambassador and Marie-Antoinette herself all had their lands ravaged.

The atmosphere of fear led to repeated calls for a general armament. Individual towns and districts, in some cases as early as 1788, armed their respectable elements and set up guards and patrols against riot and brigandage. Amidst what appeared to be a breakdown of law and order (despite the infliction of exemplary punishment on rioters apprehended by the regular authorities), urban communities increasingly took the law into their own nervous hands.

The general pattern of disorder had been quelled temporarily by only one thing – the opening of the Estates-General at the royal palace of Versailles, outside Paris, in the first week of May. Here over a thousand representatives chosen by the three Estates came together to resolve the problems of the kingdom, and were almost immediately thrown into stalemate. The Third Estate steadfastly refused to do any work unless the three Estates merged to form one body. By mid-May, suspicion between nobility and 'commons' (a new label eagerly picked up by the Third) was growing, and by the end of the month it was clear that the former were determined to defend privilege and the latter to end it. On 9 June the last attempt at reconciliation failed, and on the 10th the abbé Sieyès proposed to the commons that the other two Estates be given a last chance to join the Third, which otherwise should ignore them (and the will of the king) and proceed to business. This motion was passed by a majority of twelve to one (493–41).

A pattern of confrontation was thus laid down which would be played out, more or less, throughout the revolutionary years. Its roots lie less in the composition of the Third Estate representation (which we will examine below), than in the nobility who were chosen to go to Versailles. The noble elections to the Estates-General were a significant victory for the sword nobility over the robe that it had come to resent. Some 26,000 nobles had taken part in elections to the Estates, of whom between 20 and 25 per cent were of the robe. Yet scarcely a tenth of those elected were of the robe, including a mere twenty-two *parlementaires* of 288 deputies in all.[8] Even in Paris, heart of the robe nobility's power, military officers and seigneurs outnumbered judges among those elected by two to one. The nobility at large thus repudiated the administrative elite of the Old Regime. Timothy Tackett indicates that at least 80 per cent of the noble deputies had pursued military careers, and had thus imbibed the code of honour and obedience that set them apart from civil society, and placed loyalty to the king and the defence of their particular social group above all else. The fact that, compared with the Third Estate deputies, most of them were spectacularly rich did not aid mutual comprehension.[9]

It would be wrong to characterise these nobles, who would be the target of so much abuse over the coming years, as all unthinkingly conservative, or to label such conservatism as a product of their background alone. The marquis de Lafayette was sociologically typical of them, if not even more distinguished than most, yet he would be a leader of Revolution, at least in its early years. Nonetheless, the cultural barriers between the majority of the nobility in the Estates and their opponents cannot be overlooked. Moreover, the fact that so few of the legal hierarchy had been elected, and that this was so clearly a rejection of them by the nobility as a whole, drove those of the robe who did enter the Estates to side decisively with the Third.

Indeed, in the composition of the Third Estate, the robe nobility would have found much that was congenial – no less than 151 judges in various courts, and sixty-seven state attorneys and prosecutors. The role of the *bailliage/sénéchausée* courts in convening the Third may well have been instrumental in seating so many judges among its representatives, but this also reflects the social prominence of such figures in provincial society. Alongside these were 181 who designated themselves as lawyers. Although for many this may have been only a formal qualification masking a basically landowning, literary or municipal career, it also included brilliant and esteemed trial-lawyers such as the Parisian Target, who would later be acclaimed as 'father of the constitution'. Provincial courts also sent some of their best legal minds to Versailles. At least two-thirds of the commoner deputies were legally-trained, to which may be added two dozen with significant administrative careers behind them, including nine who had advised at the highest levels. Of the remaining 200 or so deputies, about half came from the various levels of the 'commercial and industrial bourgeoisie', the remainder split between landowning groups and the forty or so who were doctors, university scholars or professional writers.[10]

Such a diverse grouping of over 600 men from all corners of the kingdom developed remarkably quickly into a coherent body. Some have attributed this to the prior influence of the 'Society of Thirty', a body of the liberal high aristocracy that produced much of the pamphlet-literature of the winter of 1788–9 and included a galaxy of current and future political talent.[11] Tackett, however, points out the extent to which the burgeoning social and political crisis of the pre-revolution had obliged provincial groups to politicise themselves. The Provincial Assemblies decreed in 1787 had incorporated 'doubling of the third' and voting by head, precisely the issues fought over before and after the Estates' convocation, and had also provided an arena in which debating and administrative skills could be honed. The abolition of the *parlements* in 1788 had produced politicised protest from the judges, and from the lawyers that served them. Since July of that year, municipalities had been drawn by the state itself into debate on the forms of the Estates.

After the events in Dauphiné already described, similar spontaneous political mobilisation took place in many other provinces.

Brittany saw bitter strife develop between a large and intransigent noble body and commoners pressing for reform (including
the recently ennobled, now scorned openly by the sword), from
which would come a group of Breton deputies at the heart of
much legislative radicalism in 1789. Franche-Comté and Provence followed a similar pattern, this being one reason why the
fire-breathing radical noble Mirabeau was chosen by the
Provençal Third Estate as one of their deputies. Most other provinces, however, saw a more congenial relationship between noble
and commoner elements, pressing jointly, as had the Dauphinois,
for a restored Estates and more local autonomy. This was still a
political education, nonetheless, and one which continued in the
hothouse atmosphere of the Third Estate's meetings throughout
May and June.[12]

Returning to the developments within the Estates-General, the
Third's vote on 10 June to proceed to business independently
rapidly bore fruit. The following week saw a trickle of clerical
deputies joining the Third to verify credentials, and on 17 June
the Third voted to take the title 'National Assembly' and to begin
the work of national reconstruction. This was a decisive repudiation of their original existence as merely one of three Estates, and
staked out a new constitutional position as a body that represented the nation, rather than merely existing to advise the king
and approve his suggestions. This was dangerously close to challenging the monarch's sovereignty. Two days later their legitimacy was boosted as the clergy voted to join the Assembly to
verify credentials.

Meanwhile, the government had not been entirely passive,
and was beginning to come out of the shock caused by the death
of the heir to the throne on 4 June. A royal session was ordered
for 23 June, at which the king would give instructions for the programme to be followed. In preparation for this, the usual meet-
ing-hall of the Assembly was closed. Upon discovering this on 20
June, and fearing the first manoeuvres of a plot, the deputies
went to a nearly indoor tennis court and collectively pledged to
remain united until a constitution was established for France. A
crowd of the common people of Versailles surrounded them and
acclaimed their resolution, as crowds had fêted them almost since
their arrival, encouraging the deputies' sense that they truly represented 'the people'. Two days later the first crack in noble resist-

ance appeared, as two Second Estate deputies joined the Assembly's session.

On 23 June, in the formal splendour of a royal session, the king overruled all that the Assembly had done, ordered the three Estates to meet separately, and dictated a reform programme that included equality of taxation, but ruled out abolition of feudal dues and tithes. In the face of this royal repudiation of their new 'national' identity, the Assembly now chose to defy the king openly, egged on by the rhetorical talents of Mirabeau, and remained in the hall, voting by 493 to 34 to assert their constitutional inviolability, and confirming their previous actions. The merit of this seemed confirmed the next day, when most of the clergy joined them, and the day after, when forty-seven nobles led by the duc d'Orléans entered.

In the face of such defiance, the king was caught between ministers who still pressed the need for reform, and hard-line courtiers who now saw the confrontation as an issue of rebellion against royal authority. On 27 June he went both ways, ordering all three Estates to unite, while beginning a concentration of troops around Paris and Versailles. The movement of troops, which could not be kept secret, seemed to many to be the final confirmation of what had been feared since mid-May – that the state would end this confrontation by force. Troops now guarded the entrances to the National Assembly's chambers and prevented spectators from entering. Over-confident noblemen warned individual deputies that 'our knives are well and truly sharpened'. The Assembly began to take more organisation into its own hands, still cheered on by crowds in the surrounding area, as did the Parisian electoral assembly, continuing to meet in the Hôtel-de-Ville (city hall), having only just completed the business of sending deputies to Versailles. Meanwhile the fear that the foreign regiments increasingly deployed in the region would be put to use magnified.[13]

On 9 July the Assembly proclaimed itself the 'National Constituent Assembly', and pressed on with its debates. Two days later the king struck, removing Necker from power and appointing a clearly reactionary set of ministers. At this point the 'plot' of the aristocratic faction began to be exposed for the veil of over-confidence that it was, but not before the fear it provoked had catapulted France into an entirely new political situation. News of Necker's dismissal reached Paris early on the 12th, where it was immediately read by all classes as the first stage in the expected *coup*. At the sites where crowds had taken to gathering for information, notably the Palais-Royal, overtly political demonstrations took place. More visceral responses erupted at the customs-barriers. Since 1786 a new wall around Paris had made the collection of various dues much easier for the *fermiers-généraux* and much more onerous for the population. Now the many gates on this wall were attacked and their offices looted and burnt. Early clashes with cavalry in the Tuileries gardens encouraged fears, and crowds armed themselves from gunsmiths' shops. By the evening the disorder was becoming general, and the electors who had been meeting at the Hôtel-de-Ville decreed the formation of a bourgeois militia in each of the sixty electoral districts of the city.[14]

The social tension within the city became manifest in this body, which by the end of the 13th had been decreed at 48,000 in number, and would soon adopt the title of National Guard. The common people were not welcomed whole-heartedly into the revolutionary process, and as the defecting royal regiment of the Gardes françaises joined with the National Guard in patrolling the city, many looters were arrested, and some executed summarily. The Guard strove to maintain respectability and concern for private property, even as renewed rumours of troop movements early on the 14th led to mass assaults on the royal armoury at the Invalides, and then to the epochal clash at the Bastille.

There is no way of telling how many were Guards, and how many mere civilians, in the taking of the Bastille, a confrontation which cost perhaps several hundred lives. Six-sevenths, but significantly not all, of those later officially recognised for their part had been there in militia units. A massive crowd had certainly gathered, and the prime goal of its most active elements was the search for weapons, a search that had already cost the Old Regime mayor, de Flesselles, his life, when he appeared to deceive a demanding crowd. When the commandant of the Bastille, de Launay, was brought out, having during the siege appeared to trick a crowd into exposing themselves to fire, he was seized by members of the crowd, beaten and then butchered, his head hacked off and mounted for all to see. Such killings would give enlightened commentators much pause for thought in future weeks, especially after the *intendant* of Paris and his son-in-law were done to death with ceremonial savagery a week later, on suspicion of a famine plot. An atmosphere of 'carnival' pervaded these killings, radically at odds with the rationalist programmes for state reform, and indeed with the whole cultural frame, of the more educated revolutionaries. The Revolution that was already being proclaimed in the name of 'the people' would not find popular violence easy to accommodate, although at this point few revolutionaries dared deny that it appeared to have saved them from the aristocrats (document 2).[15]

The next three days marked a fundamental shift of power in France. On the 15th the king personally informed the National Assembly that troops would be moved away, having been warned that the native French regiments were no longer reliable. In Paris on the same day, the assembly of electors officially transformed itself into a new Commune, or ruling council for the city. Jean-Sylvain Bailly, astronomer, historian, and elder of the National Assembly, became mayor, and the liberal military aristocrat Lafayette became commander of the National Guard. On the 16th Necker was recalled to office, and on the 17th the king went to Paris to greet the new authorities. Their ritual signs of obedience to him could not disguise the truth of the new power-balance, as he placed in his hat a cockade of the new revolutionary colours: blue and red (for Paris) split by the white of Bourbon royalty. Meanwhile, the most intransigent aristocrats, including the king's brother, the comte d'Artois, left the country vowing to return only to destroy the Revolution, the first of many *émigrés* (emigrants) who would become its most feared enemies.

Paris in July marked only the most significant point in a widespread 'municipal revolution', which saw most major towns in France exchange their Old Regime institutions for either power-sharing with or complete takeover by various forms of 'revolutionary committee' drawn from the politicised Third Estate. In Rouen, for example, a bourgeois militia and a revolutionary committee, which shared power with the former municipality, were formed simultaneously with action in Paris, while Marseille had actually had a much earlier takeover by a committee in February. Ousted by troops later in the spring, this institution revived in the summer to force action on the older authorities. Of thirty cities with populations of over 20,000, four were taken over entirely by new forces, and sixteen saw power-sharing with some vestige of the older order left in place. Ten retained their older institutions unchanged, though doubtless with a new perceived balance of forces. It is reasonable to assume that this seizure of power was replicated at lower levels in the urban hierarchy, and the summer of 1789 across France clearly marked a profound redefinition of political power in French towns. The autonomy and self-interest of urban communities was to become a decisive factor in the re-ordering of the territory of France that was to follow, although the new authorities were often as concerned as the old to head off continuing popular disorder and food riots (document 3).[16]

The urban response to the crisis of the summer was partly occasioned by activities at the centre, but also owed a great deal to the alarming general situation of France in mid-1789. Ongoing fears of disorder culminated through much of rural France from the middle of July to the end of the first week in August, in what has come to be known as the 'Great Fear' (*Grande Peur*). Spreading from seven obscure original alarms, rumours of roving bands of brigands and aristocratic rebels flowed across the country, sometimes at speeds almost beyond rational explanation. With the whole country tense and primed for the outcome of the confrontation at Versailles, the smallest hint of unknown figures on the road, the rumour of disturbance in a neighbouring town, could become a reported horde of marauding, crop-burning, pillaging bandits. As communities responded to these fears by arming themselves and setting out on patrol, they could then trigger new rumours of armed bands, and so the tales spread.[17]

This Great Fear, though it has captured the imagination of historians, should not obscure the ongoing rural social conflict of 1789. Peter Jones points out that many duly-elected peasant representatives had found themselves excluded from the *bailliage* assemblies, which were limited by law to 200 participants. Manoeuvred out by more pushy urban representatives, disgruntled peasants bombarded Necker with letters denouncing the feudal regime in terms sometimes stronger than any of the *cahiers*. Those assemblies which had had rural participation often dispersed to carry away the impression that stating abuses had ended them, and that feudalism was over. Anger that returned when authorities tried to demonstrate that this was not so led on to direct attacks on seigneurial property, symbols and records.[18]

We have already seen that anti-seigneurial violence had engulfed several areas by the spring, and it spread in the summer to take in Alsace and Lower Normandy, and to see renewed violence in Franche-Comté, the Dauphiné and the far north. An analysis of such risings indicates clearly that they were not the work of suspicious outsiders, but of a social cross-section running from a rank and file of various kinds of labourer, to substantial tenants or independent farmers and rural artisans (document 4).

John Markoff has speculated on the basis of cross-analysis of rural disorder with *cahiers* complaints that it was in areas where the rural community was most united against external pressures that revolt was most likely. He notes that, for example, expression of grievances about communal rights came more strongly from areas that did not revolt. Such communal grazing or gleaning rights were likely to become an issue only where there was dispute in the community over how they should be used. Wealthy, middling and poorer residents might have entirely different priorities for their retention, modification or abolition. Areas that revolted tended to compose *cahiers* that focused on the 'big issues' of taxation, the role of the Estates-General, justice and the Church, and thus were clearly turned outward to the state of the country, rather than inward to their own squabbles. This is a further argument for recognising the significant quality of peasant insurrection in 1789.[19]

The response of the deputies of the National Assembly to the extent of unrest was the famous 'Night of 4 August'. During the first days of August, as news came in from the provinces of a rapidly rising tide of peasant violence, combined with reports from towns of tax riots, burning of customs-barriers and other disorder, a sense of crisis prevailed at the centre. Something had to be done to calm the country, and it was clear that 'feudalism' in all its ramifications was a central target of the unrest. Thus, in a chaotic and highly emotional overnight session, the rights of seigneurs, both honorific and financial, were declared abolished. With them, in a escalation of goodwill (or spite, depending on who was putting forward the proposals), were to go the tithes that funded the Church, all venality of judicial and municipal office, all fiscal privileges, and all the privileges and distinctions which marked one province, town or community from another.

In this way, the core structures of Old Regime society were cast aside, often by their own representatives. Some have seen this as a sign of the 'sublime' commitment to the nation that was being made, but this may be over-optimistic. Certainly when word reached the provinces of what had been done, not all were happy – Bretons, Alsatians and many others had exchanged a relatively privileged position on taxation for a totally unknown quantity. Discontent on issues such as this would take much of the next year to die down, and the loss of privileges would be used later in the decade against the Revolution. The issue of 'feudalism' in the countryside would be a source of conflict, and frequently of violence, for years to come.[20]

For the meantime, however, the decrees that followed in the week after 4 August to codify its measures seemed to serve their calming purpose, accompanied as they were by measures to intensify the surveillance of disorder from the lower orders, and to regulate the repression of 'seditious gatherings' (document 5). The deputies could thus press on with their mission to write a new constitution. After some debate, it was agreed that a Declaration of Rights would precede that document, and what was intended to be a provisional version was published on 26 August. Its first three articles codified a new political order:

1. Men are born and remain free and equal in rights. Social distinctions can be based only on public utility.
2. The aim of every political association is the preservation of the natural and imprescriptible rights of man. These rights are liberty, property, security and resistance to oppression.
3. The source of all sovereignty resides essentially in the nation. No body, no individual can exercise authority that does not explicitly proceed from it.

With these words the deputies were declaring null and void the traditions of the French monarchy and the entire aristocratic-corporate social order that underlay it. The remainder of the document guaranteed personal liberty under the law, rights to political participation, fair trials, freedom of expression and consent to fair and open methods of taxation. It ended at article seventeen:

Property being an inviolable and sacred right, no one can be deprived of it, unless legally established public necessity obviously demands it, and upon condition of a just and prior indemnity.[21]

Overall, the document was a profound and decisive repudiation of the Old Regime. Royal sovereignty yielded to the nation, the 'private law' of privileged groups was replaced by uniformity and legal equality, and a single definition of property emerged to replace a maze of customs and practices. However, building a new society on 'revolutionised' foundations was less straightforward than the production of this brief text. The elevation of property as a central right would challenge the pursuit of equality, at first in relation to feudal dues, and later in clashes with more radical conceptions of the body politic. Liberty and resistance to oppression would prove difficult to reconcile with property and security when issues of economic justice and survival were at stake.

Three days after passing the Declaration, the deputies restated their elite preoccupations by liberating the grain trade once more, and two days later, on 31 August, the Paris charity workshops that had been absorbing some of the tide of unemployment were closed. On the same day, a Parisian crowd determined to march on the 'bad citizens' holding up progress at Versailles had to be halted by the National Guard. Disruption of the food supply and economic hardship would re-emerge as an issue in the coming months. Emigration continued to create unemployment amongst the classes of servants and luxury artisans, alongside that provoked by general economic uncertainty.

The tide of purely political change nonetheless swept on. Late August and September saw a series of confrontations in the Assembly between a group, the *monarchiens*, who wanted a balanced constitution on the British model (a hereditary upper house, a royal veto on legislation), and those who took a more absolute view of the powers of elected representatives. Although committed radicals were a small minority of the total, the *monarchien* plans for an upper house were defeated through debate, aided by divisions amongst the nobility. In debates on the royal veto, a more compromise position was reached. The king was allowed a 'suspensive' rather than an 'absolute' veto, which was in effect a *monarchien* victory, as it would allow him to delay measures for up to six years. Meanwhile, under the present arrangements, the king's signature was necessary to promulgate the Assembly's decisions officially, and political stalemate set in when on 15 September Louis refused to sign either the decrees abolishing feudalism or the Declaration of Rights.

This caused considerable consternation, but there was little the deputies could do but press on with their debates. However, two weeks later news reached Paris that an 'orgiastic' banquet for a newly arrived royal regiment had been held in the presence of the king and queen on 1 October, at which the tricolour cockade had been stamped on amidst protestations of royalist fervour. Coming in the midst of turbulent demonstrations over the food supply in Paris, including threats by female consumers to lynch the municipal leaders, this provoked a massive response. Further demonstrations by women on 5 October were deflected by radical leaders towards Versailles, and the National Guard, in a state of near-mutiny, obliged Lafayette to lead them in the same direction.

The news from Versailles thus united the hungry crowd and the Guard, who had endured some ugly clashes in previous weeks. The cold, tired and wet crowds spent an uneasy night at Versailles, during which the Assembly itself was invaded by some of them, and some conservative and clerical members were harassed. The original women's march had been joined by men later in the day, and after their arrival more vehement elements in the crowds led a dramatic assault on the royal apartments, killing two Swiss Guards and almost reaching the queen. In the aftermath of this, Lafayette pulled off a remarkable political reconciliation, and amid cheers the duress of the crowds was masked as an agreement that the royal family would move to Paris. The king also agreed to pass the various measures he had been delaying, and the Assembly voted to follow the exodus to Paris on 9 October.[22]

The 'October Days' illustrate the delicate balance in the relationship between the people and the monarchy. If the middle classes were wrestling to find a new kind of national sovereignty through their stoic models, it would appear that the common people had little difficulty in simply adopting the sovereignty practiced by the crown, and by the seigneur in the countryside. The symbol of both royal and feudal authority, as it impinged on the peasant or labourer, was the gallows, and the right of punishment, as de Flesselles and de Launay had been punished, would be cherished by crowds throughout the Revolution. Hostile observers would use such practices as fuel for condemnation of popular irrationality, characterising crowds' alleged lack of control as 'effeminate' and hence dangerous, and indeed would emphasise the role of women to show this. Even commentators more sympathetic to popular action in general were nervous of female involvement, and attempted through various pamphlets published after the October Days to direct women back into a wholly passive role. We may note, however, that as men in general tried to exclude women systematically from the public sphere, they would continue throughout the Revolution to use the subsistence issue to reinsert themselves. Those who queued for bread, and watched their children starve, would not be silenced easily.[23]

Advocates of 'popular sovereignty' would continue in later years to have great difficulty with how the people saw that phrase in action. Where the paradox really lay in the early years of the Revolution, however, was in the co-existence of this model with the acknowledgement of the king. Not only was a constitutional monarchy the only political system really considered at this time, but even violent protestors showed no real hostility to his role. In the face of perceived injustice or recalcitrance, a violent mood could easily generate, but it overlay a basic willingness to believe good of the king, an acceptance of his paternal role, and a hope that he would fulfil the new role placed on him of 'restorer of French liberty'. In October 1789, as at later times, most would blame Marie-Antoinette and her advisers rather than Louis himself. At this point, the belief that his personal presence would also be a guarantee of the food supply to Paris was also strong, and borne out in an improved situation as the autumn wore on.

The latter improvement did not come, however, before further food riots had seen a baker lynched in front of the Hôtel-de-Ville on 21 October, leading to the execution of two supposed ringleaders and the immediate passage of a draconian Martial Law statute for use against dangerous crowds. The disorders of the summer were growing less and less tolerable to the majority of the political class, who saw the Revolution as nearly over, and popular grievances as increasingly unjustifiable in the new order of things. Within a week of these events, the Assembly had agreed that not all would participate in the future political life of the country. Notwithstanding the Declaration of Rights, in order to be entitled to vote, an individual had to fulfil certain residence qualifications, not be a domestic servant (regarded as too 'dependent') and crucially show that he (it was, naturally, always 'he') paid direct taxes equal to at least three days' wages for a labourer in his locality, a sum to be determined by municipalities. These criteria marked out the 'active citizens' from those 'non-active'. A payment of ten days' wages in tax was necessary for eligibility to stand for public office, and a larger contribution still (a *marc d'argent*, 52 *livres*, perhaps four or five weeks' wages by the criteria used) to stand as a deputy for the next Assembly.

In the week after passing these measures, the Assembly again swung to dramatic radical acts to resolve the problem of the public finances. Loans advertised in August had conspicuously failed to find many prepared to lend to the state in its present condition, and the 'patriotic contribution' decreed early in October as a voluntary 25 per cent tax on income did not seem likely to do better. The Assembly was unwilling to contemplate a national bankruptcy, a fact some attributed to the influence of financiers who would lose out (document 6). The deputies on 2 November decreed instead that the vast property-holdings of the Catholic Church in France would be put at the disposal of the nation. Estimates place this resource at 6–10 per cent of all land, and from December its value would be drawn on by issuing *assignats*, a form of paper currency designed to be redeemed in exchange for the lands, which were to be auctioned off as 'national property' (*biens nationaux*). At first the *assignats* would only be issued in very large denominations, intended to pay off state creditors who would treat them as a kind of government bond. They put France on a slippery slope towards inflation, however, as the state conspicuously failed to improve its income in future years, and the issuing of more *assignats* rapidly became a substitute for money it did not have. Meanwhile, the ideological implications of removing the independent resources of the Church, and in return offering state salaries to the clergy, were profound, but seemed to bother the Assembly little, as it concluded the year in optimistic mood with debates on the administrative re-ordering of France.

Notes

1 A. de Tocqueville, *The Ancien Regime*, Everyman edn, trans. J. Bonner, London, 1988, p. 114.

2 G. V. Taylor, 'Revolutionary and Nonrevolutionary Content in

the *Cahiers* of 1789, an Interim Report', *French Historical Studies*, 7, 1972, pp. 479–502.

3 See the summary account in W. Doyle, *Origins of the French Revolution*, 2nd edn, Oxford, 1988, pp. 154–7.

4 J. Markoff, 'Peasants Protest: The Claims of Lord, Church and State in the *Cahiers de Doléances* of 1789', *Comparative Studies in Society and History*, 39, 1990, pp. 413–54; pp. 416, 428–9. This work, and much more, has been incorporated into his *The Abolition of Feudalism: Peasants, Lords and Legislators in the French Revolution*, University Park, PA, 1996.

5 Information on harvests and weather from 1785 to 1799 is tabulated by C. Jones, *The Longman Companion to the French Revolution*, London, 1988, pp. 284–5. On the effects of the 1786 treaty see the case study by B. T. Ragan, 'Rural Political Activism and Fiscal Equality in the Revolutionary Somme', in B. T. Ragan and E. A. Williams (eds), *Recreating Authority in Revolutionary France*, New Brunswick, NJ, 1992, pp. 36–56.

6 G. Lefebvre, *The Great Fear of 1789: Rural Panic in Revolutionary France*, London, 1973 (orig. pub. 1932), p. 14.

7 *Ibid.*, pp. 14–23 *passim*, esp. p. 21.

8 R. M. Andrews, *Law, Magistracy and Crime in Old Regime Paris, 1735–1789*, vol. 1 *The System of Criminal Justice*, Cambridge, 1994, pp. 197–8. Figures given by T. Tackett, *Becoming a Revolutionary: The Deputies of the French National Assembly and the Emergence of a Revolutionary Culture (1789–1790)*, Princeton, 1996, pp. 32–3, differ slightly, as there remains uncertainty about accreditation and precise social identities, but the import of Tackett's figures is the same.

9 Tackett, *Becoming a Revolutionary*, pp. 29–31.

10 *Ibid.*, pp. 34–8.

11 As Tackett discusses, *ibid.*, pp. 89–90, this is the attribution of writers as diverse as Lefebvre and Doyle. The 'Thirty' included Duport, d'Eprémesnil (who would soon switch to ardent conservatism), Lepeletier, Lafayette, the Lameths, Condorcet, Dupont de Nemours, and Mirabeau. The following discussion is drawn from *ibid.*, pp. 82–8.

12 See *ibid.*, chapters 4 and 5.

13 See Lefebvre, *Great Fear*, pp. 59–61.

14 The classic account of these events, still not beaten for detailed narrative, is J. Godechot, *The Taking of the Bastille*, London, 1970, from which much of the following information is drawn. However, for the specific events of 12 July, see P. Spagnoli, 'The Revolution Begins: Lambesc's Charge, 12 July 1789', *French Historical Studies*, 17, 1991, pp. 466–97, which contradicts many traditional accounts through rediscovered eyewitness testimonies.

15 On the topic of reactions to such deaths, see C. Lucas, 'Talking About Urban Popular Violence in 1789', in A. Forrest and P. Jones (eds),

Reshaping France: Town, Country and Region during the French Revolution, Manchester, 1991, pp. 122–36. An interesting, if perhaps over-complex, explanation for their theatricality may be found in B. Singer, 'Violence in the French Revolution: Forms of Ingestion/Forms of Expulsion', in F. Fehér (ed.), *The French Revolution and the Birth of Modernity,* Berkeley, 1990, pp. 150–73.

16 The classic account of this is L. Hunt, 'Committees and Communes: Local Politics and National Revolution in 1789', *Comparative Studies in Society and History,* 18, 1976, pp. 321–46.

17 Lefebvre, *Great Fear,* documents this process in painstaking detail, pp. 137ff. For a more recent case study, see C. Ramsay, *The Ideology of the Great Fear: The Soissonais in 1789,* Baltimore, 1992.

18 See P. M. Jones, *The Peasantry in the French Revolution,* Cambridge, 1988, pp. 62–71.

19 J. Markoff, 'Peasant Grievances and Peasant Insurrection: France in 1789', *Journal of Modern History,* 62, 1990, pp. 445–76, esp. pp. 461–8.

20 See the summary account in P. M. Jones, *Reform and Revolution in France: The Politics of Transition, 1774–1791,* Cambridge, 1995, pp. 181–6. A longer discussion of these events can be found in M. P. Fitzsimmons, *The Remaking of France: The National Assembly and the Constitution of 1791,* Cambridge, 1994.

21 This translation is taken from K. M. Baker (ed.), *Readings in Western Civilisation 7: The Old Regime and the French Revolution,* Chicago, 1987, pp. 237–9.

22 See the excellent and subtle account of social and political interactions around these events in B. M. Shapiro, *Revolutionary Justice in Paris, 1789–1790,* Cambridge, 1993, pp. 84ff. A rather more scathing account of the intervention of the 'mob' is contained in S. Schama, *Citizens: A Chronicle of the French Revolution,* London, 1989, pp. 466ff.

23 See the documents on the aftermath of 5–6 October in D. G. Levy, H. B. Applewhite and M. D. Johnson (eds), *Women in Revolutionary Paris, 1789–1795, Selected Documents,* London, 1979. For a more general overview, which particularly focuses on the political implications of women's subsistence demands, see O. H. Hufton, *Women and the Limits of Citizenship in the French Revolution,* Toronto, 1992, chapter 1, 'Women and Politics', pp. 1–50.

4

The reconstructive project and the political landscape in 1790

1790 has been described as the 'Peaceful Year' of the Revolution, but that is a term that can only be applied relatively.[1] Although the year saw no major political crises or insurrections at the centre, and the agenda of constitutional and administrative reformation went on apace, the wider body politic of France continued to experience convulsions, and old and new faultlines marked the political landscape. Only a pessimist, however, could have looked back from the end of 1790 and not have seen a year of achievements – iniquitous taxes had been officially abolished, and the institutions of nobility and Church taken in hand. Moreover, the recasting of France as a constitutional and (relatively) democratic state had acquired visible shape in the new administrative units and assemblies spreading across the country.

It was in the remaking of the administrative geography of France that the Revolution left its firmest mark – whatever else was done by subsequent regimes, none tried to do away with the pattern of *départements* that was laid over France in 1790, and these county-sized units persist to this day, the vast majority with the same borders they were given in the Revolution (see map, p. viii).[2] The remaking of local administration was a crucial issue for the deputies of the National Assembly, as they saw the old provinces as bastions of aristocratic power, where particularist privileges and interests worked against the wider public good. So firm was the desire to eradicate this system that the first plans put forward would have carved up the nation in almost geometric fashion, ignoring landscape and settlement in the interests of overall uniformity, a characteristically Enlightenment approach.

Others proposed instead merely subdividing the old provinces in various ways to obtain uniformity without denying history. The map shown to the Assembly in October 1789 was a compromise between a grid-like arrangement and the retention of the borders of many of the more significant provinces. However, in many places the shadow of the provinces did not survive the intense rivalries between towns that immediately broke out over the spoils of the reorganisation. This contest over local interests, perhaps more than many of the earlier reforming plans, ensured that the *départements* as laid out represented a radical rethinking of the map of France.[3]

There were eighty-three *départements*, as finally decreed on 26 February 1790, with eighty-three capital towns (or *chefs-lieux*) to be allotted. At a rough count some 200 towns had a claim on that role, and the additional trade, population and income, not to mention prestige, that it would bring. The process of finalising the new administrative map had been given to committees of Assembly deputies from each region. What followed in the course of their deliberations was in some cases bitter argument, in others what can only be called 'horse-trading'. Conflict might be diffuse – nine towns contested for the *chef-lieu* of the Seine-et-Marne before it went to Melun – or represent a more direct rivalry. Long-standing tensions between, for example, Vienne and Grenoble, Sarlat and Périgueux, and Cahors and Montauban revived over this issue. Aix was made *chef-lieu* of the Bouches-du-Rhône, leaving Marseille nursing a grudge that would be expressed after the fall of the monarchy, with suitable political justifications, by kidnapping the administration and bringing it to Marseille.[4]

The departmental names mentioned above also illustrate the concern of the Assembly to escape old patterns. Old provincial names were rejected, and so too was an initial naming after the *chefs-lieux* – too many resentments would have festered at that. Almost without exception names were taken from rivers or other geographical features. Although this suggests a concern with 'natural' boundaries, the deputies were not experts enough (and perhaps too much townsmen) to give much unity to the agricultural landscape of *départements*. Georges Lefebvre counted six separate agrarian zones in the narrow strip of the Nord *département*, as well as a French/Flemish linguistic divide. When civil war came to France in 1793, lines of conflict often ran through *départements*, following the margins of different landscapes and settlement patterns. In this way, the conflicts of an older France continued to show through, but perhaps it was because the map of *départements* ignored this so resolutely that it survived so well.

While it was Assembly deputies who made the final decisions, urban communities had begun to petition for their interests as soon as the issue of a repartition of the country had been raised. This process would continue through much of 1790 with the allocation first of departmental, then district capitals, and finally the smallest *chefs-lieux* for *cantons* (which had no distinct council, but were the sites for electoral assemblies in rural areas). A pyramid of judicial institutions also required geographical distribution, and for all of these competition was intense. Hundreds of written representations came to the Assembly, often accompanied by 'special deputies' from the communities concerned. Many stressed the extent to which towns in the Old Regime had relied on the income brought by an administrative and judicial population, and would be ruined if they were deserted. Naked self-interest from these communities was often on display – some might plead their destitution if deprived of a replacement for an Old Regime centre, then in a fresh petition claim that their booming business community made them an ideal site for a new Commercial Court. When towns submitted maps showing their central place in the local population structure, they left off roads and villages near neighbouring towns, and marked up every track and hamlet near their own. Although the tone of many of these submissions may have harped on potential misfortune, they clearly show both that the goal of remaking France was taken up throughout the country, and that urban elites retained a healthy self-interest about the outcome. 'Urban' may in this case be an oversimplification. Centres of population at the lowest level could replicate the strife between major towns and, as shall be seen later, use their new-found autonomy in pursuit of other agendas too.

That autonomy had come when, as if to counter-balance the radicalism of the *départements'* formation, in early December 1789 the Assembly decreed that every place of habitation that had had an administrative identity under the Old Regime would form a municipality, or commune, in the new order. This resulted in the creation of some 44,000 communes, many of which were minute, but which had the virtue of extending a democratic and uniform administration into every corner of France (and of directly offending no one). Each commune had a General Council (*Conseil général*), the size of which depended on the size of the commune, but which included an elected mayor and *procureur* (legal officer), as well as a number of ordinary members (*notables*).

Larger towns and cities had essentially similar arrangements, but with the addition of a distinction between the full *Conseil général* and a *Corps municipal*, a subset of that body, which met more regularly. Cities were also divided geographically into sections, where electoral assemblies met, and which also elected their own neighbourhood administrators. The number of sections varied with population – from five or six up to twenty-four in Marseille, twenty-eight in Bordeaux, thirty-two in Lyon, and forty-eight in Paris.

Elections took place for municipal posts in January and February 1790.[5] Here for the first time the active citizenship and eligibility requirements came into force. The electoral assemblies in which the voters gathered could be bearpits of factional manoeuvring, or, as for example at Bayeux, show the problems of demanding new levels of political participation. Bayeux was a declining town in the late eighteenth century, dominated by the Church, as the centre of one of the country's richest dioceses, but with little independent vitality as a community. It had 629 active citizens in 1790, of whom 352 were eligible for office. In the electoral process, the repercussions of the disorder and hostility shown to tax-gathering officials throughout 1789 were visible. Only half the electorate bothered to vote for the mayor, and the choice fell on the bishop, representing traditional authority and stability. In the subsequent election to fill the six *notables'* places on the council, only 294 voted. Four of the six men with the highest votes refused to serve. Only one of the next four down the list accepted, and one of the next three after that. To fill the fifth and sixth places, they had to go thirty places down the list, first to a lawyer with seventy-seven votes, and finally to a minor noble with under twenty. The men elected spent much of the next six months prevaricating about their responsibilities, bearing out their political nature as a conservative, even reactionary group, while pleading the impossibility of raising independent revenues. They refused to reinstate the municipal customs-dues on the city gates in the firm belief that the result would be a massacre by resentful locals.

Such reluctance and helpless (or truculent) inaction was far from the whole story of the new municipalities. For example, in Lille the same elections saw the commercial bourgeoisie swept to power with fourteen of the seventeen council seats, and keen once in office to retain municipal customs-posts, from which a healthy revenue was collected.[6] It has been estimated that the rounds of municipal and departmental elections in 1790 saw an average turnout of between 40 and 50 per cent of active citizens, a figure concealing wide variations, but a higher one than recorded at any later point in the Revolution. What is also noticeable about the figures is a distinction between urban and rural patterns of turnout. As Malcolm Crook has summarised, 'the bigger the commune, the smaller the vote and vice-versa'.[7]

There are a variety of plausible reasons to account for this. One of the most obvious is that voting in a small rural *canton* or municipality was a relatively simple matter – with a few men to be chosen, and relatively few electors, the business could usually be done in a day. It has also been suggested that a relative continuity with Old Regime rural governance via the convening of heads of households aided rural turnout, unlike the sharp break with previous urban assemblies convened on corporatist lines. The novelty of the urban arrangements for neighbourhood gatherings was compounded by the relatively cumbersome procedure decreed in late 1789, under which urban elections could take several days, if not a week or more, a substantial disincentive in itself.

The conscientious urban elector in 1790 would be contained in a temporary assembly-hall, usually a church, and obliged to write out his list of preferred candidates on his ballot paper. Voting went through several rounds as an overall majority was sought for every place to be filled. As lists could not be prepared in advance, but had to be composed while standing at the voting-table, it was a test both of the memory of each voter and of the patience of the collectivity. Yet more taxing was the task of nominating twice as many names as there were places to fill. Parisian electors, to take the extreme example, had to write a list of up to seventy-eight names, and although this was done in section assemblies, with several hundred voters present this could leave the tellers with 20,000 votes to transcribe on each round of voting. Poor handwriting, the eighteenth-century habit of knowing people only by their surname, and the variability of spelling many names, led to further confusion. Given that candidates were not allowed to declare themselves or solicit support, voters were left to judge who might be worthy of office – hence the long 'tail' of nominees at Bayeux, and thirty mayoral candidates at Toulon on the same occasion. Of course, lobbying and factional campaigning did go on, but its enforced behind-the-scenes nature could only add to confusion.

The example of Bayeux also shows another flaw in the system – those chosen might not wish to serve, and in a few cases might even have been elected out of malice. This problem could lead to yet further new elections, although the procedure of simultaneously electing *suppléants*, or substitutes, mandatory for national deputies, was sometimes adopted as a local insurance for other posts. When, to crown the difficulties, electoral assemblies had to select their own presiding officers, and this in itself could take up all the first day of meeting, it is more surprising that so many voted, than so few.

The enthusiasm for the local autonomy and empowerment offered by the Revolution's innovations is here clearly demonstrated. However, as the process was repeated seven or more times over the following two years, in times of growing strife and ultimately of war, that enthusiasm declined markedly. Moreover, the keen initial seizure of municipal power in rural areas, discussed further below, was followed by a very sharp drop in participation from 1791, so that urban voters, except in the largest cities, were soon outpolling the peasantry. In this the very 'urban' nature of revolutionary political development is confirmed, and was underpinned by the broad socio-economic features of the body of elected officials.

Once the municipal and departmental elections were complete (the latter not until the summer of 1790, the first repeat of the voting procedures), a multi-layered 'political class' – of municipal councillors, electoral college members, and departmental officers – was installed in revolutionary France.[8] In several fundamental ways, it is impossible to deny this group the label 'bourgeois'.

They were overwhelmingly non-noble, very rarely did they work with their hands, by definition they paid substantial taxes, and they were essentially town-dwelling property-owners. Even in highly rural *départements* rural landowners were outnumbered on councils by lawyers and/or merchants. Those who had bought royal office before the Revolution, a large proportion of the more prosperous non-nobles, showed up strongly in early elections, although fading from view later (perhaps because of disenchantment or replacement by 'new men', perhaps because such office-holding was later concealed as insufficiently revolutionary). In the four large towns of Amiens, Bordeaux, Nancy and Toulouse, between two-thirds and three-quarters of municipal council members in 1790 were either lawyers or merchants, with the latter making up half the council in the first two of these. The strong representation of merchants in trading cities was a gain for them over the pre-revolutionary situation, often coming at the expense of *noblesse de robe* elites now fading from sight. It was also an exception, as generally it was lawyers and other professionals who made up the bedrock of the new political class.

There are obvious reasons for this – there were very many lawyers in pre-revolutionary France, servicing the maze of now-abolished jurisdictions, or simply living from rental incomes while enjoying the social status that legal accreditation to an important court gave. Office above the municipal level required permanent or periodic absence from home. For this, professionals, and especially those whose 'profession' concealed a landowning or investment income, had a freedom denied to most merchants, to almost all shopkeepers and artisans, and to anyone active in agriculture. They were also used to the procedures and frustrations of administrative and deliberative business, and to the paperwork attendant on both. Lawyers did not take over France at the Revolution, but they were available, and perhaps necessary, to fill many of the new posts the new order was creating. The shift from a wide rural participation at the base to an urban dominance at higher levels, already marked in the elections to the Estates-General in 1789, would, despite its very practical origins, pose significant political problems for the revolutionary administration in years to come.

The 'political class' was to mutate over time (while not losing its urban nature), for a variety of reasons, but as its members took up their places in 1790 in the network of new revolutionary institutions, continued disturbances marked resistance from those who would undo all the Revolution's work. Many of these centred, inevitably, around the socio-political agenda of royalty, nobility and Catholicism, the heart of what was coming to be ever-more clearly defined as 'counter-revolution'.[9] February 1790 saw, for example, the decrees intended to dissolve France's monastic establishments, and also the execution after a long trial of the marquis de Favras, ringleader of an *émigré* plot to 'rescue' the royal family from Paris. In southern France, tensions between the Protestant population, often merchants and employers, who had welcomed the Revolution, and Catholics who did not (and might even see it as a plot to oppress them) were rising, and could be played on by *émigré* conspirators and their sympathisers.

There was a rash of counter-revolutionary revolts across the south in the spring and summer of 1790. Some were demonstrations by a conservative elite, such as the abortive rising by the National Guard of Toulouse's wealthy St-Barthélemy quarter in April. Others, like those at Montauban in May, were attacks by Catholics on Protestants. Most significant of these was the so-called *bagarre* (brawl) at Nîmes in early June. It was a brawl that left several hundred dead, as social, political and economic tensions led Catholic workers to rise against their Protestant employers, whose organisation via the local National Guard turned defeat for the Catholics into massacre. These events were fomented, at least in part, by *émigré* agents, as clearly was the *camp de Jalès* in August, where 20,000 met and agreed a counter-revolutionary manifesto declaring the work of the Revolution void, criminal and treasonous. National Guard units dispersed the assembly without difficulty, but simple repression could not make the fact of determined opposition to all that '1789' stood for go away.

France's second city of Lyon had seen insurrection in February, and disorder broke out more extensively in July – episodes which have also been claimed for the influence of the counter-revolution. Recent work on that city, however, suggests a more complex socio-political dynamic to these events.[10] The ennobled oligarchy that controlled the city before 1789 had combined with mercantile interests to head off more popular and radical forces in that year, notably by forming a 'Volunteer Corps' out of the propertied, their sons and employees, to police the city during wide-spread disorders in July. This socially exclusive force was kept in being into 1790, reneging on promises to dissolve them into a more inclusive National Guard establishment, itself only created at the end of January 1790 after protests. The power to locally set the cash value of the active citizenship qualification was also used to keep the franchise as narrow as possible. These issues were the focus for tensions between the conservative elite and the wider body of artisan workers. This group centred around a large and relatively homogeneous silk-weaving community, with long-standing grievances about the unjust organisation of their trade under the merchants' control. The political elements of their grievances, although not necessarily their socio-economic complaints, were supported by elements of the city's professional classes who defined themselves as the 'Patriots'.

It appears that the conservative leaders may have gone out of their way to provoke violence, seeking to disrupt the passage to a new municipality attendant on elections in February. Thus on 7 February their deployment of a large force of Volunteers to the central Arsenal, in the face of National Guard protests, led to rioting and a popular seizure of the Arsenal, followed by the distribution of its weapons and attacks on municipal leaders. In the face of this, the Volunteers were disbanded almost at once, and the franchise was lowered sufficiently to admit perhaps half the male population over twenty-five, and to nearly double the numbers eligible for office.

A relatively conservative municipal council nonetheless emerged from elections later in February – perhaps the popular violence had indeed encouraged voters to seek stability. The 'Patriots' had thus not gained anything from a tacit support of insurrection, a support which was itself hedged around with entirely typical bourgeois fears about the dangers of disorder to property. Political hatred between 'Patriots' and conservatives grew increasingly venomous, while the concerns of the wider population went unanswered. Central among these concerns were the municipal customs-dues, denounced in the *cahiers* of 1789 as a burden on industry and the poor, but continued for want of a reliable new source of income. Throughout the first half of 1790, 'Patriot' pamphleteers campaigned for their swift replacement, calling special attention to their role in financing a municipal debt which had relieved the old oligarchy of taxes. Naturally such pamphlets did not advocate direct action, but when concerns rose amongst the population about bread prices in the summer, the people did not need pamphlets to encourage them to resume a pattern of *taxation populaire* in June. This escalated to collective invasion of the council chamber in early July calling for the customs-posts' abolition, followed rapidly by direct armed attacks on the posts. The council suspended the dues, and did not dare comply with National Assembly orders to reinstate them until 21 August, with the backing of a large garrison of regular troops.

By that time it was clear that, although National Guard units from popular areas may have participated in insurrection, the majority of the Guard had thrown in its lot on the side of property and order. When sniping came from a popular district on 26 July, the response was an invasion on the 28th by 1,800 troops and Guards from wealthier quarters to disarm the area. This house-to-house procedure involved smashing furniture, ripping up mattresses and the gratuitous destruction of unfinished weaving – a direct attack on workers' livelihoods. Even before this last act, popular voices were being heard condemning the richer citizens as *muscadins* – idle, luxurious, and thus immoral and counter-revolutionary.

Meanwhile both conservatives and 'Patriots' sought to explain popular discontent as resulting from agitation – by self-interested stirrers of the barbarous mob on the one hand, counter-revolutionaries and dangerous foreigners on the other. In this respect, many of the beliefs and attitudes underlying the politics of Lyon were typical of those of the whole country. The rhetoric of a united people created before and during 1789 required that political and social divisions be discounted as fomented from outside this 'people', even while clear signs were available that crowds and protestors did not necessarily share this vision. The vigour and vitriol of contestation in Lyon at this point was not typical of France in 1790, and both the city's sharply divided social structure in general, and its future political trajectory, were likewise unusual. However, Lyon's troubles reveal openly what was largely concealed elsewhere, and provide us with a clear example of the socio-political tensions fundamentally unresolved by 1789, and for which the constitutional project of the Assembly offered little relief.

Nonetheless, as such upheavals continued, the work of the Assembly moved on. The salt tax passed into history in March, the grain trade was freed (again) in April, and in November the internal customs-barriers were abolished. Municipal customs-posts, thanks to the accessibility of their revenues, would however continue operating into the following year. November also saw a land tax agreed as a basis for a new fiscal regime. Between August 1790 and January of the following year, the judicial system was overhauled: its seigneurial and provincial structures replaced by civil and criminal networks and hierarchies conforming to new boundaries, its privileged judges replaced by elected officials. All the Old Regime courts, including the *parlements*, were suppressed officially from September. Thus the *noblesse de robe* passed into history. Even more momentously, hereditary nobility itself had been abolished in June, with remarkably little clamour, although the subsequent alienation of the nobility doubtless helped to root developing opposition even more deeply. The Civil Constitution of the Clergy was agreed in July, reorganising the Catholic Church in France and subordinating it to the state which had taken away its independence in seizing its property.[11] This could be fairly held responsible for much, if not most, of the Revolution's future violence, as we shall see, but in 1790 there was still a political will to conciliate the wider Catholic hierarchy. For this reason, the Assembly declined at this point to annex the enclave of Papal territory in the south, around Avignon, despite a successful pro-French insurrection there in June.

Meanwhile in Paris, enthusiasm for the Revolution's promises could also be read as a challenge to the new revolutionary order. The Assembly's debate in May about the power to make war and peace (eventually divided awkwardly between king and legislature) had seen riots in Paris against right-wing publications. The same month also saw lynchings of thieves, seized from escorting National Guards on the way to detention, after rumours had spread that corruption (itself implicitly counter-revolutionary) was allowing criminals to escape the law. Such tokens of popular justice were read by the press and the rulers of the city as disorders provoked by counter-revolutionaries for their own purposes. The final form for the government of the city was also decided in May, and the suppression of the sixty electoral districts led to outcry from radical democrats, who had seen their meetings and scrutiny as an important check on the exercise of municipal power. A centre of this concern was the District des Cordeliers, home to a nucleus of influential radical politicians, most notably Danton, Desmoulins and Hébert. In response to the loss of the district (merged with a more conservative area to form the Section du Théâtre-Français), radicals established the Society of Friends of the Rights of Man, soon better-known as the Cordeliers Club. Here doctrines of political equality were preached, along with a far more direct form of democracy than was practised under the active-citizenship rules. Soon this club, which allowed both women and members of the lower classes access to its debates, was to become a role model for others, and after the turn of the year its politics would lean increasingly to republicanism.[12]

Although that spectre still lay mostly in the future, the authorities were not taking any chances with the sentiments of the capital. The National Guard commander Lafayette and his associates in the municipality sponsored anti-seditious pamphleteering throughout the summer, partly in the belief that the duc d'Orléans planned a rabble-rousing return from temporary exile. Parisians volunteered *en masse* to prepare the site for a 'Festival of Federation' on 14 July, and welcomed thousands of National Guards from around the country. In return they were treated to a quasi-military, quasi-religious display, centred on a Catholic mass and the presence of the king, which emphasised unity and clearly subordinated enthusiasm to order. Six weeks later a forceful reminder of this agenda came from the garrison city of Nancy, where a regiment of Swiss troops, in dispute with its officers, was fiercely repressed following orders from Lafayette. The Assembly approved these actions a few days later, to the anger and dismay of radicals. There were many sincere revolutionaries, however, who saw the disciplining of the army as crucial. Soldiers in many regiments had been defying their 'aristocratic' officers, who frequently responded by emigration, leading to a steady degradation in fighting capacity, while the powers of Europe were sheltering overt counter-revolutionaries and were permanently on a war-footing. Memories were still strong of the Prussian invasion that had ended revolution in the Dutch Republic in 1787, and insurrection would be crushed in the Austrian Netherlands (modern-day Belgium) in November 1790. Real war was not yet on the political agenda, but the threat was there, and many saw good reason to value order and unity above concessions to ignorant crowds or misguided humanitarians.[13]

Of course, the fact that valuing social order above radical demands made perfect sense seen from the Assembly did not mean that it appealed to the bulk of the population, who had their own situation to worry about. The example of Lyon shows that urban groups nursed a power-keg of political and socio-economic grievances, and the rural majority had equal reason to be dubious about the Revolution's claimed benefits. The force of rural demands from 1789 on has been seen as 'a gigantic centrifuge ... spinning the centralised state into smithereens', and it might equally well be argued that this machine also tore apart all efforts to reconcile the 'feudal question' with the rights of property.[14]

Rural communities replicated the larger urban struggles over sites of administration during 1790. The *cahiers* of 1789 had in many cases already expressed fierce local rivalries, in some cases over issues of prestige, such as the siting of churches and parish boundaries, in others a variety of issues linked to the distribution of taxation and the availability of justice. These were key tenets of life in the eighteenth century for a rural population burdened with a multiplicity of taxes and jurisdictions, and inclined to dispute both. The autonomy offered by the decree creating the municipalities was seized by the peasantry as an unprecedented empowerment. Hamlets of a handful of households declared themselves municipalities in the Aveyron, while in other areas what was at stake was shown by the reports of violence threatened to neighbouring communities over boundaries and elections. Rivalries between communes forced to come together into a *canton* assembly for elections might lead to fights, boycotts or secessions – the latter sometimes officially sanctioned as the safest way to avoid deep-seated disputes.[15]

Older disputes might be compounded by new ones, as once communities had become communes, this freedom became part of schemes to do down rivals and to better themselves. It was evident to the peasantry that a *bourg* with the status of district *chef-lieu*, or failing that the centre of a *canton*, would have material gains. The site of a court (and every *chef-lieu de canton* would ultimately have a magistrate in residence) was bound to benefit from partiality in decisions, especially in tight-knit communities. The occasional go-ahead municipality even managed to shift themselves across departmental borders in pursuit of more agreeable local alliances.

This was one side of the centrifugal power of rural politics in the Revolution. Given the chance to free themselves from the burden of central administrative tutelage, peasant communities seized it with both hands, and would later yield only grudgingly, and sometimes at the cost of blood. Another side was the ongoing reluctance to pay anything to any authorities, which was to dog the finances of the state throughout the Revolution, and which at this point effectively sabotaged the Assembly's plan to redeem feudal dues.

Overt violent anti-seigneurialism, which had been such a feature of 1789, had still not died out in 1790. A wide rural zone between Bordeaux, Montauban and the Massif Central saw a revival of attacks on châteaux between December 1789 and March 1790. Armed expeditions came in waves from various *pays* in over a hundred separate incidents, involving over 300 communities. In the classic pattern already evident the year before, oppressive lords or their stewards were singled out for vengeance, with Church institutions also coming under attack, either as feudal landlords or as titheholders and hoarders of supplies. Peasant action was not always brutal, and seldom chaotic – in one case a particularly hated *seigneur* was obliged to watch as the contents of his château were publicly auctioned, and this area saw the widespread planting of 'may-poles' as symbols of revolt, which would evolve into a revolutionary cult of the 'liberty-tree'. Such acts nevertheless spread fear and hostility among the property-owning classes, who often took part in National Guard expeditions to quell unrest, and intensified the urban–rural split already visible in revolutionary politics. A similar outbreak led to assaults on some thirty châteaux in Upper Brittany in late January 1790, and lower-level unrest and resistance was widespread (document 7).[16]

One of the provocations for the south-western revolt in 1790 was the attempt by some seigneurs to enforce feudal obligations at law, and the realisation by peasants that this was still possible. The decree of 11 August 1789 which 'destroys in its entirety the feudal regime' did no such thing as far as the financially most burdensome elements were concerned, and indeed allowed them to be collected as usual. Moreover, when in March 1790 the Assembly decreed definitively on the subject, its social conservatism was fully on display. A spurious hard-and-fast division was invented between a few 'relics of serfdom', which could be erased, and a system of 'charges on the land'. These latter were held to be a justifiable form of private property, including elements such as milling and baking monopolies. The drafters of the legislation clearly valued property over liberty in the Rights of Man, ruling that none of these 'charges' should be revoked without compensation to the owners. The definitive blow to peasant hopes came in early May with the publication of the terms for redemption of these dues – twenty times the annual value for cash dues, twenty-five for those paid in kind. Even this was protested as too low by some seigneurs. No state aid was available, and arrears had to be paid off first. The Assembly made a slight concession to those whose feudal overlord was the now-nationalised Church. They could redeem annual and casual dues (i.e. occasional, such as on the sale of land) separately; all others had to redeem all at once, or not at all. Even this last concession was not granted until November, by which time the failings of the planned system had already become apparent.

With the passing of the March decree, seigneurial aggression had resumed in the countryside. Seigneurs, now often renaming themselves 'fief-owners' to emphasise their property-rights, pursued claims for dues in kind owing from the 1789 harvest, often timing them for when the cash price of grain was peaking. Others continued the intrusive practice of revising their feudal land-registers, a practice formally forbidden by the Assembly. When the new district court system was established in November 1790, some of its first plaintiffs were fief-owners pursuing defaulting vassals, and often winning judgments against them. Needless to say, the seigneurs were not the only ones taking action on this issue. As Peter Jones notes, a range of tactics was open to peasant communities: 'they quibbled over details, they demanded access to title-deeds, they bombarded the authorities with petitions [against the redemption-payment levels] … and they took up arms'.[17]

In all of these aspects rural communities can be seen acting collectively on this issue. Administrative petitioning and querying of details (such as who should pay for the transport of payments in kind to seigneurs' stores) were almost always acts of communities, or indeed communes, drawing on their official existence to add authority to their claims. The demand for access to original title-deeds to prove liability for dues was another notch in the escalation of rural assertion. Over the northern two-thirds of France where the legal doctrine of *nul terre sans seigneur* (no land without a lord) held sway, fief-owners had never needed to prove their 'primordial title', and the legislation of 1790 made no change to this. In fact, it allowed seigneurs who had had their land-registers destroyed, or who had renounced their rights under pressure in 1789, to reclaim them. Nevertheless, through 1790 reports grew of rural communities obstinately delaying payment until such titles were produced, and equally often using the demand as a thin cover for brazen refusal to pay. Local authorities and envoys from Paris attempted various compromise arrangements, but the harvest of 1790 stayed resolutely away from fief-owners' barns. Over the next two years peasants were generally to ignore the whole mechanism of redemption – in most cases, they could not pay, and where they could, they would not.

The willingness of peasants to resort to insurrection, throughout the crisis that ended the Old Regime, and as we have seen continuing into 1790, marks out clearly the vital nature of the interests at stake in the battle over feudal dues. The area of the south-west that saw violence at the beginning of the year, identified by Peter Jones as bearing a particularly heavy burden of dues, was enflamed again after the May redemption decrees. The new *département* of the Lot saw the worst strife, provoked from August when the departmental authorities came out with official pronouncements of the need to pay dues. By November, armed expeditions against châteaux had resumed, and in December local law and order broke down in the district of Gourdon. Five thousand armed peasants sacked the houses of seigneurs and other wealthy inhabitants over three days, the local National Guard defecting to join them. Nobles in response formed vigilante bands, one of which attacked a crowd, provoking further attacks on châteaux as rumours of aristocratic plot swept the locality. Similar incidents occurred elsewhere, in some cases setting the pattern for years of intermittent conflict.

It should not be thought, however, that this violence was the product of an underclass or a rural proletariat. The National Guards who joined protests had purchased their own equipment, and the communes that voiced peasant demands were made up of solid taxpayers. It is unlikely that when events turned to violence a whole new social group should take over. In many cases the poorest in the countryside had no stake in the 'feudal' issue – if they owned no land and gathered no harvest of their own, the vast majority of such exactions would not have touched them. Of course, when a community jointly expressed its grievances in direct action, it is probable that this mobilisation reached across socio-economic lines, as the privileges of the seigneur in a general sense weighed on the whole community. The core of grievances, however, rested with small property-owners and tenants who saw the 'feudal system' as an injustice that threatened their livelihoods. This attitude directly clashed with those more distant from its effects who saw the loss of legitimate revenues as an injustice, as well as a threat to good order and the rights of property in general (document 8).

A further dimension was added to the rural troubles of the Revolution by the question of the distribution of land. Here social and political differences over definitions of property, and major regional differences in land-use, would thwart every attempt at a uniform settlement of several pressing issues. The most abiding problem was the two-pronged issue of collective rights and common land. As has been mentioned, rights such as *vaine pâture*, free grazing of livestock on harvested fields, were widespread in eighteenth-century France, but acceptance of their status was far from uniform. Poorer peasants tended to want to see such rights preserved, along with others that gave them access to resources, such as firewood, not easily obtained otherwise. Richer peasants, and larger farmers and landlords, might see such rights as hindering more systematic 'modern' land-use.

Alongside this went the vexed question of whether or not commons should be divided up and enclosed for crops. In some regions, the Revolution saw an immediate seizure of seigneurial 'wastes' by poorer peasants who divided them up for their own uses; in others, peasants might break down seigneurial enclosures to restore common grazing. Common lands in France had been in decline for some time, as royal decrees of the 1760s and 1770s had allowed processes of enclosure to begin, but many peasants clung to a 'customary' conception of property, in which their collective rights strongly counterbalanced their desire to own land for themselves. The sale of Church lands as *biens nationaux* (national property), which began in 1790, ran head-on into this attitude, relying as it did on an absolute definition of private property in land. For the rest of the decade, peasant conceptions of the land would clash first with the seigneurs, and then with bourgeois purchasers of land, not to mention the social and political prejudices of the political elites.[18]

Here, from 1790, new conflicts were cutting across the Revolution that had begun as a united attack on 'privilege'. Amongst both the urban and rural populations, those higher groups in control of substantial property would close ranks against those who had little or none. The difficulty of reconciling property and equality, and the violent consequences of failure, would dog the revolutionaries as long as the popular voice was able to make itself heard. As the active citizens and elected authorities of France wrestled to define the operation of a democratic body politic, this kind of fundamental conflict of interest underlay and reinforced the more visible menace of counter-revolution. By the end of 1790, and increasingly in the early months of 1791, that menace was taking firmer shape, compounded by growing religious strife, socio-economic instability, and rising political confrontation. A hint of what was to come can be seen in Aix-en-Provence in mid-December. Local nobles and royalists had proposed forming a monarchist political club, part of a brief wave of such formations at the end of the year, in response to which local radicals held a march to demonstrate their united opposition. As it passed the main square, this procession was shot at by a royalist, and a riot ensued. Two days later he and two other royalists, one of whom had been detained with correspondence from the *émigrés*, were ceremoniously lynched on the same main square.[19] 1790 was the last year of the Revolution when it might appear to have been possible to 'end' it peacefully, but the evolution of events and attitudes in that year, and indeed before, had effectively ruled out such a consummation. If it would take pessimism not to acknowledge great achievements in 1790, it would have taken a good dose of optimism as that year ended not to see problems ahead in 1791.

Notes

1 The term is applied, and critiqued, by S. F. Scott, 'Problems of Law and Order during 1790, the "Peaceful" Year of the French Revolution', *American Historical Review*, 80, 1975, pp. 859–88.

2 For this, and the following paragraphs, see I. Woloch, *The New Regime: Transformations of the French Civic Order, 1789–1820s*, New York and London, 1994, pp. 26–36; and T. W. Margadant, *Urban Rivalries in the French Revolution*, Princeton, 1992, pp. 84–140.

3 For a regional case study of this process, see A. Forrest, *The Revolution in Provincial France: Aquitaine, 1789–1799*, Oxford, 1996, chapter 3, evocatively titled 'The Loss of Innocence'.

4 Margadant, *Urban Rivalries*, pp. 242–3, tabulates the alliances and rivalries between representatives of towns that formed within the Assembly's committees. Marseille was defeated by a coalition of every other significant town in its vicinity.

5 Paris here, as in so many ways, was an exception – its municipal government was not finalised in form until May 1790, with a third layer of sixteen elected officials forming a *Bureau municipal* with the mayor above the *Corps municipal* and the *Conseil général*, which included the other two bodies and comprised 144 members in all.

6 See O. H. Hufton, *Bayeux in the Late Eighteenth Century: A Social Study*, Oxford, 1967, pp. 155–7; and G. Bossenga, *The Politics of Privilege: Old Regime and Revolution in Lille*, Cambridge, 1991, pp. 109–10.

7 M. Crook, *Elections in the French Revolution: An Apprenticeship in Democracy*, Cambridge, 1996, p. 62. The tables on pp. 60–1 indicate between 11.7 and 72.1 per cent turnout in a sample of areas, the highest figures always in rural *cantons*.

8 The term, and the basis of the following discussion, is taken from Lynn Hunt, *Politics, Culture and Class in the French Revolution*, Berkeley, 1984, chapter 5, pp. 149–79.

9 See C. Garrett, 'The Myth of the Counterrevolution in 1789', *French Historical Studies*, 18, 1994, pp. 784–800, which argues that it was in 1790, not before, that this concept was clarified in revolutionaries' minds.

10 For the following paragraphs, see his *Jacobinism and the Revolt of Lyon, 1789–1793*, Oxford, 1990, pp. 40–62.

11 The debates on these topics, often acrimonious, are discussed by T. Tackett, *Becoming a Revolutionary: The Deputies of the French National Assembly and the Emergence of a Revolutionary Culture (1789–1790)*, Princeton, 1996, chapter 9, esp. pp. 288–96.

12 Little meaningful research has been done in recent years on this form of radicalism. R. B. Rose, *The Making of the Sans-culottes: Democratic Ideas and Institutions in Paris, 1789–1792*, Manchester, 1983, is the most accessible work, but now appears rather naïve in its political assumptions.

13 This issue is discussed by Scott, 'Problems of Law and Order', pp. 863–71, which also includes a more detailed account of the motives for the conflict at Nancy – as in a variety of other incidents, justifiable complaints of financial mismanagement by officers of soldiers' benefit-funds were present.

14 P. M. Jones, *The Peasantry in the French Revolution*, Cambridge, 1988, p. 169. Material in the following section draws on chapters 4 and 6 of this work.

15 See Crook, *Elections*, pp. 73–5, for examples of this.

16 Jones, *Peasantry*, pp. 70–1, 111. On the maypoles/liberty-trees, see M. Ozouf, *Festivals and the French Revolution*, Cambridge, MA, 1988, chapter 9, esp. pp. 233ff.

17 Jones, *Peasantry*, p. 105.

18 *Ibid.*, chapter 5, examines this aspect of the Revolution in detail.

19 P. R. Hanson, 'Monarchist Clubs and the Pamphlet Debate over Political Legitimacy in the Early Years of the French Revolution', *French Historical Studies*, 21, 1998, pp. 299–324, esp. pp. 305–7.

5

Dissent, radicalisation and the descent to war, 1791–1792

The first few weeks of 1791 saw a profound rupture in the revolutionary body politic, described by Timothy Tackett as 'the first great parting of the ways ... a great and lasting schism across the political allegiance of the entire population'.[1] In late December 1790 the king had sanctioned an Assembly decree requiring all serving priests to swear an oath of allegiance and obedience to the Civil Constitution of the Clergy. This codified the fundamental reordering of the French Church that had taken place over the previous year. On the one hand it dissolved all the old bishoprics, creating new ones matching the boundaries of *départements*, and similarly reformed parishes in line with smaller communities. On the other hand it demanded that new priests and bishops, as paid state servants, be chosen not by their superiors, but by the local electorate.

The extent to which this had become a divisive issue was demonstrated when most of the clergy sitting in the Assembly itself, the allies of the Third Estate against noble privilege in 1789, refused to swear the oath. Only seven of the 136 bishops across the country took the oath, and over 45 per cent of all parish clergy refused it. Priests were forced to make hard choices about their relative allegiance to their Church and their nation. Many took the oath with a clear conscience, seeing it as part of a tradition of relative independence from Rome, as what was desired by their congregations, or as an inevitable sign of the times. Many others fervently resisted the invasion of the Church hierarchy by state funding and lay election, their reasoning varying from complex

89

theological justifications, to reliance on papal authority, to conspiracy theories about Protestant plots against the true faith.

Oath-taking and refusal formed a complex map of the politico-religious sensibilities of France, a map that was to be reflected in patterns of more violent dissent in the future. Some districts, notably in the Parisian basin, the centre and to the east of the Rhône valley, saw over 80 per cent oath-taking (Paris itself was much more evenly split); others, especially in the west and south-central France, often saw less than a quarter of clergy willing to swear. From the very beginning of oath-taking controversies, violent emotions and actions were never far from the surface (document 9). The French people maintained a complex and often ambivalent set of attitudes towards the Catholic clergy, attitudes reflecting the extent to which the Church had been intertwined with their own spiritual and material lives, and with the Old Regime systems of privilege.

The Catholic Church's ability to extract revenues from its landholdings, feudal rights, and tithes, and often apparent failure to put these to any worthwhile use, had made it widely resented, and a target as soon as rural violence had begun. From another perspective, it is noteworthy that the fornicating priest was possibly the leading stock character in the pornographic literature that flourished behind the scenes of late eighteenth-century cultured society. The clerical vow of celibacy was widely regarded as a cover for every form of sexual licence, whether practiced with each other, with innocent young girls (and boys), or with respectable women for whom they acted as confessors and spiritual directors.[2] At the same time, however, men in holy orders could also be respected political philosophers – such as the abbé Sieyès, and others of the Enlightenment such as Mably, Morellet, Raynal and Condillac. A modern viewpoint might see such men's political and philosophical preoccupations as little less odd than others' alleged debauchery, but by the late eighteenth century many educated people would have seen it as alarmingly fanatical to worry about whether or not a cleric believed in God. Talleyrand, bishop of Autun, had to be coached in order to say the mass at the Festival of Federation in 1790, and the Church had long been seen as a valuable career-path for younger sons of the nobility, bourgeoisie and even peasantry.

At the critical moment in 1791, however, it was revealed that not only did many priests have genuine theological commitments, but that many parishioners believed quite profoundly in their God and his Church, or at least in their own interpretations of religion as central to their lives. In the St-Roch parish in Paris, for example, the parish priest and many of his assistant priests defied the oath, provoking near-riot on several occasions, and a group of female parishioners attempted to organise a petition of women for his retention. Journalistic commentary turned this into a 'plot', and much else that the priests and their supporters undertook was to be seen in a sinister light. Nonetheless, over the spring of 1791, as the scale of clerical resistance became clear, the revolutionary authorities at the centre had to back down from their original hard line. When it was clear that so many priests were resisting, they had to be asked to retain their functions temporarily, for want of sufficient oath-taking ('juror') priests to replace them. In some cases, especially where non-juring was common, this temporary situation endured for over a year. Moreover, not only would non-juror (or 'refractory') priests be pensioned off, but from early May they were officially allowed to hold religious services for dissident congregations in church buildings.

By that time, Paris, like many other areas, had seen a clear polarisation of opinion on this issue. Priests, monks and nuns had been obstructing the continued religious life of parishes, for example by refusing premises to catechism classes, or not taking school classes to mass with a juror priest. March and early April saw angry crowds of parishioners invoking police aid to restore normal service, not always successfully. Crowds of both sexes vented their anger, stirred by inflammatory press reports, in the second week of April, breaking into convents and whipping nuns in rituals of public humiliation. In mid-April, Easter services by non-jurors in hired churches were attacked by large crowds, driving out the mainly female congregations. Later in May, the priest of the Bonne-Nouvelle parish, which was due to be amalgamated with a neighbouring one under the revolutionary rationalisation, was arrested as a danger to the public peace. He had held an assembly of some 250 female parishioners, which was in itself regarded as dangerous, even had he not also talked of giving them a political education as to which Assembly decrees were good and bad.

The standard hostile construction of this as 'women led astray by priests' is challenged by an incident from the far south of France, dissected by Timothy Tackett from the lengthy enquiry that followed it. In the town of Sommières, halfway between Nîmes and Montpellier, crowds of women and some men attacked municipal officials whom they feared were coming to enforce the oath on their priests. Although the organisation of this disturbance seems to have owed something to a political factionalism especially strong in the south-east, it was also clearly not a priest-led 'party'. Indeed, the clergy themselves tried to intervene to stop violence, but were shouted down by women determined to defend 'their religion' and, if necessary, actively to prevent clergy taking the oath.[3] The participants seem to have partaken of an oral culture in which the clerical oath had easily been assimilated to folk-memories of earlier strife. The rioters appeared to believe that 'the Protestants' were likely to raid the town, while simultaneously assuring local Protestants, 40 per cent of the population, that they meant them no harm and were responding to the threat to religion from 'bad Catholics'.

The particular sectarian divide present in the Midi no doubt added to the alarm in this region, which had already seen the Revolution associated with inter-communal violence, such as at Nîmes the previous June. In many other parts of France, however, equally complex issues were played out within entirely Catholic communities. The balance of forces that made priests individually or collectively decide whether or not to take the oath hinged on many factors. These included the density and prosperity of clerical institutions in an area, the social origins of priests themselves, their relations with parishioners, the prior history of local Church–state relations, personal views on both theology and the Revolution, the level of influence of local bishops (and their inclinations), and the degree of support or antipathy from local authorities. In parts of the west, where a dense and prosperous network of locally reared priests nurtured relatively isolated communities suspicious of anticlerical urban influence, the oath was rejected by many. Such priests were then able to count on the support of their faithful, protecting them and following their services even when held away from churches or habitation. In other areas, though the withdrawal or flight of priests caused consternation, parishioners seemed more concerned that the ritual life of the community should go on, and that spiritual protection should be spread over their fields and flocks. Later in the Revolution, such communities would even conduct services for themselves, investing the act itself with power, rather than the priest.[4]

This attitude is mirrored in the Parisian reaction to the priests' resistance. Here the role of the Church seems to have been to give services to the population – to baptise, educate, marry, confess, absolve, bury them – rather than to exercise a spiritual authority over them. The idea that there might be good theological reasons for refusing to continue these services seemed as absurd to many 'good Catholics' as had the Church's attempt to stop 'good priests' practicing several decades earlier, just because they were theologically tainted with Jansenism. There were many other 'good Catholics' who accepted the priests' word that they should shun the oath-takers, but in the major urban centres these were clearly in a minority, and tended to be those women whom local prejudice had long condemned for being under the thumbs of the priests.

Though urban populations turned against obstructive priests, on a broader canvas the clerical oath began a new process of popular discontent directed against the actions of the Revolution itself, and not merely against its shortcomings, unlike, for example, the rural violence of 1790. It also ignited a fresh burst of conscience in the mind of Louis XVI, especially after the pope attacked the Civil Constitution and the whole Revolution in March and April 1791. On Palm Sunday, 17 April, the king took communion from a non-juror priest. News of this reached the open spaces of Paris via National Guards in attendance, and caused serious disquiet. The royal family were due to leave for the château of Saint-Cloud, some way outside the city, the next day, there to spend the summer, and incidentally evading the need to make a public appearance in church on Easter Day. Louis's two maiden aunts had already caused concern across the land by leaving for Rome in February, and rumour at once escalated the Saint-Cloud trip to a full-scale escape attempt. Consequently, on Monday 18 April, the royal family was effectively blockaded in the Tuileries palace by crowds. National Guard units refused to clear a path for the coaches through the alarmed, but not overtly hostile, Parisians. Their spokesmen stressed the desire to protect the king from plots to spirit him away, but the experience of that day confirmed his, and especially Marie-Antoinette's, view that they were effectively prisoners of Paris.

The popular disquiet catalysed by the religious issue had been stoked further by the development of a network of radical popular societies within Paris since the end of 1790. Often led by educated members of the Cordeliers Club, such groups as the Fraternal Society of the Two Sexes, the Society of the Halles (the main market area), the Society of the Indigents, and the Societies of the Carmes and Minimes (two convents that provided meeting-places), gave a new dimension to Parisian politics. Admitting women and men to their meetings for a small subscription, the societies echoed forms of political sociability that had developed rapidly among the more educated. What had begun in 1789 as a 'Breton Club' of Assembly deputies from that region, and then become the 'Society of the Friends of the Constitution', was soon commonly known as the Jacobin Club of Paris (like the Cordeliers, named for its monastic meeting-place), and had grown to a virtual assembly of left-of-centre political activists in the capital. This body had created a new forum for the unofficial, but increasingly authoritative, discussion of political agendas. This pattern of gathering spread rapidly into the towns of France, as did the habit of corresponding with the 'mother society' in Paris. From some twenty provincial affiliated clubs in January 1790, there were over 300 by January 1791, and the affiliations continued to accelerate to over 900 by July, and thousands in later years.[5]

Members of the Jacobin movement in the Revolution's early years were exclusively male, and drawn almost entirely from the middle orders of society. Even the Cordeliers Club had not particularly sought a popular following, though it found one, but the newer Parisian societies created a body of several thousand members from all ranks of society, increasingly permeated by the intemperate egalitarianism of radical journalists such as Marat and Fréron. Their political views mutated rapidly. In late 1790 the Fraternal Society could produce a pamphlet praising Lameth, a moderate leader, for standing up to aristocracy, but by the late spring of 1791 the political agenda of Lameth and his fellows was being condemned vociferously by the same society.

The authorities sought to clamp down on the political 'interference' of such societies, passing a decree on 10 May 1791 forbidding collective petitions to the Assembly, the most common protest tactic of such groups. Rumours of plots and shady manoeuvres swept over the city almost every day, conveyed by word of mouth and by a press and pamphlet literature that poured out, seemingly from almost every pen that could write and every broken-down hand-press that could be put into action. Literally hundreds of new journals were founded in the first two years of the Revolution, and if many folded after a few days, weeks or months, many more became influential, read on the streets of Paris and subscribed to by provincial individuals, clubs and communes. In the capital, the press formed part of a dense and frequently chaotic panorama of public interaction, and across France provided much of the raw material for political development.[6]

The development of a new political sociability was not confined to Paris. In Lyon an even more dense network developed from mid-1790, based on strong traditions of neighbourhood (*quartier*) solidarity. Each new municipal section had a club, and these all sent delegates to a Central Club. Unlike Paris, however, this network rapidly developed internal tensions. The clubs were not held together by a single political agenda, but tended to split according to the social composition of their *quartiers*. At the same time, despite these tensions, few of the clubs showed the signs of thorough-going radicalism shown in Paris – their social scope reached somewhat less far down, and none admitted women to full membership.[7]

In Bordeaux, the club situation was more simple. Only two explicitly political clubs were visible in 1790–2, and both of these were basically middle-class. The National Club was more radical, and already by December 1790 had been censured by the local authorities for over-zealous pursuit and condemnation of perceived counter-revolutionaries. Even so, this group was recruited amongst the professionals and lesser merchants of the great port, and the more conservative Friends of Liberty and Equality exercised a much greater influence, with its membership drawn from the higher ranks of the law and commerce.[8] Such unofficial political organisations, where definitions of patriotism and counter-revolution could be worked out in response to local agendas and particular readings of national politics, would become ever-more significant as the revolutionary situation continued to grow more intractable.

As the rest of the country still wrestled with the consequences of the clerical oath, the Parisian crowds were swept up with repeated alarms – fighting between National Guards and customs-men outside the city in January 1791, rumours of plots at the fortress of Vincennes and an aristocratic invasion of the royal palace at the end of February, the Easter royal crisis, and from April a series of bitter strikes and pay disputes, in which employers and workers used the language of aristocracy, faction and plot to condemn each other in published exchanges (document 10). As the municipality and National Guard struggled to contain the waves of criticism in print and speech, rumours flew in mid-June that the royal family would attempt another escape. Newspapers carrying such reports from previous days were on the streets when it was discovered on 21 June that Louis, Marie-Antoinette and their immediate family had been spirited out of the palace, and the city, during the night.

This 'Flight to Varennes' (the place where the royal family was soon apprehended) had a number of consequences. On 24 June a petition declaring liberty and royalty to be incompatible was handed to the National Assembly, bearing some 30,000 signatures gathered by the radicals of the Cordeliers Club. Overtly republican opinions were soon common on the Parisian streets, but the Assembly could not envisage France as a republic, and fell back on the implausible theory that the king had been 'abducted'. After some soul-searching (and delicate negotiations with the royal pair), and strong objections from a few radical deputies, on 15 and 16 July the Assembly cleared the king of complicity, decreed him personally inviolable, and declared that his reinstatement would follow on his acceptance of the new Constitution. The 15th saw a dramatic split in the Paris Jacobins – all but the most left-wing deputies departed to another monastic building, from which they began a new 'Feuillant' Club. The Feuillants discovered, however, that their authority as deputies could not usurp the moral authority of the consistently radical Jacobin position, and the original Club eventually retained the vast majority of provincial affiliations. In Lyon, the club movement also split, as a strong groundswell of republicanism led to expressions of intemperate social radicalism and conservatism, and secessions in some clubs. The Central Club petitioned the Assembly to declare a republic, while some clubs split from it. They accused radicals of misconduct, while radicals charged that the rich were usurping popular organisations and deceiving their poorer neighbours.[9]

Meanwhile, since word of the Assembly's moves on 15 July, the radical clubs in Paris had begun to organise more petitions, demanding a referendum, or at least some form of national consultation, before the king was allowed back on the throne. Meetings to sign these petitions took place on the 'Altar of the Fatherland' on the Champ de Mars, site of the Festival of Federation. Over the 16th and 17th, the meetings grew larger and more alarming to the authorities, with upwards of 20,000 estimated on the latter day, though many of those who flocked along were probably spectating rather than agitating. On the 17th, the National Assembly, Paris Municipality and Lafayette's headquarters decided that the time had come to face off the rabble of popular radicalism, which they viewed as largely stirred up by paid agitators for the duc d'Orléans or the *émigrés*. A Martial Law proclamation was made, on the pretext of the lynching of two men earlier in the day. The general alarm was sounded in the afternoon, and large bodies of National Guards mustered and marched to the Champ de Mars. The crowd declined to disperse, stones were thrown and allegedly shots fired, and the Guard fired back before closing in with musket-butts and bayonets.[10]

In this 'Champ de Mars Massacre' (which may have killed between a dozen and fifty people) the socio-political tension within the capital, latent since July and October 1789, was made remarkably evident. In the days to come, crowds exchanged stories of the casual brutality of the 'bourgeois' Guards, while the latter hunted down anyone seeking to criticise their actions or authority. However, a language of social tension, which overtly challenged the idea of a single revolutionary 'people', was not allowed to surface for long. Suspects were stigmatised as vagrants, brigands and paid agitators, no matter that they might actually be National Guards themselves, or in stable employment. The press, including its most radical elements, seemed content to follow this pattern, though some asserted that the authorities and the brigands were in league against the 'true' people. Meanwhile, the radical clubs were harassed, and decrees and new laws reinforced penalties for sedition and riot. As part of a longer backlash, the organisation of the National Guard was definitively closed to non-active citizens, and the property-requirements for political participation were tightened in August and September.

The divisive aftermath of the 'Massacre' was nonetheless rapidly overshadowed by the wider troubles of the Revolution. The situation of the army became critical, as a fresh wave of emigration followed the king's flight. Within six months, over 60 per cent of its officers would be abroad. The very day of the flight's discovery, the Assembly ordered battalions of 'National Volunteers' into existence – men from the National Guard were enlisted for one year only, at double pay-rates. Twenty-six thousand were allowed for, but by August over 100,000 had signed up, perhaps demonstrating fervent patriotism, perhaps also escaping economic collapse. Mid-August saw further restrictions on the priesthood, and an official demand for all *émigrés* to return within a month. On the 27th, Austria and Prussia responded with the 'Pillnitz Declaration', threatening military intervention to protect Louis. The external menace was counterbalanced by a sense of renewal, as the National Constituent Assembly concluded its business, elections took place for a new regular Legislative Assembly, and the king accepted the Constitution on 13 September. An amnesty followed for all those guilty of revolutionary violence since 1788, and the country seemed to believe for a while that all would be well.

Unfortunately, nothing had yet been done to alter any of the basic divisions within France. Particularly in the west, tensions over the clergy had already been growing dangerous in the summer. Anticlerical urban elites in control of *département* administrations set out to vigorously purge non-jurors, defying permissive legislation from the centre and closing down rural chapels that might be used for non-jurors' services. In a region where the Church was often the only centre of peasant sociability, the driving out of the non-jurors, who were the vast majority of clergy here, hit hard. Peasants sometimes took to trekking long distances for clandestine services, and as early as 16 July one district declared Martial Law to disperse approaching processions from fourteen parishes. By the autumn, violence had broken out over these issues, sufficient to warrant an investigation by the new

Assembly (document 11).[11]

In the neighbouring area of Calvados, in Normandy, there was a different type of trouble with priests. Claude Fauchet, a radical cleric who had made a name for himself as a public lecturer and municipal politician in Paris, was installed as bishop in Bayeux in May 1791. By the next month, he had begun to build up a radical 'party' through ecclesiastical appointments and influence with local popular societies. This group set out to combat the resolutely conservative authorities of the Bayeux municipality and Calvados *département*. In June, Fauchet ordered priests to denounce the arrest of two local radicals from their pulpits, provoking skirmishes between radicals and National Guards. In July, he threatened to move his episcopal seat to the more 'patriotic' city of Caen if Bayeux did not learn more appropriate attitudes. The municipality obtained an order for Fauchet's arrest from the district tribunal. This caused furious splits and faction-fighting, and ultimately in August, referral to the Assembly. Although he finally found himself isolated, and had to apologise to the Bayeux municipality, this did not hinder Fauchet's bid to be elected to the Legislative Assembly. He departed for Paris in September, leaving behind a strong radical faction which gained more power over the coming months. Fauchet's status was exceptional, but this episode exemplifies the growing political strains in France even before the Constitution was properly put into effect.[12]

The Constituent Assembly had barred its members from election to the new body, in a move proposed by Robespierre, aiming to give the new system a 'clean slate', and thereby exclude some more conservative elements. The new Assembly was composed of the products of politics throughout France since 1789, the pinnacle of the new 'political class' being created through the expansion of elective office. It was a remarkably uniform body, in which the landowning and frequently legally trained revolutionary bourgeois dominated. Fewer than twenty of the clergy had seats, and around the same number of ex-nobles, leaving over 700 'commoners'. Among these, there was also a sharp decline in the number of Old Regime office-holders – under 6 per cent of the total – while almost two-thirds had held elective office since the start of the Revolution.

The Legislative Assembly therefore embodied a clear rejection of older centres of power in favour of the new order, and lost no time in making clear its opposition to those forces that did not agree. However, while the Assembly repeatedly took action through the autumn and winter against *émigrés* and non-juror clergy, and asked the king to warn off the hostile European powers, Louis, restored to his constitutional powers, repeatedly vetoed punitive measures. While publicly complying in foreign policy, the king secretly informed the Holy Roman Emperor of his support. Suspicion of these moves aided a continued radicalisation of Parisian politics. Mayor Bailly resigned, worn out by factional fighting, and Lafayette was defeated in elections to replace him by Pétion, a far more radical figure, and one of the few ex-Constituent Assembly deputies to stay with the Jacobins after July 1791.

Rising tensions continued into the new year, as the country experienced the consequences of another poor harvest, and general disruption in the economy. It had already become clear in 1791 that both state finances and the general circulation of money in France were in crisis. By the best estimates, the French were only paying around a quarter of the taxes needed to meet state expenditure, while the *assignat* paper-currency was provoking inflation. People basically distrusted it, and by the summer of 1791 if one wanted good solid coin, one had to exchange *assignats* for only some 80–85 per cent of their face value. Both coin and paper were in grave shortage, and many local banks were established to issue small-denomination notes as a substitute, covered by deposits of large-denomination *assignats*. Forgeries began to proliferate, and suspicion of forgery to run even higher – there were, after all, some sixty-three different kinds of paper-money circulating in Paris late in 1791. Doing business in such circumstances became fraught with risks, and when in February 1792 the tax offices refused to accept non-*assignat* notes, again through fear of forgery, there was renewed panic. The inflation could only accelerate, since thanks to the tax-evasion of the majority, the state could only fund its spending through printing more paper. This economic dislocation would underpin the social experience of the French for the remainder of the decade, and it was not until the new century that some semblance of order would return to fiscal and monetary affairs.[13]

Meanwhile, immediate concerns pressed on the population, who responded in time-honoured fashion. In the autumn of 1791 price-fixing riots had affected many regions of northern France, in some of which radical egalitarian views had been expressed (document 12). In January and February 1792 Parisian crowds protested the shortages of sugar and coffee, apparent 'luxuries', but actually staples of the lower-class diet. Through February and March food riots were widespread across France, including an incident at the town of Étampes where the mayor was lynched for refusing to control market prices. He would become a martyr in the eyes of social conservatives. In the countryside itself, shortage of food and anti-seigneurialism inflamed the agrarian regions south of Paris (document 13). Fief-owners continued to demand repressive action against peasants, who carried on attacking and destroying the signs and documents of feudal obligation. Château-burning had re-erupted in the south-west too, and by early spring 1792 broke out in a wide area of the south-east centred around the Ardèche and Gard.

Conspiratorial activity by counter-revolutionary local nobles was amongst a wide range of motives for this action, which was on a scale equal to the major risings of 1789. This region had already seen some of the most overt manifestations of counter-revolutionary resistance, and was also the site of some of the most dramatic social inequalities in the country. The destruction of feudalism here began to overlap with more explicitly socio-economic demands, such as for the sale of Church lands to smallholders and division of commons, as well as with price-fixing riots, while on the other hand known 'patriot' nobles had their castles and papers spared. Local communes sometimes paraded their National Guards with drums and colours to take part in attacks, while also accusing *département* authorities of concealing decrees from Paris sanctioning the action.

The spreading network of Jacobin clubs was particularly active in this region, where the population was concentrated in small towns rather than spread in villages. Radical activity was often driven by the propaganda and 'missionaries' of the Marseille club, and this helped to inject protest with a political dimension, as fief-owners were painted as aristocrats and counter-revolutionaries. Nevertheless, some ambiguities should be noted about all these risings and riots. The redistributive and occasionally proto-socialist demands of rioters, heard notably in the apocalyptic sermons of some popular priests in the north, had nothing in common with the political culture of the Legislative Assembly. If Robespierre and some Parisian radicals denounced the mayor of Étampes as a food-hoarder, neither they nor any other politician had any constructive response to the kind of issues being raised by such actions.[14] The single opposition between Revolution and Counter-revolution would continue to dominate political discussion, but the population of France often had other things on their minds.

We can observe further here that this division was not the only gross over-simplification that would cripple politicians' perceptions of the real state of France through the 1790s. The Constituent Assembly had set out to reform the entire structure of social relations, including replacing the byzantine structures of charity and aid that Church and state had erected over the centuries, and which helped to support perhaps as many as one in five of the population in some way. In addition to some 55,000 nuns, a large proportion of whom were devoted to healthcare, charitable or educational work, there were perhaps as many as 150,000 women in religious 'congregations' or 'communities' who had taken lesser vows, but nonetheless devoted themselves to similar tasks in their localities. Such groups were a vital agency of redistribution of resources in the Old Regime, but their existence came under attack in the new order from several directions. Enlightenment rationalism, and views on the nature of woman, demanded an end to the enforced celibacy of the convent. Increasingly, after the clerical oath, religious women would be seen as a central element of the counter-revolutionary threat, though as 'mere women' they were rarely seen as individually dangerous and were seldom accorded the persecution meted out to priests.

In structural terms, the Assembly deputies who formed Ecclesiastical and Poverty Committees to explore these issues saw the Church as perpetuating poverty. The encouragement of charitable giving was seen as anti-social, because such giving itself was selfish (aimed at personal salvation). It allowed, in their view, the development of a class of indigent social parasites who knew that the Church and the Hospital (in the eighteenth century less a place for healing than for the incurably sick and old) would help them regardless of their own efforts. The Committee on Poverty (*comité de mendicité*, which is more literally 'beggary') also firmly believed that two working parents could support themselves and at least two children, though larger families might need supplemental aid. The possibility that wage-rates in some areas were simply too low for this they rejected out of hand – the free market would provide, though the state might have to make some unskilled work available in emergencies. These attitudes would paralyse effective reform, as the Revolution ground on in what amounted to a permanent economic crisis. Increasing hostility to the Church would see its personnel manoeuvred out of all their roles (except where they were able quietly to take on a 'civic' identity), while no effective frameworks were ever found to deal with poverty, or indeed education or healthcare. In these respects, the Revolution's aspirations to create a nation of equal citizens did less for the most needy in society than did the supposedly problematic charity of the Old Regime.[15]

The effects of the limited perspectives of the revolutionary politicians can also be seen elsewhere. One of the last issues that had been tackled by the Constituent Assembly was the question of slavery. For a Revolution founded on liberty and equality, this was to prove a remarkably problematic issue, and one largely dealt with by ignoring it.[16] Much of France's pre-1789 economic growth had been based on the colonial trade, which was itself based on slave-grown sugar from the Caribbean islands of Guadeloupe, Martinique, and, largest of all the sugar-islands, Saint-Domingue (present-day Haiti). Every group in these islands had grievances that the Revolution might have addressed. The white planters wanted autonomy from the rigid trading rules imposed by France. The slaves obviously wanted their freedom, and between the two, a class of free blacks and mixed-race subjects wanted equality with whites in local politics. Events in 1789 had stirred up the demands of all these groups, but they were in conflict with each other as much as with the state. Both whites and the free non-whites had protested violently by mid-1791, and in August the situation sharply deteriorated as a massive slave revolt broke out on Saint-Domingue. In the final sessions of the Assembly, the slavery issue was bitterly debated, but in the end it was decided to leave such matters to the whites-only colonial assemblies – a recipe for further bloodshed. Having washed their hands of the Caribbean, the deputies were happy a few days later to vote the abolition of slavery within France itself, an almost meaningless measure. In early 1792 the new Assembly would order a non-racial constitution for the colonies, and slavery would be abolished outright at the height of the Revolution's radicalism in February 1794, but this would be too late to prevent civil war in the Caribbean. Ironically it was this neglect, and later overt hostilities, which drove the 'Black Jacobins' of the Saint-Domingue slave revolt to form and successfully defend the world's first black republic of Haiti.[17]

A further irony in the constitutional arrangements made in 1791 was the backward step in the status of women implied in the project for a law on adultery set out in Article 13 of the new Constitution. Although this measure was not finally enacted, it provided for the right of the husband to imprison his adulterous wife for up to two years, and to take control of property she had brought to the marriage. The article clearly stated that the charge of adultery 'can be pursued only by the husband' – there was no provision to charge a man with the same crime, although the male accomplice in a wife's offence could be fined and imprisoned for three months. Sarah Hanley has noted how this would have stripped women of their rights to sue for separation and to claim equal rights in marriage, abilities which had been struggled for in the courts for centuries. Although not decisively won in the Old Regime, persistent recourse to the 'tribunal of public opinion' had made wives' rights at law sufficiently arguable to deter some of the more brutal practices of the traditional absolutist husband.[18] The Revolution threatened to remove this convenient vagueness, and although the adultery measure fell, and in 1792 a divorce law was passed, even this was not 'egalitarian' between men and women. More than two-thirds of actions under this law over the next decade would be brought by women, but they still faced disproportionate penalties if the law found against them, including loss of their property (and thus, effectively, of their civil existence). For those enslaved by race or sex, there was little to be happy about in the Constitution of 1791.

Nonetheless, in what the revolutionaries clearly saw as a more important struggle, the escalation of tensions with the European powers continued into 1792. The faction known as 'Brissotins' or 'Girondins' had been calling for aggressive international action since late 1791. Centred around Brissot, a radical journalist and Parisian politician, and a group of deputies from the Gironde *département* around Bordeaux, their rhetorical leadership in the

Assembly had carried a hard line against *émigrés*, and by early March they were attempting to impeach the king's foreign minister for concealing the war preparations of the Holy Roman Emperor. In mid-March, some of their supporters outside the Assembly were called by the king to form a ministry, and international hostilities escalated further. The Brissotins believed that only decisive military action could sweep the *émigrés* from the frontiers, and that the military might of the liberated French would be invincible. This coincided ominously with Louis's and the Court's wish to see the Austrians and Prussians march to their aid, and on 20 April war was declared on 'the king of Bohemia and Hungary' – that is to say, Francis II, Austrian ruler and Holy Roman Emperor.[19] France went to war almost gaily, and Robespierre was almost a lone voice in the Jacobins denouncing this confluence of opposing interests and its inevitably terrible consequences. Other German powers, most notably Prussia, would join the Austrian side over the coming months, as Europe passed into warfare that would not end for a generation. The war and its conduct would raise up popular forces unimagined in 1789, transforming the social landscape in the battle for national defence, while in the political arena an unparalleled violence would be unleashed. Few of those on the political stage in the last months of peace would survive the coming storm.

Notes

1   T. Tackett, *Religion, Revolution and Regional Culture in Eighteenth-Century France: The Ecclesiastical Oath of 1791*, Princeton, 1986, p. 3. This is the fundamental modern study of this episode, and of the roots of the divisions it revealed.

2   Titles such as *Venus in the Cloister* dated back to 1682; other classics included the *History of Dom B[ugger]* (1741), set in a monastery, or *The Ecclesiastical Laurels* (1748). Many others followed. See R. Darnton, *The Forbidden Best-Sellers of Pre-Revolutionary France*, London, 1996, esp. pp. 85ff., and the extracts from *Thérèse the Philosopher* (1748), *ibid.*, pp. 249ff., esp. pp. 256–62, for one such 'spiritual director'.

3   T. Tackett, 'Women and Men in Counterrevolution: The Sommières Riot of 1791', *Journal of Modern History*, 59, 1987, pp. 680–704.

4   See T. Tackett, 'The West in France in 1789: The Religious Factor in the Origins of the Counterrevolution', *Journal of Modern History*, 54, 1982, pp. 715–45; and S. Desan, *Reclaiming the Sacred: Lay Religion and*

Popular Politics in Revolutionary France, Ithaca, NY, 1990, esp. chapter 3.

5   C. Jones, *The Longman Companion to the French Revolution*, London, 1988, pp. 181–6. See M. Kennedy, *The Jacobin Clubs in the French Revolution: The First Years*, Princeton, 1992; *The Jacobin Clubs in the French Revolution: The Middle Years*, Princeton, 1988.

6   The revolutionary press has a well-developed historiography. For an introduction see J. D. Popkin, *Revolutionary News: The Press in France, 1789–1799*, Durham, NC, 1990.

7   W. D. Edmonds, *Jacobinism and the Revolt of Lyon, 1789–1793*, Oxford, 1990, chapter 3.

8   A. Forrest, *Society and Politics in Revolutionary Bordeaux*, Oxford, 1975, pp. 62–6.

9   Edmonds, *Jacobinism*, pp. 97–101.

10   There is a detailed account in G. Rudé, *The Crowd in the French Revolution*, Oxford, 1959.

11   See Tackett, 'West in France', and P. M. Jones, *The Peasantry in the French Revolution*, Cambridge, 1988, pp. 198–201.

12   See O. H. Hufton, *Bayeux in the Late Eighteenth Century: A Social Study*, Oxford, 1967, pp. 178–85. On Fauchet's political career, before and after the Calvados episode, see G. Kates, *The Cercle Social, the Girondins, and the French Revolution*, Princeton, 1985.

13   For an overview, see F. Aftalion, *The French Revolution: An Economic Interpretation*, Cambridge, 1990. This is rather a diatribe against the revolutionaries' economic incompetence, but the situation could hardly be painted much blacker than it was.

14   See Jones, *Peasantry*, pp. 120–2; and D. M. G. Sutherland, *France 1789–1815: Revolution and Counter-Revolution*, London, 1985, pp. 139–44.

15   This issue is discussed in summary by O. H. Hufton, *Women and the Limits of Citizenship in the French Revolution*, Toronto, 1992, chapter 2, 'Poverty and Charity: Revolutionary Mythology and Real Women', pp. 51–88. See also her *The Poor of Eighteenth-Century France, 1750–1789*, Oxford, 1974; and A. I. Forrest, *The French Revolution and the Poor*, Oxford, 1981.

16   See D. Geggus, 'Racial Equality, Slavery, and Colonial Secession during the Constituent Assembly', *American Historical Review*, 94, 1989, pp. 1290–308.

17   The classic account of the black movement is C. L. R. James, *The Black Jacobins*, New York, 1973. See the recent collection of essays, D. Gaspar and D. Geggus (eds), *A Turbulent Time: The French Revolution and the Greater Caribbean*, Bloomington, 1997, esp. chapters 1, 2, 4.

18   S. Hanley, 'Social Sites of Political Practice in France: Lawsuits, Civil Rights, and the Separation of Powers in Domestic and State Government, 1500–1800', *American Historical Review*, 102, 1997, pp. 27–52.

Note that the husband and the monarch had consistently been linked, both literally and metaphorically, in the seventeenth and early eighteenth centuries, but qualms over the adultery litigation made the image of the father seem less problematic for the king in the later eighteenth century.

19 T. C. W. Blanning, *The Origins of the French Revolutionary Wars*, London, 1986, goes into great detail on the international and diplomatic calculations around this decision, but for most observers within France it was a political and 'revolutionary' issue.

6

War and the Girondin Republic, 1792–1793

The first months of the French Revolutionary War seemed closer to fulfilling the desires of Louis and Marie-Antoinette than those of the Brissotins. A French general was killed by his own troops after one of the first unsuccessful skirmishes, in the belief that he had betrayed them. By May 1792 the three main army commanders were urging peace-talks, not wanting to risk throwing disorganised armies into battle. June saw them ordered onto the offensive, but rapidly driven back. This sequence of disasters only spread more panic within the political class. By late May, Brissotins were openly denouncing an 'Austrian Committee' operating within the Court, more measures were enacted (and vetoed) against non-jurors, and the 'aristocratic' royal bodyguard was dissolved. In early June Louis vetoed plans for 20,000 *fédéré* troops (volunteers from around the country) to be gathered near Paris, and subsequently dismissed the Brissotin ministers, substituting a more conservative group associated with the Feuillant Club.

Added to this situation, the internal threat remained real. Since the *camp de Jalès* and other troubles of 1790, it had been clear that counter-revolutionaries were active throughout the country, and the religious troubles that began the following year had compounded their impact. Conspiracies and attempted risings added to the anxiety of patriots. On 31 May 1792 a secretary of the marquis de La Rouerie was arrested, carrying papers which compromised a sweeping plot to arm discontented Breton ex-smugglers, seize the cities of western France, and declare for the king as foreign armies attacked from the east. Investigations into this 'Breton Association' would continue through the following year, and it can be linked both to the later insurrections in the west and to *émigré* and internal aristocratic networks. A similar network was known to exist in Normandy. Meanwhile in the south-east a second *camp de Jalès* in late February 1792 had been broken up by the authorities, and an attempt to gather a 'Catholic Army of the Midi' at Jalès in July led to the deaths of several hundred royalists, as the local authorities deployed National Volunteer battalions to destroy the rebels. In this region too, aristocratic and *émigré*-funded networks would continue to agitate throughout the following year.[1]

With such activities as a background, radicals pressed furiously for more decisive action. It was in this context that the Parisian sections began to present their new identity as *sans-culottes*, of which more later, and to demonstrate before the Assembly with the pikes of popular militant patriotism. Left–right conflicts in politics became entwined with issues of the war effort (document 14). On 3 June the mayor of Étampes was given a state funeral in Paris, an event used as a 'Festival of the Law' by Brissotin and Feuillant deputies, and vigorously opposed by Jacobin supporters. Lafayette, now commanding an army, called for Jacobin clubs to be suppressed as a danger to order. On 20 June, in what was in effect an unsuccessful insurrection, a crowd of civilians and National Guards managed to press into the royal palace, confronting Louis with demands to lift the veto on the *fédéré* camp and the anticlerical measures of May. A week later, Lafayette, back in Paris, demanded the suppression of the Jacobins again, and the punishment of these demonstrators. He was backed by a wave of provincial protest against Parisian excess (document 15). The Legislative Assembly, however, was moving towards a more radical stance in the face of royal intransigence, as Parisian radicals pressed for further action (document 16).

On 2 July the Assembly decreed the creation of the *fédéré* camp over Louis's veto, and on 5 July created emergency powers to be used if *la patrie en danger* ('the fatherland in danger') was decreed. Faction-fighting continued – on 6 July the authorities of the Paris *département* unseated Pétion for not stopping the 20 June demonstration, and on the 10th the Feuillant ministry quit under severe political attacks. The next day, as it became clear that Prussia was about to launch itself into the war, the Assembly used its new powers, declaring *la patrie en danger*, allowing it to ignore the royal veto, calling all administrative bodies into permanent session, and uniting the National Guard with the army. On the 12th it called for another 50,000 volunteeers to join the army (as with the 1791 volunteers, this would be massively over-subscribed, some 200,000 registering), on the 13th it reinstated Pétion, and on the 17th it decreed the sale of *émigré* property that had been subject to seizure since February.

With emergency powers in the hands of the Assembly, the fate of the king began to look grim. He had been cut out of the legislative loop, and effectively out of the executive as well. By the last week of July a petition from the Jacobins and *fédérés* (now gathering in Paris) had called for his removal. Parisian politics themselves continued to radicalise. The forty-eight sections were authorised to keep their general assemblies in permanent daily session, and by the end of the month, to open their National Guard battalions to non-active citizens. Some also began to allow non-actives to take part in the assemblies. The rhetoric of absolute political equality that had been the vocabulary of the popular societies over the last two years was now put into practice and helped to expand the forces confronting the monarchy (document 17). By now, radicals from the clubs, sections and municipality were already meeting to plan the overthrow of the king, plans given more urgency as news reached Paris that the enemy's 'Brunswick Manifesto' threatened death to civilians who resisted them, and to Parisians if the royal family came to harm.

On 3 August forty-seven of the Paris sections officially petitioned for the overthrow of the king. For a tense week, the Assembly adjourned the issue, then fudged it in debate on the 9th. Over this period the Brissotins had begun to compromise themselves in the eyes of radicals, as they attempted to get themselves into ministerial office while arguing that it was too dangerous to change the form of the executive in a crisis. As they were the ones who had denounced the 'Austrian Committee' in the Tuileries in the first place, such moves smacked of self-serving hypocrisy. An 'Insurrectionary Commune' of radical leaders formed itself on the 9th, co-opting authority from the regular city government, and on 10 August Parisian and *fédéré* National Guard battalions (most notably that of Marseille) stormed the

Tuileries palace. They and their supporting crowds massacred the defending Swiss Guards while the royal family took refuge in the chamber of the Assembly. With this stimulus the Assembly voted to suspend the king, and to order the summoning of a 'National Convention' to decide on a new constitution. All vetoed decrees were enacted, and a Provisional Executive Council was established to watch over government.[2]

Elections took place over the next month for the Convention, a body that would declare a Republic, re-make all the institutions of France, re-start the calendar at Year I, and seek to reform human nature. The period of the Convention would also be the period of the Terror, when death would often seem the only solution to political disagreement. Before considering how it was that French society was plunged into this new world, it would be well to draw up a balance-sheet of the changes that had taken place since 1789, and the issues yet to be resolved or arisen anew since then.

The visible structures of French society had quite clearly been remoulded. The maze of privileges and jurisdictions that passed for an organic social body had been replaced by a pyramid of rationally apportioned responsibilities in which only a few clear-cut divisions – active and non-active citizenship, the eligibility thresholds – were supposed to distinguish equal citizens from each other. Estates, orders, provinces had all passed away unmourned by the majority, even if the nobility had been reinvented as the 'aristocratic' enemy of all that had been done.

Of course, little had been done to change many basic features of French society. Private property, even if redefined, had not been challenged. Poverty and insecurity had not been effectively diagnosed, let alone confronted, and gender roles and their attendant inequalities had if anything been reinforced. Institutional change could not quickly affect basic agricultural forms, and such change as there was in the agrarian and industrial economy was mostly in the direction of dilapidation and dislocation, worsening underlying economic problems. Disputes in Paris early in 1791 showed that abolishing urban guilds still left both workers and masters determined to distort the free market with corporatist practices. The rage with which peasants continued to pursue their seigneurial persecutors showed the limits of peaceful change without radical redistribution. Yet those actions themselves were the product of remarkable developments. While it might plausibly be argued that the Old Regime was discredited in its last years, it took the process of involvement in Revolution to invoke a new dynamic centre of loyalty for the French. The assurance of citizenship in the Declaration of Rights was taken seriously, and applied in ways that did not always match its authors' preconceptions (including the attempt by a few to extend it to women), while the profusion of elected authorities marked a seizure of autonomy from the lowest levels. This was counter-balanced by a sense of active nationhood, and the waves of voluntary enlistment in 1791 and 1792 showed that many men were willing to place themselves on the national stage.

The political rhetorics of nationhood, citizenship and popular will that had shaken the surface of Old Regime politics were now ubiquitous, and a genuine militant patriotism animated many in the face of aristocratic and foreign enemies. Such a situation already had its paradoxes, however, and the tension between fighting for a unified nation and resisting outside intrusion would ultimately create a situation close to general civil war. The rhetoric of nation and patriotism simply did not allow for the differences of perspective created by socio-economic, geographical and cultural disparities, or by the evolution of revolutionary events themselves.

The period of the Republic and the Terror would show that the creation of a citizen-state under such circumstances led not to inclusion, but exclusion. If the citizen-body was expanded by manhood suffrage, it was contracted by the definitive proscription of priests and their believers, by hostility to those in the countryside who resisted the urban demands for cheap food, and by the exclusion of all those either too rich or too poor to behave like 'good citizens'. Women's insubstantial grip on a claim to citizenship, advanced by a small step in September 1792 with the legalisation of divorce, would be denied definitively as they proved insufficiently masculine to meet the prevailing tenets of political virtue. All of this can be condemned as a programme of repression, but it was the consequence of a desperate struggle for survival against those who rejected every principle of the Revolution, and that element of it cannot be overlooked.

The first weeks of the new order were a time of panic fear. The enemy armies crossed the frontiers of northern France on 19

August, and swept towards the fortress-towns that guarded the roads to Paris. In the face of this threat, the new rulers made a series of attempts at consolidation. Even before 10 August, some municipalities and *départements* had begun arresting or expelling non-juror priests. The right of all authorities to arrest suspect individuals was one of the first powers voted after the 10th. In a series of further measures, a new oath was imposed on all functionaries, including priests, public religious ceremonies were banned, the teaching and nursing orders of monks and nuns were formally abolished, and finally priests who refused the new oath were ordered to quit the country. Priests had already fallen victim to popular alarm – two were lynched and beheaded in Bordeaux in July, for example, and a potential major massacre was averted at Port-en-Bessin in late August when the Bayeux National Guard rescued a hundred emigrating priests from a crowd gathered on rumours of a British attack.[3] In the west anti-revolutionary sentiment in the countryside was already causing open conflict (document 18). More general rural unrest was tackled first with an abortive order for the division of common lands, then more decisively with the complete abolition of all feudal dues for which seigneurs did not have clear title-deeds. This was effectively an encouragement for peasants to continue destroying such deeds, and marked a shift of emphasis in dealing with this intractable problem. Across the country, radical factions kept down under the monarchy reshuffled or overturned more conservative municipalities, districts and *départements*, a 'second revolution' given retrospective legitimacy by the Convention on 22 September.

Meanwhile the first house-to-house searches for arms and suspects were authorised in Paris, which within a few days filled the prisons with nobles, priests and anyone else felt to be dubious by suspicious neighbourhood authorities. They joined a cross-section of the pre-10 August local elite, many of whom had for years been accused by radicals of connivance with aristocratic forces. By the beginning of September, it was clear that Verdun, the last fortress before Paris, could not long withstand siege. Alarm redoubled in the capital about the mass of enemies now rounded up, but ill-contained in the poorly guarded and possibly corrupt prison system. Patriotic volunteers from the National Guard were preparing to quit the city to form new defensive lines, and did not want to leave the city full of enemies behind them. Thus between 2 and 6 September, well over 1,000 inmates of the Parisian prisons were put to death. Local activists seized control of the buildings, sometimes co-opting prominent radicals to act as judges, and demanded decisions on the fate of prisoners. Not for the first time, or the last, a dramatic black-and-white view of politics was put on show – those adjudged no threat were released, embraced, welcomed into the people; those deemed guilty, men and women alike, were butchered.

The 'September Massacres' were yet another step in the consolidation of absolute opposition between the Revolution and its enemies, and a decisive step towards opposition between Parisian radicals and more moderate republicans. The Girondins who had fought for war to deal with counter-revolution would shrink from the butchery it now appeared to imply, blaming radical journalists such as Marat for inflaming popular bloodlust, and painting the massacres as part of a factional plot by Robespierre and the Commune to seize national power (document 19). The municipality of Lyon, closely linked to the Girondins by the presence of its Patriot leader, Jean Roland, at the Interior Ministry, faced a similar popular rising. Lyon lived in even more constant fear of counter-revolution than Paris, being closer to the borders, and the reputed refuge of fleeing seigneurs from most of southern France. On 9 September, with the inspiration of Parisian events, a popular crowd stormed a prison and butchered three non-juror priests and eight cavalry officers held on suspicion of attempted emigration. The following week, an even more remarkable rising took place, illustrating the continued relevance of material demands. For a week the city's streets were virtually given over to crowds from the common people. Policed by women calling themselves 'female police commissioners', and guided by printed lists, a massive exercise in popular price-fixing occurred. Goods of all descriptions were seized and sold from shops and warehouses, only ending as shops emptied and peasants and wholesalers declined to send goods into the city. The National Guard was powerless, especially after one was hacked to death for firing at a crowd on 17 September.[4]

In Marseille, which had repeatedly set itself up at the forefront of revolutionary activism, participating in armed conflict over the papal enclave around Avignon in both 1791 and early 1792, for example, counter-revolutionaries were hunted down with renewed vigour after 10 August. The *département* administration, allegedly in thrall to the unpatriotic business interests of large merchants, was conducted under armed guard from Aix to Marseille. Counter-revolutionary suspects had been killed publicly in July, and four conspirators were lynched in September. Going a step further, a 'Popular Tribunal' was set up by the Marseille patriots to judge accused conspirators. This had no official status or central approval, and while it was symptomatic of the city's advanced attitudes in politics, and a grand example of the autonomy that urban communities had extracted from the Revolution, such developments were not well-regarded from the centre.[5]

In Paris, the new revolutionary assembly, the National Convention, was gathering. It had been elected with the same two-tier mechanism as the Legislative Assembly, although in a democratic concession no level of payment was set to restrict the basic franchise. Voters did, however, have to be male, over twenty-one, and possessed of an income, and domestic servants were again excluded because of their dependent status. This gave an electorate of some six million, half as many again as in the 1791 Constitution.[6] In the turbulent atmosphere of September, some elections were troubled by political conflicts, and Jacobins in particular were becoming less averse to naming lists of approved candidates (and those to avoid). This was still not a prevalent practice, however, and the elections did not produce a sharply divided body. It might be fairly said, however, that those who opposed the result of 10 August were unlikely to be enthusiastic voters.

Socially the Convention remained dominated by lawyers, those in official or private practice making up almost 48 per cent of its 749 members. A wide range of other middle-class groupings had between 5 and 10 per cent each of the seats: farmers, businessmen, civil servants, doctors, and academics and writers. There remained a significant group of clergy, 7.3 per cent, and military officers, 4.8 per cent, but all of these would have to be seen as firm revolutionaries. Overall, some 86 per cent of the *conventionnels* had already served the Revolution in some form of office. The violent divisions that would emerge within the Convention were between men whose political views would have

115

seemed indistinguishable, and all equally outrageous, five years previously. Politically, over 500 of the *conventionnels* can be classed as no more than the relatively passive supporters of any significant 'party', and at least half of these were firmly neutral.[7] Unanimity and disinterestedness would continue to be prized in politics, even as factional strife accelerated in the months ahead.

The Convention began to meet on 20 September, and on the 21st unanimously voted to abolish the monarchy, formally declaring a Republic the next day. By the end of the same week, however, Girondin deputies were calling for a new force of *fédéré* troops from around the country to protect them from Parisian excess. Meanwhile, the fortunes of the new Republic saw a dramatic improvement. On the day of the Convention's first meeting, the French and Prussian forces met at Valmy. Expecting to meet a leaderless rabble, the Prussians instead confronted a well-motivated army of regular and volunteer battalions, and withdrew after an exchange of artillery fire. This victory galvanised the Revolution's troops, who pushed north and east, liberating French territory and going on to the offensive. Breaking the sedate rules of eighteenth-century warfare, campaigning on into winter, substituting fervour and mobility for the rigid discipline of their enemies, these volunteer armies conquered the Austrian Netherlands (present-day Belgium), parts of the German Rhineland, Basle in Switzerland and Savoy to the south-east.[8]

Revolutionary politics, however, continued to generate new conflicts. The Girondins became clearly opposed to the Jacobin Club, which expelled Brissot in October. In return, attacks on the personal integrity of radical figures such as Danton, Robespierre and Marat became common. However, it was increasingly these men who held the initiative, balanced between the social caution of the Girondins and the intemperate demands emanating from the spokesmen of the population of Paris. Like other urban centres, Paris was suffering from the declining value of the *assignat*, which added to economic instability already provoked by war and suspicion. Although the paper currency rallied to some 70 per cent of its face value in the autumn of 1792, after falling below 60 per cent in the spring, the following six months would see it plunge below 50 per cent, a collapse from which it would never recover.[9] In the face of this, and renewed rural disorders over food prices south of Paris, the Girondin-controlled administration insisted on liberalising trade in grain again in December 1792. From this point on, however, there was no longer truly to be any 'normal' economic life for the country. Long before official economic controls were put in place in 1793, urban and rural districts were set against each other in the pursuit of subsistence. Municipal authorities, given responsibility for feeding their populations, did not hesitate to use force, and peaceable private commerce became a thing of the past.

Meanwhile, the emblematic process of the winter of 1792–3 was the trial and execution of Louis XVI. Secret correspondence discovered in a concealed cupboard in the Tuileries palace left little doubt that he had betrayed the Revolution, and some radicals insisted that a trial was not even necessary before his execution. The question was vigorously debated in the last two months of 1792, and the distance that sentiments had moved since the early years of the Revolution was visible in many speeches. The king was denounced as a monster, inhuman by his royal nature. The young Jacobin Saint-Just put the matter brutally: 'this man must reign or die ... One cannot reign innocently ... Every king is a rebel and a usurper. Do kings themselves treat otherwise those who seek to usurp their authority?'[10]

The Convention, with its heavy load of lawyers, nevertheless went through the motions of formal trial proceedings. Louis's guilt was agreed unanimously, but a substantial body of deputies, including many Girondins, were reluctant to take the final step – some wanted a referendum to obtain popular consent, but this was voted down. The vote for Louis's execution, and a subsequent one which turned down a reprieve, both had majorities of under a hundred. The guillotine, in use since April 1792 as a humane mode of execution, despatched 'citizen Capet' on 21 January 1793. The death was counter-pointed by the assassination of Lepeletier de Saint-Fargeau the previous day, a Jacobin *conventionnel* killed by a counter-revolutionary fanatic. Over the next six weeks, the new Republic set itself still further against all of Europe, declaring war on Britain and Holland, various Italian states, and Spain, in the belief (largely accurate) that they were already secretly working against France.

The Revolution now approached its greatest crisis. Declaring war on Britain added a seaborne blockade to France's economic troubles, a hardship felt particularly strongly in the great mercantile cities. Meanwhile, the troops who had signed up as volunteers in 1791 and 1792 had begun to go home, as was their right. On 24 February, in response to this and to the widening of the war, the Convention decreed a levy of 300,000 men for the army – no longer a call for volunteers, but the setting of quotas for every *département*, district and municipality to meet as they saw fit. This was to have dramatic repercussions, as revolutionary politics continued to experience division and crisis.

Since 1789, France had effectively been fragmented. The waves of local autonomy had washed away chains of command and administrative hierarchies, and as political polarisation had intensified, both long-standing and newly provoked antagonisms had become strongly felt. The overriding war effort was able to suppress the signs of division in the country from some perspectives, but especially when it came to food, necessity overrode the rhetoric. Lyon is a case in point. The months after 10 August had seen a tenuous but ferocious hold on power taken by radical Jacobins. Looking to the Paris club for a lead, this group spouted bloodthirsty rhetoric and claimed to offer solutions to the city's subsistence problems, but found itself paralysed by the lack of effective repressive legislation, and by a desperate lack of funds as the *assignat* plunged in value by nearly half in the first few months of 1793. Severe economic dislocation affected the city, and the urban population, supposedly the Jacobins' 'natural' supporters, grew disenchanted. Jacobin actions did not match their rhetoric in the face of urban hunger, and their violent denunciation of figures such as Roland clashed with a widespread view of him as the city's tribune and a 'man of the people'.

In Jacobin rhetoric, opposition to them from below could only be a symptom of aristocratic infiltration or of an 'incivic' concern with luxury (Lyon's artisanal base was after all the silk industry), and they could not see why their 'natural' role as spokesmen of popular sovereignty was being scorned.[11] By the spring of 1793 the club movement in the sections of Lyon was riven with splits and faction-fighting, and a challenge to the Jacobin municipality was being mounted by groups in some sections founding rival societies, imitating by various subterfuges the permanent sessions of the Parisian sections. By March, a body of regular troops and several Parisian representatives were in the city attempting to prop up the Jacobins. Parisian opinion by now saw in Lyon a dangerous haunt of counter-revolution, and future events would do nothing to dispel that image.

As deeper and wider war engulfed France, more social and political divisions were emerging within the country. Deportations of priests, continued emigrations, arrests and massacres had thinned the ranks of declared enemies of the Revolution, but the patriotic unanimity that ought logically to follow was lacking. Ever since the defeat of the *monarchiens* in the autumn of 1789, doing away with their vision of a balanced constitution, the revolutionary political system had been built on the idea of a single sovereign will, a single guiding force in politics. This was the ironic heritage of the years of monarchical absolutism, supplemented by the elevation of public opinion into a 'tribunal' in the pre-revolutionary decades. Nothing in the aristocrats' behaviour since the 1780s had led revolutionaries to believe that the kind of mixed constitution that pandered to vested interests was an acceptable substitute for concentrated power. However, the form of 'popular sovereignty' invoked to replace royal authority raised far more problems than it solved.

It had been that sovereignty which had made the position of the king untenable. The transfer of sovereignty away from him rendered his position meaningless, in Old Regime terms, and hard to grasp even within the discourse of the Revolution. He became essentially a scapegoat for the inability of the body politic to function efficiently around him. With the king disposed of, however, the internal problems of popular sovereignty became even more manifest. Since 1789, crowds had implicitly claimed the punitive rights of the sovereign, in the face of educated observers' repulsion, but there were more aspects to the problem than merely containing violence. For a start, there was the issue of representation. With whom did power actually lie? Attributing it to the 'Nation' in 1789 meant little when the active citizenship requirement was put in place, although that problem had been swept away in August 1792. Theoretically after that every adult male was an equal part of the sovereign. Sovereign power, however, (if it was not to be left to mobs) had to be wielded through some form of organs. By late 1792 this had become a clearly divisive issue. The Girondins preached obedience to regularly constituted authorities – that municipalities should yield to districts, districts to *départements*, and all to the Convention and the rule of law. This also meant that the centre, or what in the Girondin view were 'factions' manipulating power in Paris, had no right to impose its views on other authorities with violence and illegal measures. Jacobinism, as espoused in the Convention and the Club and its affiliates, was more intemperate. Not only did it refuse to denounce popular violence (when directed to appropriate goals), but it insisted that constituted authority had to yield to political virtue. The voice of 'the people', provided it was expressed by spokesmen who followed a Jacobin line, was to be listened to in preference to authorities who might be tainted with insufficiently politically or socially virtuous personnel.[12]

This tendency had been clear in some areas before the crises of 1793 – Marseille, for example, saw itself as in the revolutionary vanguard, and Jacobin-inclined local leaders did not hesitate to overturn other local authorities in a region 'known' to be riddled with counter-revolutionary plots. The problem was, of course, that sooner or later issues arose which led the centre to reassert its possession of the unified authority that 'popular sovereignty' was held to represent. And that unified authority did not take notice of the particular situations in which large portions of the 'sovereign people' found themselves. Jacobinism as expressed from Paris was above all a centralising tendency. The French Republic had been proclaimed 'One and Indivisible' in the face of various centrifugal tendencies, but Jacobinism was blind to the social and political realities behind those outward pulls. We may also note here that the kind of radicalism that was growing amongst Parisian local militants was just as inward-looking as the views of any other town, but its location and its vehemence pushed the Jacobins of the Convention into alliance with it.

Between March and May of 1793 France passed from a state of high internal tension, in which popular protest and counter-revolutionary activity were intermittent, to a condition of civil war. The first blow came in the west, where the levy of 300,000 men was the spark for widespread resistance to what was effectively revolutionary conscription. The area had not really been pacified since the clerical oath had inflamed it in 1791, and a wide variety of new and long-standing general and intra-regional disputes and grievances made these new demands the final straw. The summer of 1792 had already seen insurrections against some local authorities across Brittany and the lower Loire, especially against anticlerical measures and efforts at recruitment. Upon news of the new levy, groups, mainly of peasants, rose up and seized local towns in the area to the south of Brittany centred on the *département* of the Vendée. From a largely spontaneous beginning, more organised forces emerged, led by overtly counter-revolutionary elements. This 'Vendéen Revolt' destroyed revolutionary authority over a wide area, and by May regular troops had had to be committed against the 'Royal and Catholic Army' that formed from the initial risings.[13]

Resistance across much of the country, notably the south, was less spectacular, but sometimes violent, and alarming to the Convention. March 1793 saw it promulgate an array of new powers and dispositions, establishing many of the mechanisms which would later be used to implement Terror. On the 10th, a Revolutionary Tribunal was established at Paris to deal with counter-revolutionary crimes; on the 19th, rebels captured under arms were decreed liable to death without trial; on the 21st, surveillance committees (*comités de surveillance*) were decreed for every commune and section, to monitor movement and issue identity-certificates to loyal citizens; on the 28th, further laws penalised the *émigrés*, rendering them legally dead and liable to the loss of their property; and on the 29th, press freedoms were formally limited, with the death penalty for incitement to murder or violation of property, or proposing the dissolution of the Convention or the re-establishment of monarchy. In this last measure, the Convention showed that it still looked two ways, against popular agitation as well as counter-revolution. This stance had been stressed on 18 March with a law decreeing death for anyone who proposed the egalitarian redistribution of land. Measures like these, coming on top of the conscription requirements, intensified yet again the contrast between a revolution of local autonomy and a revolution of republican unanimity.

Between March and May over eighty largely Jacobin-oriented deputies were sent out from the Convention as 'representatives-on-mission', authorised to take all necessary steps to stabilise the political situation and assist military recruitment. What such steps were taken to mean can be gauged from the record of two deputies, Chabot and Bo, in the *départements* of the Aveyron and Tarn. In the month of April alone, they imposed the following measures: various special delegates and commissioners were appointed to oversee recruitment and disarm 'suspects', a 'war tax' was extorted from aristocrats and the wealthy 'moderates', elections were annulled and all local bodies purged of unreliable members, such 'incivic' citizens were disarmed and the National Guard was reorganised, and a military force was formed to pursue non-juror priests and *émigrés*. The new surveillance committees were filled with suitably reliable patriots under the deputies' guidance. By the end of the month, 'suspects' were being held as hostages in district *chefs-lieux*, lists of charges were being compiled for Parisian scrutiny, and house-to-house searches had been authorised wherever necessary. This extensive list of actions is not typical of all such missions at this time, but its components were common enough. Many such measures remained technically illegal, and subject to vigorous denunciation by more moderate Girondins in Paris. They left swathes of the country under effectively paramilitary rule in the hands of one political faction, even as the deputies took the road back to Paris by the end of the spring.[14]

This internal conflict coincided with a reversal in the wider war, one reason for the vigour of the action. A spring offensive into Holland had left the French vulnerable, and the Austrians had by April counter-attacked and driven them out of Belgium. As well as adding new urgency to a wave of further punitive measures adopted against *émigrés* and suspects, this intensified the hostility between Girondins and Jacobins in Paris. The latter were now led by a group in the Convention identified as the 'Montagnards' or 'Mountain', because they habitually sat high up on the tiered benches of the assembly-hall. The defeated Girondin-linked general Dumouriez was suspected of having betrayed the army, and the war minister and four Convention deputies were sent to arrest him. He handed them over to the Austrians, then after unsuccessfully calling on his army to march on Paris, fled to the enemy on 5 April. On the same day, Marat, as president of the Paris Jacobins, sent a circular to provincial clubs, calling on them to campaign for the removal of the deputies who had sought a referendum on the king's fate. His subsequent impeachment, trial and acquittal by the Revolutionary Tribunal further polarised relations between the Girondins and Parisian radicals, in the Jacobins, the sections and the Commune.

Such radicalism took several forms. Most vocal in the spring and early summer of 1793 would be the *enragés* (literally 'madmen', a label applied by their opponents), a small group of extreme radical spokesmen and journalists who drew support from the poorest sections of the city and from some of the more radically egalitarian popular societies. These included the 'Society of Revolutionary Republican Women' led by Pauline Léon and Claire Lacombe. The members of this group were amongst the most militant feminists to emerge during the Revolution, even demanding the right to bear arms in defence of the Republic. They also launched a violent attack in May 1793 on another prominent female activist, Théroigne de Méricourt, for her Girondin sympathies. *Enragé* figures such as the priest Jacques Roux had been prominent in food riots in February, and implicated in attacks on Girondin printers in March.[15] Like Marat, they extended the label 'aristocrat' to all those who seemed to resist the goal of an egalitarian society, and more directly, to threaten the people's subsistence (document 20). Their influence, however, was challenged by the more organised 'popular movement' based in the section assemblies, which looked to radical municipal politicians such as Hébert for leadership, and tempered their views on subsistence issues with an eye to the political agenda of the Jacobins. Divisions between these groups would emerge to greater effect later in the summer.

In the spring, however, Parisian radicalism presented a relatively united face against the Girondins, while radical agendas continued to be expressed in new legislative measures, reflecting the fluid nature of political initiative within the Convention, and the lack of a solid partisan divide. On 21 April the Convention authorised the deportation of any priest, even an oath-taker, who was denounced by six citizens. April also saw the creation of the Committee of Public Safety (*salut public*, which has connotations of 'public salvation'), drawn from the Convention, charged with oversight of government and the running of the war effort. Over the next year this body would increasingly become the effective government of France. On 4 May, responding to Parisian demands voiced since February, the Convention voted to regulate the price of food grains by setting a 'Maximum'. On 20 May a forced loan on rich citizens was decreed for the war effort. Yet the political struggles went on. On 18 May the Convention had named a Girondin-packed 'Commission of Twelve' to investigate

the subversive intentions of their Parisian opponents, and a fortnight of vicious political infighting followed. The resolution of
this conflict would show the Jacobin and Girondin conceptions of
sovereignty in action, and plunge France, already racked with
warfare, into further turmoil.

Notes

1 See J. Godechot, *The Counter-Revolution: Doctrine and Action,
1789–1804*, Princeton, 1971, pp. 207–10, 231–5.

2 There has been little specialist work in English on this insurrection. It was a time of great confusion and hesitation for many political
figures, though there was also a broad view that the monarchy could
not last: see L. Whaley, 'Political Factions and the Second Revolution:
The Insurrection of 10 August 1792', *French History*, 7, 1993, pp. 205–24.

3 See A. Forrest, *Society and Politics in Revolutionary Bordeaux*, Oxford, 1975, pp. 60–1; O. H. Hufton, *Bayeux in the Late Eighteenth Century:
A Social Study*, Oxford, 1967, pp. 193–4.

4 See W. D. Edmonds, *Jacobinism and the Revolt of Lyon, 1789–1793*,
Oxford, 1990, pp. 124–6.

5 See W. Scott, *Terror and Repression in Revolutionary Marseilles*,
London, 1973, pp. 29–31, 40–3.

6 See M. Crook, *Elections in the French Revolution: An Apprenticeship
in Democracy 1789–1799*, Cambridge, 1996, pp. 79ff.

7 Debate over the political make-up of the Convention is a long-
standing historiographical issue. The figures here are taken from
C. Jones, *The Longman Companion to the French Revolution*, London, 1988,
p. 168, which uses A. Patrick, *The Men of the First French Republic: Political
Alignments in the National Convention of 1792*, Baltimore, 1972. For other
views, see for example the 'Forum on the Girondist Faction in the
French Revolution', *French Historical Studies*, 15, 1988, pp. 506–48, and P.
Higonnet, 'The Social and Cultural Antecedents of Revolutionary Dis-
continuity: Montagnards and Girondins', *English Historical Review*, 100,
1985, pp. 513–44.

8 See T. C. W. Blanning, *The French Revolutionary Wars, 1787–1802*,
London, 1996, pp. 74–80, for an account of Valmy, and *passim* for a
purely military account of the war.

9 There was a 'recovery' to just over 60 per cent in the spring/sum-
mer of 1794, but this was when economic activity was most closely controlled by Terror.

10 On the correspondence, see A. Freeman (ed.) *The Compromising
of Louis XVI: The Armoire de Fer and the French Revolution*, Exeter, 1989.

On the trial of the king in general, see M. Walzer (ed.), *Regicide and Revolution: Speeches at the Trial of Louis XVI*, London, 1974, and David P. Jordan, *The King's Trial: The French Revolution vs. Louis XVI*, Berkeley, 1979.

11 See Edmonds, *Jacobinism*, pp. 138ff.

12 It can be noted in passing that both these attitudes were placed in a situation of paradox by the Girondin appeal for a referendum on the king: on that question the Jacobins insisted on the absolute sovereignty of the representative assembly, whilst the Girondins sought to refer the matter back to the 'sovereign people' they represented.

13 The literature on the origins and nature of the Vendéen revolt is voluminous, and often vitriolic. A good introduction is C. Petitfrère, 'The Origins of the Civil War in the Vendée', *French History*, 2, 1988, pp. 187–207.

14 P. Jones, *The Peasantry in the French Revolution*, Cambridge, 1988, pp. 232–3. See pp. 217–30 for more detail on the Vendée and general resistance to recruitment.

15 For a highly sympathetic picture of the *enragé* group, see R. B. Rose, *The Enragés: Socialists of the French Revolution?*, Sydney, 1968. Roux committed suicide in prison early in 1794, while the other leaders faded into obscurity.

7

Terror and the Jacobin Republic, 1793–1794

The split in the National Convention between Girondins and Montagnards was resolved on 2 June 1793 by a purge of the Convention, voted by its members under the threat of surrounding armed forces from the Commune, sections and Paris National Guard. Two ministers and twenty-nine deputies were removed and placed under house arrest, and the power of the Girondins was broken. For the previous two days a more bloody outcome had appeared possible, following a more explicitly popular demonstration on 31 May, influenced by the *enragés*, which had surrounded the Convention but had not managed to force it to act.[1] The subsequent illegal coercion of the legislature was justified in Jacobin and Montagnard eyes as an act of popular sovereignty, liberating the Convention from a faction which had itself tried to eliminate leading radicals. It was read in many other parts of France, however, as the surrender of legitimate authority to dangerous Parisian 'anarchists'.

In Lyon the news from Paris was particularly unfortunate, as the sections there had just held a similar rising, but in an opposite political direction. Indeed, news of this event reached Paris on 2 June, in time to harden Jacobin attitudes there. The extreme Jacobin municipality of Lyon, which had proved unable to alleviate the city's considerable problems of subsistence and employment, and had increasingly threatened to unleash a reign of terror against wide sections of the population, had been overthrown on 29 May by a sectional movement linked to Girondin perspectives. Marseille had entered into similar conflict – its sections had been contesting power with its Jacobin club and deputies sent from Paris throughout the spring. Already at the beginning of May, the deputies had fled and declared the sections to be counter-revolutionary. The sections had declared themselves to be resisting oppression, as guaranteed in the Rights of Man, and had suppressed the club and repudiated policies pursued by it (document 21).[2]

Events in Paris on 31 May and 2 June left these cities, and others with Girondin sympathies, with little choice. As the proscribed deputies and their sympathisers evaded their rather loose arrest and fled, Lyon and Marseille, along with Bordeaux and Caen, declared themselves to be legitimate centres of popular authority, while Paris was now in the hands of a 'faction' which preached anarchy and destruction, and threatened to leave France in the hands of counter-revolution. This was in effect to impose a second civil war on the one already raging in the west, but the alternative for Lyon and Marseille was to release the dangerous men they had just detained, and to await their vengeance. In Bordeaux and Caen (where many Girondins gathered) the immediate situation was less critical, but in their view the assault on the national representation had to be opposed (even if, ironically, one response was to arrest Convention deputies on mission in their areas).[3]

Much debate has gone on about the social character of this division. The Jacobins at the time played on the idea that the cities that rose up were haunts of commercial luxury, that the rank and file of opposition were being cruelly misled by a debauched 'aristocracy of wealth' bent on their own selfish ends. Likewise the Federalists, as the various rebels were labelled, stressed the rootless, demagogic, socially indeterminate and hence dangerous qualities of both local and national Jacobins, who again were thought to lead the common people astray. Such assessments obviously cannot be taken at face value, and in any case it is apparent that the Federalist cause was not uniform. In Lyon, the 'popular' silk-workers were instrumental, at least in the early stages of revolt, whereas in Bordeaux politics seemed to remain the preserve of those more generally 'middle-class'.

One social dimension to these conflicts is that stressed, or perhaps overstressed, by Richard Cobb – that Jacobin supporters, 'Terrorists' as they soon became, were outsiders. This was inevitable, considering the political evolution of the previous half-decade. Communities, accustomed both to the irritating yoke of absolutist centralism and to the pervasive localism that underlay it, embraced their own interests vigorously when offered the chance to do so by Revolution. In the increasingly dangerous and divisive political climate of the following years, communities (and more specifically powerful groups in those communities) dealt, or failed to deal, with social and political issues in their own ways. Autonomy was the order of the day, whether that led to the expansionist revolutionary pride of the Marseillais, the internal strife of Lyon, the domineering radicalism of Paris, or a multitude of other potential responses.

In general, prior to 1793, communities were left to work out their own destinies within the general parameters of 'revolutionary' behaviour, albeit with an increasingly hectoring lead to local radicals from the Parisian Jacobins. Groups with substantial local power-bases were those most successful at maintaining control, regardless of how an outside observer might construe their political complexion. By 1793, however, this balance of power between centre and communities was under threat. The war and its needs had sent increasing numbers of commissioners from the centre into the regions. Such men tended to see issues from an exclusively national perspective, to which must be added their largely Montagnard allegiances. To affronted local elites such men might be seen to have a narrowly 'Parisian' perspective, and to condone disorder in the name of revolution. Coming from outside, predisposed by tales of conflict reaching Paris to find 'counter-revolution', the agents of central government read local autonomy as threatening, and sought out those less complicit in its maintenance to combat it. In Cobb's eyes, such men were often 'the obscure, frustrated, rancid thirty-five-year-old', now licenced to take out his frustrations on those who had kept him down.[4]

Lynn Hunt has noted this tendency, but also describes a more complex and ambiguous relationship between insider and outsider in local communities. French towns in the 1790s usually had a substantial group of 'outsiders', given the very high rates of migration prevalent over the previous decades, and which were raised still further by the Revolution. Such people might actually be chosen as local representatives, rather than imposed from outside. For an electorate unsure of who to select, such men had a number of advantages. On the one hand, they were bound by no long-standing family ties, and thus there would be fewer repercussions if they had to be repudiated later. On the other hand, they might bring connections with other places and sources of power and influence. Their status as more than just another 'local' offered to those who chose them a sense of participation in a national movement, especially as such 'outsiders' often enthusiastically pursued such links. The members of the Jacobin Club of Marseille, for example, were over 50 per cent immigrants to the city in its early years, and over 70 per cent in the later years of its existence. (Although one should note that nearly half of all Marseillais were not natives of the city.)

The outsider might be defined in geographical terms, or by religious or social differences; cynically one could see many impoverished educated men taking up the revolutionary cause for the job it offered them. However, an outsider, prey to no long-standing vendettas, could also mediate successfully between his adopted community and the outside world, be it the demands of larger neighbouring communities or the rigours of national politics. There are many senses in which the world and personnel of the Jacobin Republic came crashing into local communities like a tornado, but there were many communities, and their 'outsiders', who learnt to bend with the wind successfully.[5]

In the summer of 1793, agents of central government moved into, and reinforced, an almost complete militarisation of public life. Even before the Federalist outbreak, local armed forces were being raised by municipalities and *départements*, drawing on and supplementing the National Guard, for use against counter-revolution or in factional fighting in the name of revolution. In addition, of course, much of the country was close enough to hostile frontiers and active battle to be effectively under military control. With the Federalist revolt added to this, full-scale armed conflict, in one form or another, occupied most of France. Brittany and Normandy, the areas around Bordeaux, Lyon, and the cities of Provence all took up arms, fourteen *départements* in the end declaring formally against the Convention, and some forty experiencing some kind of disturbance.

Federalist revolt, and a small Girondin 'army', was put to flight in Normandy in July, and progress was made by the Convention's forces against the southern cities. Lyon showed its defiance and executed the Jacobin leader Chalier in the same month, and in August was put under siege. The Lyonnais moderates had chosen to make common cause with royalist elements in the city, exacerbating the Jacobin determination to destroy them. Marseille was retaken at the end of August, precipitating the holders of the nearby military port of Toulon to hand it over to British and *émigré* counter-revolutionary forces. Meanwhile, the Vendéens won a string of victories through June and July, leading to a decision in August to deploy more regular troops there, and to enforce a scorched-earth policy. On all of France's land-frontiers, her troops were defeated, her earlier gains lost, and desperate defensive actions fought.

In the face of this peril, the Montagnards now ruling in Paris could see little option but to continue to tighten their line of doctrinal purity. Although committed to popular sovereignty, they were now sure that the Convention embodied the will of the sovereign people, having been purged of suspect elements, and all resistance to it was no less counter-revolutionary than the Vendéens or the Austrians. Some of the ambiguities of popular sovereignty were embodied in the new Constitution, which had been published in June for ratification by electoral assemblies. It codified the 'right of insurrection' – that the people could rise up against their government if it violated their rights. This was termed 'the most sacred of rights and the most imprescriptible of duties', but it risked being either a meaningless token or a recipe for chaos. Voting for the Assembly was to be annual, and by 'acclamation' rather than ballot – in accordance with ideas of popular unanimity, but a licence for intimidation of a kind radicals had already proved adept at exercising, for example in the Parisian sections.

This Constitution was, in any case, never implemented, although it became a totem for later radical groups. Its approval by popular assemblies provided a useful morale-boosting exercise, and the demonstration of moves to restore regular political institutions helped to dissipate Federalist resistance outside the main urban centres. Jacobin desire to use the Constitution as a stabilising device led to growing hostility towards *enragés* who continued to agitate over popular subsistence and against the 'unpatriotic' rich (document 22). Nonetheless, overwhelming approval of the Constitution by the people was announced as part of the festivities for the anniversary of the king's fall, but the process of elections for a new legislature was put off, and in October it was suspended 'until the peace'. Government was to be 'revolutionary' until then, and what that meant was already becoming clear.

By this point, the Revolution had officially entered a new phase. Terror was declared 'the order of the day' on 5 September 1793, after a march by Parisian sectional activists on the Convention. It came hot on the heels of news of Toulon's treachery, and two weeks after the revolutionary state's grip on society had been tightened by the decree of the 'Mass Levy' (*levée en masse*), a measure which put all resources of society, and all individuals, at the disposal of the Republic for the war effort. At the height of its impact over the next year, this would see tens of thousands of workers employed making war materials, while France fielded an army of over 800,000 men, with well over a million notionally under arms – a force without precedent in history.

Fighting in the Vendée, and against Lyon, Marseille and Bordeaux, had already led to several thousand deaths in the previous months. The move to go beyond even this, and officially declare a reign of Terror on the Republic's enemies, represented the working-out of a variety of agendas agitating the Convention and the Parisian radical movement through the summer of 1793. Laws passed in the weeks following 5 September included a systematic internment of suspect individuals (the 'Law of Suspects'), political purges of administrative committees, and expansion of the work of the Revolutionary Tribunal. Added to this political agenda were the introduction of comprehensive controls on prices (the 'General Maximum'), payment for 'poor citizens' who attended section meetings (although such meetings were limited to twice a week), and the establishment of a 'Revolutionary Army' (*armée révolutionnaire*), an instrument of Terror manned by urban radicals, designed to force food-growers to supply the cities, and to weed out lurking counter-revolutionaries in rural communities.

Most of these measures had been present in Parisian demands as early as 31 May. At that time, however, they were largely the cause of the *enragés*, rather than of the broader Parisian 'popular movement'. The social identity of this 'movement', long thought of as unproblematic, is now something of a historical conundrum.

Its roots were in the sections, rather than the radical clubs that had been in existence since 1790, and it was thus a more masculine and neighbourhood-based grouping. Through the spring of 1793 sections where committees and local assemblies had radical majorities coerced neighbouring more 'moderate' ones into electing radical leaderships by the process of 'fraternisation' – intimidatory expeditions to section assemblies, which then voted by acclamation for new committees. Clearly this was no more than a façade of democracy, but those who were now calling themselves *sans-culottes* believed that they had revolutionary virtue on their side – they were 'the people', for whom all necessary measures were justified.

The *sans-culottes* – those who did not wear the knee-breeches of the respectable classes – played on their distinction from the educated and wealthy. Their archetype was the 'Père Duchesne', a stock character from eighteenth-century popular theatre revived as the crude, vulgar but honest mouthpiece for a number of revolutionary newspapers.[6] By 1793, the journalist and municipal politician Hébert had established his version of this figure as definitive, and the image of this foul-mouthed independent artisan craftsman, father of a family, shouldering responsibilities for politics at home while his sons fight on the frontiers, proclaiming his straightforward radical views on political issues, gave the *sans-culottes* a focus for their ideas (document 23). However, as this suggests, the idea of the *sans-culotte* was at least as much an invention of journalists and politicians as a reflection of some social reality. Michael Sonenscher has argued that practically every aspect of the *sans-culotte* image was invented in order to give the educated politicians a way of conceptualising how 'the people' should behave in a modern republic, as opposed to the ancient ones they knew from their classical studies.[7]

Richard Andrews has gone further and claimed that the 'popular movement' in Paris actually had social control as its goals – for example, that the General Maximum and the *armée révolutionnaire* allowed popular anger over the economic situation to be displaced onto rural suppliers rather than urban employers. Actual *sans-culotte* activists in the sections often prove to have been relatively wealthy players in the artisan economy – still close enough to their popular roots to give an image that matched the Père Duchesne, but with capital behind them, and considerable local influence. Their battles against Parisian 'moderates', often portrayed in social terms, can in this version be seen as the translation onto new political circumstances of older oppositions, neighbourhood feuds, even perhaps disagreements within Old Regime guilds. In this analysis, the *sans-culottes* are seen as a section of the lower bourgeoisie pursuing their own interests in social stability and the victory of the Republic, not the admittedly petty-bourgeois leaders of a movement with a 'popular' heart, as in the classic Marxist analysis.[8]

It is certainly the case that, in the summer of 1793, the idols of the *sans-culotte* movement resisted the attention to social issues that the *enragés* put on the agenda, particularly about the food supply. Both Marat's and Hébert's papers were quick to condemn attempts to keep food on the agenda of debate on the new Constitution in June, seeing this as counter-revolutionary destabilisation. Marat was assassinated on 13 July, and in the wake of this several *enragés* took up his journalistic mantle as 'friend of the people' or 'defender of the Republic', and pressed the case for economic regulation in the name of the hungry crowds. By August the *enragés* were being denounced in the Jacobin Club by Marat's widow, and by Robespierre, the great 'Incorruptible' Montagnard leader. However, by the end of August both the Jacobin and *sans-culotte* leadership had moved towards admitting the need for such policies, and soon made them their own. Thus 5 September saw the results of a great 'popular' *journée*, while on the same day Jacques Roux, radical priest and most prominent of the *enragé* journalists, was arrested as a counter-revolutionary suspect. In actions like this, it becomes hard to distinguish a 'popular movement' from a political faction. One may also note, for example, that two members added to the Committee of Public Safety on 6 September 1793, under '*sans-culotte*' pressure, Collot d'Herbois and Billaud-Varenne, were both extremely radical, but far from being 'men of the people'.

The politics of 'sans-culottism' were particularly visible in the War Ministry from April 1793, under Bouchotte. This former professional soldier enlarged the Ministry, bringing in supporters of Hébert and the Cordeliers Club, which persisted in giving a lead to the 'popular movement'. Other significant figures in this grouping included Ronsin, a failed playwright who became a National Guard officer and club orator, and Vincent, a clerk and long-time Cordeliers member. Ronsin was sent to the Vendée, from where he agitated for stronger measures against the rebels, while Vincent brought a heavily 'Hébertist' politics to the internal workings of the Ministry. Although this policy did include aspects such as recruiting *sans-culotte* fathers of families to work in the Ministry, in place of single clerks who should be at the front, it is hard to isolate many more 'social' aspects of their approach. Men such as these, none of whom had genuinely risen from the people of Paris, were nonetheless the most visible figureheads of Parisian radicalism in 1793–4.[9]

The measures of September 1793 were taken out to the country at large by growing numbers of 'representatives-on-mission', who had since April accumulated ever-wider powers to purge administrative bodies, direct the effort against external and internal enemies, secure food supplies, and punish counter-revolution. Over the following months administration was streamlined, and authority at local levels shifted from *départements*, many of which had supported Federalism (at least verbally), downwards to districts, whose smaller jurisdiction could be better monitored by the centre and its agents. The General Maximum and the Mass Levy were co-ordinated by a Subsistence Commission established on 27 October, a bureaucracy which sent its own agents into the field alongside the representatives, taking control of all economic activity. A ruthless approach by such men succeeded in saving France from the looming disaster of the summer. The autumn saw the recapture of Bordeaux and Lyon, along with victories on the northern and eastern borders. By December, the British had been driven out of Toulon, liberating the south, and after a vicious campaign with several significant battles, the Vendéen army was crushed and put to flight (though it continued a guerrilla campaign).

The cost of such victories was the terrorisation of much of the population. It was in the period of the Terror that the contradictions at the heart of the Revolution were most clearly exposed. The Revolution that the Convention and its agents sought to save was one seen from the centre, where nothing was more important than the purity and unity of the revolutionary people. They had created a Republic, which to their minds, filled with the ideals of ancient Rome and the works of Rousseau, was a community of masculine citizen-warriors dedicated to the collective good. The Revolution that most of the population had wanted was one at the grass-roots, that freed them from arbitrary burdens, from the politics of individual privilege and influence, from the claims of particular rights acquired through incomprehensible tangles of law. Seen from below and outside, the period of the Terror saw the reinvention of much of this, even as the Republic strove to make its people virtuous. The pressing need to supply Paris with food, for example, created for its outlying communities the spectre of an unaccountable, brutal, external *armée révolutionnaire*, empowered to descend upon them and appropriate their livelihoods (not to mention killing and raping them, as was reportedly widespread).[10] In the provinces, the weight of repression might be brought down against populations that did not even speak French, let alone grasp the jargon of Republican virtue that was increasingly in use (document 24).[11] For many communities, especially in the west, the republicans, *les bleus* ('the blues', from the colour of their uniforms), were also *les intrus*, the intruders, aliens to be repelled.

Just as the Vendée had now become a zone of guerrilla war, so many parts of Brittany and Normandy became prey to the anti-revolutionary brigands known as *chouans*. In the provinces, the attempts of some representatives-on-mission to recreate a 'Parisian' revolutionary fervour added to the sense of interference and hostility. The Law of Suspects could be applied to intern any potential enemy, and was used against relatives of *émigrés*, regardless of age, against supporters of the priesthood, against those who had held office under earlier, discredited phases of the Revolution, even against those who had displayed insufficient enthusiasm at news of revolutionary events. Often only those who had been driven to extreme positions by exclusion from the political mainstream now appeared untainted. In the areas of worst conflict, Cobb's view of the Terrorists is borne out, as embittered and marginal individuals were given free rein to impose their version of punitive justice on their communities (and thus frequently to pursue personal vendettas under a new guise). In the Vendée and the Federalist cities of the south-east, representatives worked with those elements who had stayed loyal, purging the local body politic with executions (document 25).

It must be acknowledged, however, that such bloodthirsty actions came in parts of France experiencing real crises, and where large sections of the population had shown active sympathy with enemy forces. Whether that in some way excuses them is a moot point, but it is also the case that in other areas, the presence of Montagnard representatives-on-mission saw a more peaceful attempt at social integration. While in the west and the south-east especially, men like Carrier, Fouché, Javogues, Collot d'Herbois and Fréron would make bloody names for themselves, in the backwaters of south-western and central France, other representatives pursued a Jacobin social agenda with less Terror, if no less vigour. Here, men such as Lakanal, Saint-André, Bo, Romme and Roux-Fazillac worked with local populations to create, rather than impose, a new vision of the social order. Jean-Pierre Gross has recently argued that their efforts deserve recognition, even if the wider context would bring their experiments in what can be called a 'republic of fair shares' to naught. In the areas dealt with by such men, communes were made to share scarce food resources without *armées révolutionnaires* to oblige them, the richer citizens had their wealth taxed progressively, but not confiscated wholesale, and employment and education were rationalised for the immediate war effort and the collective future.[12] Although we may suspect that the threat of repression aided such men in obtaining co-operation, the contrast between the tone of their efforts and those of the more bloody Terrorists remains worthy of note. Whatever must be said about Jacobinism as a frequently autocratic and intolerant political doctrine, it was also committed to the goals of justice and equality, and should not merely be seen as a monolithic creed of violent rule.

In the personnel of politics overall, there is little doubt that the more radical period of the Revolution saw an opening of the 'political class' to those below them. The classic Parisian or provincial *sans-culotte* was an artisan, shopkeeper or tradesman, and such figures undoubtedly were better-represented in politics in this period, and not necessarily as a consequence of overt Terror. In Bordeaux a doubling of the proportion of such figures on the municipal council did go along with a political purge after the Federalist defeat, and over 300 executions ordered by a commission of local radicals. In Amiens, Toulouse and Nancy, however, similar proportional increases, usually at the expense of lawyers' seats, were not linked with any particularly bloody episodes.[13] Such an opening can be identified as occurring right down to the level of villages, where local artisans and poorer peasants appeared as administrators in 1793–4. Although such processes inevitably resulted in tensions with the displaced wealthier members (and it might be argued that Federalist revolt in some centres had been an elite response to signs of democratisation after elections in 1792–3), there is no suggestion that communities in every corner of France were terrorised from within. For every town or village where antagonisms led to violence in this year and the next, and there were many, there were others where the Terror was a difficult period to be survived as a community, and doubtless still others where interventions by national politicians aided survival in what was a desperately difficult subsistence situation.

Regardless of such activity elsewhere, at the centre the political process increasingly came to resemble a desperate pursuit of purity. This was made explicitly gendered in the trial of Marie-Antoinette in October 1793, in which her alleged lesbianism and incestuous assaults on her son were made part-and-parcel of her political depravity and treason. She was executed on 16 October, and all women were banned from taking part in political meetings a fortnight later, with Rousseau invoked as philosophical authority, and the disruptive efforts of the Society of Revolutionary Republican Women to impose a 'revolutionary' dress-code on female Parisians as a practical pretext. For the next month, the executions of leading Girondins (now labelled Federalist rebels and traitors) were interspersed with those of Olympe de Gouges, an outspoken (albeit royalist) feminist, Louis XV's mistress Madame du Barry, and Madame Roland, the female intellectual widely reviled as a Girondin plotter. The fact that Marat had met his death at the hands of Charlotte Corday, a young woman of noble descent and Girondin sympathies, was grist to this mill. In the official emblem of the Republic, the people personified as Hercules replaced the female figure of Liberty (documents 26 and 27).[14]

It is ironic to note that at this very time, the Jacobins were striking a blow for gender equality in their policies on family and property. Laws passed in October 1793 and January 1794 required that property be passed on to all children equally, male and female (and including illegitimate ones). This overruled a wide variety of regional customs which allowed property to be bequeathed to one, normally male, heir, and produced a spate of legal assertions by formerly disinherited daughters of their new-found rights. This move was seen in the legislators' eyes, how-ever, as less about the gender of the children, than about reducing the authority of the father to behave in inegalitarian ways.[15]

To further the cause of renewal, a Revolutionary Calendar was introduced in late October 1793, counting from the establishment of the Republic, and renaming the months after meteorological, rather than mythological, features.[16] This was now, therefore, the 'Year II', and it is under that name that the worst excesses of the Terror were remembered. Equality became the central virtue to be pursued in this period (except, of course, between men and women). From 1 November (11 brumaire II), official correspond-ence abandoned the use of the polite *vous* form for 'you', replac-ing it with the familiar *tu*, previously reserved for intimate friends, children or inferiors. Likewise, it became mandatory to address individuals as 'Citizen', rather than 'Monsieur' or 'Mad-ame', erasing the lingering trace of feudalism in such words.[17] Thus language abandoned hierarchy, or so the Jacobins hoped. A further radical break with the past developed through Novem-ber. On 5 November (15 brumaire II) the Revolutionary Calendar was elaborated with the addition of a range of civic festivals, and over the next four days the Convention voted to allow munici-palities to renounce the Catholic faith, and the archbishop of Paris was persuaded by radical activists to abandon the priesthood. On 10 November (20 brumaire II) a 'Festival of Liberty' saw the cathedral of Notre-Dame redesignated a 'Temple of Reason'.

This was the first central manifestation of a wave of 'dechristianisation', emerging simultaneously from the work of some representatives-on-mission and from the 'Hébertist' left of the Parisian political spectrum. In many areas of France it was marked with what would soon be termed 'vandalism': the out-right destruction of church art and property, the effort to erase the Christian past, and its links, as revolutionaries saw it, to tyr-anny. Many town and village names that incorporated religious figures were changed, 'Saint-Marie' becoming 'Saint-Montagne', 'Bonnet-Rouge' or 'Marat', for example. Individuals renamed themselves after Roman republican heroes, while the move away from saints' names for children produced a brief flowering of botanical offspring, along with those named for *sans-culotte* vir-tues or republican victories.[18]

Dechristianisation was the issue that first revealed serious splits in the Montagnard leadership. On 21 November (1 frimaire II) Robespierre condemned it as 'aristocratic' and immoral, sharing Rousseau's belief that some kind of 'supreme being' was necessary as a moral focus if men were not to become depraved. On 4 December (14 frimaire II) the Terror was codified and bureaucratised, and almost all executive power was put into the hands of the Committee of Public Safety, partly to restrain local radicals and representatives-on-mission. The twelve members of this committee did not always see eye-to-eye, but nonetheless worked to a punishing schedule to control the revolutionary effort, and acted as the central machinery of government from this point until the summer of 1794. Since his election to it in July 1793, Robespierre had increasingly been its guiding spirit, his Rousseauist political philosophy, appetite for work, and personal morality adding rigour to its actions as the wider situation became more complex.[19]

As the winter wore on, the pursuit of purity seemed to be becoming ever-more difficult. Fraud was revealed amongst Convention deputies in the dissolution of the French Indies Company. A 'foreign plot' began to emerge which tied other deputies, and agents of the War Ministry, to foreign bankers and corruption. Opposition to the continued intensity of Terror began to be heard from circles around Danton, another hero of the Revolution, while from the Hébertists the cries for more Terror were so extreme that they began themselves to seem suspect (document 28). In the spring, the Committee of Public Safety struck. The prominent Hébertists were arrested in mid-March (late ventôse II) along with 'foreign plotters', and all went swiftly to the guillotine after a sketch of a trial. At the end of the month (16 germinal II), the group around Danton followed them, denied even the right to speak at their trial for fear of Danton's oratory. Later in April (24 germinal II), the widows of Hébert and Camille Desmoulins, Danton's associate, would share their husbands' fate as part of another batch of allegedly dangerous dissidents. Meanwhile, the independence of the Parisian 'popular movement' was stripped away, the *armée révolutionnaire* dissolved, the *sans-culotte* mayor Pache arrested, and the sectional societies pressured into dissolving themselves (document 29).

Parallel processes occurred everywhere that the crises of 1793 had brought *sans-culotte* militants to the fore. This was the logical outcome of the Terror's bureaucratisation. By the winter of 1793–4, the governing committees were coming to see the shadow of a 'new Federalism' in uncontrolled popular radical activity, as the *armées révolutionnaires* and groups of local activists pursued agendas driven by local circumstances and conflicts.[20] All such groups offered alternative centres of loyalty to the Convention and the Committee of Public Safety. They had challenged, or potentially challenged, the idea of 'the Republic One and Indivisible', and the intimate link that Robespierre had established between Terror and virtue in a speech 'on the principles of political morality' in early February 1794 (17 pluviôse II).[21]

In this speech Robespierre declared virtue to be the 'soul of democracy' and the 'mainspring of popular government', and announced that the 'purity' of the Revolution's bases 'rallies against us all men who are vicious', along with those who 'embraced the revolution as a livelihood and the republic as if it were an object of prey'. Thus in revolutionary times Terror must be added to virtue – without virtue, Terror is 'fatal', but virtue would be 'impotent' alone. In a long argument, he essentially justified everything the Revolution had done (and was going to do) in terms of virtue, the possession of this inner quality rendering legitimate what would otherwise be horrific.

Robespierre clearly believed himself to be the possessor of such virtue, and was thus able to claim the right to make the crucial decisions about who should remain within the circle of virtuous citizens. Within this speech itself are encapsulated the key elements which drove the Terror beyond being merely the response to circumstances. If the Republic by its very nature attracts those who seek to exploit and despoil it, republican existence can only be an ever-more bitter struggle, in which the line between good and evil grows perpetually thinner, and the circle of the virtuous ever smaller. This is indeed how things appeared in Paris by the summer of 1794. Despite the fact that the shadow of defeat had by then lifted from the French borders, the Committee of Public Safety pressed for ever-more efficient despatch of all those who did not measure up to Robespierre's standards.

Of course, the Montagnards continued to believe that there were many in France who did measure up, and that particularly the 'poor patriots' had to be supported through the time of national struggle. On 1 February (13 pluviôse II), just before Robespierre's speech, 10,000 million *livres* of poor relief was authorised for distribution to *départements*. The sum was enormous, but even with the General Maximum in place it would not go far. A more concrete measure was proposed by Saint-Just on 26 February and formalised on 3 March (8 and 13 ventôse II). He recommended that the property of those incarcerated suspects who were judged 'enemies of the Revolution' should be confiscated and used to 'indemnify' poor patriots. Communes were instructed to draw up lists of those who might qualify for this allocation, but although some lists were made, no mechanism was ever put in place to actually seize suspects' lands, and the measures faded from sight.

The 'Ventôse Decrees' were the high-point of a radical rhetorical commitment to social equality and redistribution that had been present since 1789, gradually coming closer to the centre of power. It remained in practice, however, largely a rhetorical commitment only. Church lands, which had since 1790 been sold in large lots by auction, were augmented after the fall of the monarchy by a second wave of such *biens nationaux* (national property), the seized lands of *émigrés*. In 1793–4 these were sold in smaller lots, and efforts were made to reach the poorer peasantry. A decree of 3 June 1793 promised indigent peasants the use of a half-hectare plot, rented from the Republic. However, even this proved too problematic, and on 13 September 1793 it was replaced with the offer of a 500 *livre* credit-voucher for the purchase of land. It is difficult to see any significant effect of this measure, and such an amount would in any case not have bought much at the prevailing prices.

Peasant demands, especially in areas north of Paris where there were extreme social differences, had already outstripped such moves, with calls as early as 1792 for the radical redistribution of lands. Common lands were frequently offered-up for division during the Revolution on a per-capita basis, but demands from the area of Picardy went further: those that had the least should gain the most, and not just the commons, but all land. For those in power in the early Republic, this had proved too much, and the law of 18 March 1793 had imposed the death penalty for those agitating for such divisions, which were referred to as the 'Agrarian Law' (*loi agraire*), after a similar scheme proposed in ancient

Rome. On 17 July 1793 feudal dues were abolished definitively without compensation, and four days later it was proposed that *émigrés'* lands should be divided amongst impoverished peasants. The former measure, however, merely acknowledged an existing reality, and the latter had little visible effect. During 1793–4 in general, the demands of feeding the towns and the armies often caused representatives-on-mission to block or reverse measures of redistribution of land or extension of collective rights, in the name of agricultural efficiency. Overall, even in its most radical phases, the Jacobin Republic neither supported nor truly understood the attitude of the peasant population to the land. Their continued distance from the perspectives of the rural majority was only one aspect of a growing divorce between Jacobinism and the people.[22]

In early May, the Convention, prompted by Robespierre, had instituted a 'Cult of the Supreme Being' to replace both Catholicism and the excesses of dechristianisation. Few apart from Robespierre and his close associates had any enthusiasm for this project, and the whispered ridicule from Convention members that emerged during the 'Festival of the Supreme Being' on 8 June (20 prairial II) was a sign of continuing faultlines in the revolutionary leadership. Nonetheless, the Robespierrist agenda continued to prevail, and open opposition became even more difficult from 10 June (22 prairial II) as the Revolutionary Tribunal was made yet more rapid and arbitrary in its operations, and the flow of bodies from the guillotine increased. Amongst the masses of suspects crammed into temporary prisons, it was easy for paid informers to foment tales of plots and planned revolts, and by this stage it was impossible to defend oneself against such accusations.

As the summer progressed, dissent within the Convention, the Committee of General Security (which handled political policing), and the Committee of Public Safety itself, began to emerge. By late July, Robespierre was hinting strongly that a new wave of purges of the Convention might be necessary. Various groups united to oppose him. The members of the Committee of General Security resented the steady flow of power from them to the Committee of Public Safety. Some returned representatives-on-mission had reason to believe that their bloodthirsty and 'ultra-revolutionary' activities, along with examples of lax personal morality, might well put them on Robespierre's list of suspects. The surviving friends of Danton and Hébert contemplated a chance for revenge. More broadly, the conjunction of military victory and relative internal order with an ever-growing prison population, and the threat of more Terror to come, no longer made sense for many moderate deputies.

Thus when on 26 July (8 thermidor II) Robespierre openly hinted at a purge during a Convention speech, his opponents hurried to depose him. Rapid and ruthless action by those who felt most threatened brought into the open the misgivings of the majority, and once Robespierre had been denounced, they flocked to condemn him. On 27 July (9 thermidor II) Robespierre, his Committee colleagues Couthon and Saint-Just, and various others were declared outlaws, accused of having planned to establish a personal dictatorship. Execution would follow automatically on their arrest and formal identification. For a few hours it seemed that the Parisian National Guard might launch a counter-coup, but most forces refused to rally. The working population of the city had been antagonised on 23 July (5 thermidor II) by the publication of a table of maximum wages, mostly below the prevailing rates. The rank and file of the *sans-culottes*, whose independent political organisations had been suppressed, and whose livelihoods were now threatened, had no reason to save Robespierre, and so on 28 July (10 thermidor II) the architect of Terror died. Over the following days, batches of his alleged followers in the Parisian authorities went to the guillotine, as the 'Thermidorians' consolidated their grip on power. The future would show, however, that simply ending the Terror was not enough to bring order to revolutionary France.

Notes

1 For a detailed study of this event, see M. Slavin, *The Making of an Insurrection: Parisian Sections and the Gironde*, London, 1986.

2 For Lyon, see W. D. Edmonds, *Jacobinism and the Revolt of Lyon, 1789–1793*, Oxford, 1990, pp. 186ff.; for Marseille, see W. Scott, *Terror and Repression in Revolutionary Marseilles*, London, 1973, pp. 88ff.

3 On the subject of sovereignty, see the debate taken up by P. R. Hanson, 'The Federalist Revolt: An Affirmation or Denial of Popular Sovereignty?', *French History*, 6, 1992, pp. 335–55.

4 See R. C. Cobb, *Reactions to the French Revolution*, Oxford, 1972, pp. 64–5, and chapter 3 *passim*.

5 L. Hunt, *Politics, Culture and Class in the French Revolution*, Berkeley, 1984, chapter 6, 'Outsiders, Culture Brokers and Political Networks', esp. pp. 184ff.

6 Père Duchesne literally means 'Father of Oak', with all that conveys of sturdiness, rootedness, etc.

7 See M. Sonenscher, 'Artisans, Sans-culottes and the French Revolution', in A. Forrest and P. Jones (eds), *Reshaping France: Town, Country and Region in the French Revolution*, Manchester, 1991, pp. 105–21.

8 See R. M. Andrews, 'Social Structures, Political Elites and Ideology in Revolutionary Paris, 1792–4', *Journal of Social History*, 19, 1985–6, pp. 71–112. The classic Marxist account is A. Soboul, *The Parisian Sans-Culottes and the French Revolution, 1793–4*, Oxford, 1964.

9 For the internal workings of the 'Hébertist' grouping, and their subsequent fate, see M. Slavin, *The Hébertistes to the Guillotine: Anatomy of a 'Conspiracy' in Revolutionary France*, Baton Rouge and London, 1994.

10 See R. C. Cobb, *The People's Armies: The Armées Révolutionnaires: Instruments of the Terror in the Departments, April 1793 to Floréal Year II*, New Haven, 1987, esp. Book 2, chapters 4 and 7 for this issue.

11 The classic study of a revolutionary 'proconsul' at work is C. Lucas, *The Structure of the Terror: The Example of Javogues and the Loire*, London, 1973.

12 J. P. Gross, *Fair Shares For All: Jacobin Egalitarianism in Practice*, Cambridge, 1997.

13 Hunt, *Politics, Culture and Class*, pp. 163–5. In 1790–1 the proportion of artisans and shopkeepers on the city councils was between 12 and 17 per cent.

14 This process is charted in Hunt, *Politics, Culture and Class*, chapter 3, 'The Imagery of Radicalism', pp. 87–119. See also L. Hunt, *The Family Romance of the French Revolution*, London, 1992, pp. 89–123.

15 S. Desan, '"War Between Brothers and Sisters": Inheritance Law and Gender Politics in Revolutionary France', *French Historical Studies*, 20, 1997, pp. 597–634.

16 The Revolutionary Calendar is explained in more detail in C. Jones, *The Longman Companion to the French Revolution*, London, 1988, pp. 425–30. I shall give revolutionary dates in brackets where appropriate.

17 'Monsieur' has its root in *sieur*, which is similar to the English 'esquire', originally indicating a gentleman or minor landowner.

18 Dechristianisation has been analysed by M. Vovelle, *The Revolution against the Church: From Reason to the Supreme Being*, Cambridge, 1991.

19 See R. R. Palmer, *Twelve Who Ruled: The Year of the Terror in the French Revolution*, Princeton, 1970 (orig. pub. 1941), a dated but still valuable study.

20 See Slavin, *Hébertistes to the Guillotine*, and N. Hampson, *Danton*, London, 1978, for the rivals who shared their fate. R. C. Cobb, *The Police and the People: French Popular Protest 1789–1820*, Oxford, 1970, pp. 118–211, is a comprehensive, if anecdotal, discussion of the kinds of people to be found as local popular militants, and what became of them.

21 This speech is reprinted in K. M. Baker (ed.), *Readings in Western Civilisation 7: The Old Regime and the French Revolution*, Chicago, 1987, pp. 368–84.

22 See P. M. Jones, *The Peasantry in the French Revolution*, Cambridge, 1988, pp. 137–66.

8

The quest for social order – Thermidor to Brumaire, 1794–1799

The first consequence of the Thermidorian coup was confusion. The population of Paris, which had been persuaded that both Hébertists and Dantonists were the enemies of the Revolution, and that the popular societies were a threat to order, had little trouble swallowing the story that Robespierre planned to make himself a Cromwell or a Caesar. As Martin Lyons observes, 'there was little popular enthusiasm left for a government of puritanical lawyers, who demanded complete unanimity, dictated the organisation of leisure time and family life, and regarded every form of popular amusement with suspicion'.[1] Parisians had learnt that the best course of action through the factional upheavals of the Terror was to place their faith in the Convention as an institution. It was also, of course, the safest path. Amongst the deputies of the Convention itself, and out in the rest of the country, it was less clear how to react.

The leading 'Thermidorians' were essentially Montagnards, but ones who had now broken with the drive and unanimity of the past. Under the shadow of Robespierre they had swallowed their anxieties at the course of events, but now found that they held a wide variety of agendas. Some wished to continue the Terror, at least against relatively clearly-defined enemies like rebels and royalists. Others saw it as time for a moderation, a return to the agenda that Danton had favoured. Some sought revenge on those who had brought down one or another faction. However, as Montagnards, they were all fundamentally associated with the rigours of the Terror, and within weeks it was clear that they

146

remained, as they had always been, a minority in the Convention. The majority of the relatively uncommitted, who occupied the so-called 'Plain' or 'Marsh', had kept their heads down until Thermidor, then backed the strike against Robespierre. It soon became clear that their basic antipathy to Terroristic measures, which they had suppressed under pressure of military necessity for so long, was reviving.

To retain any influence, the Thermidorian Montagnards had to go along with the majority's demands for an end to the most severe Terrorist measures. On 1 August (14 thermidor II) the 'law of 22 prairial' which had made the Revolutionary Tribunal into a killing machine was repealed, and between 5 and 10 August large numbers of detained suspects were freed from Parisian prisons. A series of restrictions on the activities of representatives-on-mission and local committees and assemblies were passed later in the month, culminating on 24 August (7 fructidor II) with a new law on revolutionary government, reversing the concentration of powers in the Committee of Public Safety and establishing a range of checks and balances in the administration.

In the provinces, a wide variety of responses followed on the news of Thermidor. Although at a rhetorical level the notion of a Robespierrist-plotted dictatorship, denounced with all the regimented enthusiasm learnt since 1793, was prevalent, what action to take was less clear.[2] As the centre became embroiled in settling scores and wrangling over future political directions, some representatives-on-mission actually intensified their 'Terrorism' in the late summer, freed from the constraints of Robespierrist supervision. Other areas, where the early summer had already seen a relaxation of tensions as the military situation eased, remained calm. Those regions where politics had always been most violent and divisive continued with the same pattern. In the south-east Jacobin administrations were purged and mass releases of suspects occurred, to be followed by a 'White Terror' of assassinations throughout the following year, often by 'murder-gangs' led by well-known royalists. In the west guerrilla royalism went on unabated (document 30).

Increasingly, as summer passed into autumn, and the new 'Year III' (from 22 September), the consequences of political relaxation became apparent. As Jacobins were already protesting, overt counter-revolution was starting to attract a new legitimacy.

Furthermore, the repudiation of 'Terrorism' extended to the persecution of what remained of the sectional movement in Paris, and to attacks on the Jacobins and the whole idea of political clubs. In early September 1794 the Jacobins had attempted to start a movement to counteract the growing laxity of political control, demanding the re-application of the Law of Suspects, a strengthened Revolutionary Tribunal, and new moves against *émigrés* and priests. This followed the expulsion of leading Thermidorians such as Fréron and Tallien from the Club, but these men now began a counter-offensive. Fréron had allied himself with what came to be called the *jeunesse dorée* ('gilded youth'). These young men, whose background was often little different from the *sans-culotte* leaders of the lower middle classes, now scorned Jacobin puritanism and *sans-culotte* modesty, roaming Paris in gangs dressed in ostentatious finery, and picking fights with alleged 'Terrorists' (document 31). With the connivance and protection of leading political figures, there were no public forces able to counter them. By early November they had begun to attack meetings of the Jacobin Club in force, and a brawl there on 12 November (22 brumaire III) was the excuse the Convention needed to order its definitive closure.

The autumn of 1794 marked a savage swing of the political pendulum against the personnel of the Terror. Ex-Terrorist Thermidorians succeeded in finding scapegoats for the past, discrediting die-hard Jacobin Terrorists by revealing the truly inhuman horrors of the Terror's worst episodes. The trial of the representative Carrier was central to this. During late 1793, in Nantes, a city packed with refugees and prisoners from a defeated Vendéen army, Carrier and a variety of 'revolutionary' committees and militias had sought to retain control through intimidation and slaughter, including infamous mass drownings, or *noyades*, in the Loire. At the same time, and like many other representatives-on-mission, it could be said that Carrier had abused his position to ensure his personal comforts while exercising unlimited powers. The long-delayed trial of the city council of Nantes, accused by Carrier of counter-revolution, held for a year in Parisian prisons and brought before the Revolutionary Tribunal in late 1794, began to bring this all to light. The revelations of this trial, in which most defendants were acquitted, led almost at once to charges against Carrier and his leading associates, which were exploited by the Thermidorians to full effect. In the weeks leading up to Carrier's execution on 16 December (26 frimaire III), the Tribunal's audience, and the reading public, witnessed a theatre of ghastliness as every imaginable cruelty was reputed to the Nantes Terrorists. Testimony over more than a month, much of it exaggerated hearsay, elevated an undoubted several thousand casualties to tens, even hundreds of thousands, and created in the public mind a vision of the Terror as an eruption of individual wickedness of monstrous proportions, helping to ensure the decisive abandonment of any political agendas associated with such practices.[3]

Thus Thermidorian politics were re-opened to all the currents that the Terror had successfully forced underground. Gradually elements that had been purged from the Convention were re-admitted, including by March 1795 the surviving Girondin and 'Federalist' members. Released prisoners had for months been introducing royalist sentiments of various kinds to social life, if not yet to overt politics. That social life also took on a new hue. The *jeunesse dorée* and their provincial parallels had shown the way to a re-adoption of old modes of ostentation and display, and under the umbrella of 'political liberty' a kind of high society not seen since the early days of the Revolution began to enjoy itself at parties, balls and salons. The stern Jacobin masculinism of public life was relaxed, and women such as Thérèse Cabarrus and the future empress Josephine de Beauharnais became renowned salon hostesses, as well as influential mistresses to a succession of politicians.

This political opening had its darker parallel in the social closure of public life. If personal iniquity was useful in condemning individuals like Carrier without implicating his colleagues such as Barras, Fréron and Tallien, then the idea of the Terror as an uprising of the hideous brutal mob was valuable in abandoning its wider agendas. 'Terrorists' of the Parisian sectional movement were purged from November 1794, and the common people had the protection of the Maximum taken from them on Christmas Eve 1794 (document 32). The Jacobin Republic had at least tried to keep the population fed, and showed its sympathies through frugality; the Thermidorian Republic rejoiced in wealth, and did nothing as the people began to starve in the winter of 1794–5, known to history in the northern patois as *'nonante-cinq'*. Colder even than the legendary freeze of 1709, that winter saw death stalking France, taking the old, the sick and the new-born in huge numbers. As peasants kept their meagre harvests for themselves, prices of food rocketed. Major cities made some relief efforts – the Lyonnais lived on a pittance of rice, and many others had to survive on half a pound or less of bread each day – but the freeze made moving what supplies there were almost impossible. There is no doubt that this was a great natural disaster, and indeed that the brutal enforcement of controls in 1793–4 had aggravated urban/rural tensions over supply. Nevertheless, during this winter the politicians had resumed the old ways of luxury and excess, as money in sufficient quantities lubricated the wheels of commerce, while they did nothing for the poor.

This dramatic contrast, redolent of the worst of pre-revolutionary ways, led in the spring of 1795 to the last popular radical uprisings of the Revolution. On 1 April (12 germinal III) a crowd invaded the Convention demanding the Jacobin Constitution of 1793 and action against hardship. They were expelled, and various Montagnards suspected of collusion were arrested in the following days. Ten days later, all 'Terrorists' were disarmed, which meant also stripped of civic rights. At the end of April there were further disturbances, and on 20 May (1 prairial III) the start of a larger insurrection. The Convention was again invaded, and the same demands put, with some Montagnards throwing in their lot with the protestors. Over the following three days these political sympathisers were seized, while troops restored order in the city (document 33). As they had in October 1789, women from the popular classes had led the attempt to take their subsistence-demands to the very top, their rhetoric condemning the idleness and cowardice of both politicians and their own menfolk.[4] Although often dismissed as disorganised and leaderless, it is important to note that these risings were against the Convention, albeit that the *sans-culottes* had no alternative leadership to put in its place. In desperation, they had found the initiative to make demands of the body that had for so long been their unquestioned political idol.[5]

Germinal and Prairial achieved nothing, however, except renewed persecution. In the week following the latter rising the sections were again politically purged, and all those merely suspected of Terrorism were disarmed. The inquiries that this involved produced the voluminous police records on which much study of the *sans-culottes* has been based. The logic of their circumstances demanded that suspected individuals play down their social standing in order to plead that they had been ignorant followers. This left a legacy that painted the *sans-culottes* as more 'popular' than they might otherwise have appeared. At the time it also helped further a discourse that associated the mob with coercion and irrationality, valuable to a propertied elite that was driving the popular elements introduced after 1792 out of politics, and rediscovering the liberal economics that had governed the Revolution before the fall of the Girondins. It is ironic that one of the few revolutionary innovations to profoundly affect the whole world, the metric system of measurement, under discussion since 1790, was adopted on 7 April 1795 (18 germinal III), just as the process of finally restricting more overtly social change was under way. The inclusive elements of republican citizenship would increasingly be abandoned in the later 1790s, and republicanism, which had seemed to stand for a total remaking of the social world, would come to mean little more than fear of a royal restoration.

This can be seen in the constitutional arrangements made by the Convention on 22 August 1795 (5 fructidor III). Although prefaced like the other revolutionary Constitutions with a declaration of rights, that of the Year III amended the formula to 'Rights and Duties', and omitted the fundamental 'born free and equal in rights' clause, while warning that violations of the law were a declaration of war on society. The basic electorate was similar to that of the 1791 Constitution, a taxpayer franchise, although no minimum tax payment was specified, and ex-soldiers were admitted by right. However, the formula of indirect election was also restored, and the 'electors' who would choose representatives had to own or rent property worth over 100 days' labour. Thus the mass of the people were excluded again from politics. Voting returned to the secret ballot, and the general tenor of the Constitution was of a liberal balance of power, protecting property-owners, in direct opposition to the centralised democracy envisaged in 1793.

Separation of powers was taken to an extreme. The unity of sovereignty carried over from monarch to National Assembly was broken down, with two chambers for the legislature: the

Council of Five Hundred to propose laws, and the Council of Ancients (250 in number, all forty or older) to approve or reject them. All of these representatives were to be subject to re-election every three years, with a third elected each year. Meanwhile, no government minister or agent could be a member of the Councils, and had to communicate with them through formal notes. To control the executive a new institution was devised, the Executive Directory. This was a body of five men elected by the Ancients from shortlists proposed by the Five Hundred. They were formally responsible for internal and external security, could suggest, but not demand, legislation, and appointed and controlled ministers (who were not part of a 'Cabinet', and were also responsible to the Councils). The Directory needed the signatures of a majority of the five to make its acts legal. They were a kind of collective representation of the role intended for the king in the 1791 Constitution, though without the veto.

The Directory and the Councils were supposed to exist in equilibrium, equally responsible for the maintenance of the Constitution, and watching over each other's activities. As the Treasury was controlled by the Councils, not the Directory, the executive's power was weakened still further, reflecting the fear of strong government produced by the Terror. This delicate and balanced set of powers might have worked in an orderly and stable society without significant immediate threats, but that, of course, was not the situation of France in 1795. External warfare continued to be relatively successful, but extremely costly, and internal threats were widespread and manifold.

In the face of this, the Convention ordained that continuity would be provided by only electing one-third of the new legislators initially; the other two-thirds would be chosen by the Convention from amongst its members. This was specifically designed to head off what looked like a real possibility by the autumn of 1795: a full-blown royalist takeover. Released suspects, agents of the various *émigré* organisations, and of the Great Powers, had all been agitating for such a move, and the Republic as such probably had very little meaningful support in the general population. However, the political leadership of the Republic could not envisage a restoration. In June 1795 the comte de Provence, Louis XVI's brother, proclaimed himself king after the (natural) death of the ten-year-old Louis XVII in Parisian captivity. As Louis XVIII, he made the 'Verona Declaration' of hard-line royalism: a restoration would bring back Old Regime privileges (and property-relations), and see the execution of all those who voted for the king's death, and doubtless many others.

Even aside from the interest of politicians in preserving their necks in the light of this statement, the wider agenda of restoration helped to provide republicanism with at least a pragmatic constituency. Fortunes had been made, and would continue to be made, in the supplying and equipping of the armies that fought against royalism; in the armies themselves, a new breed of professional officer was arising, attuned to political influences, and also stained by years of combat against royalism. They too had lives, and sometimes fortunes, ill-gotten or otherwise, to defend. Across the country, the property of the Church, and later of the *émigrés*, had been seized and sold as *biens nationaux*. The many peasant purchasers may not have had a political voice, but the larger investors who took a majority of the land by value certainly did, and they too had a vested interest in the Republic.

This Directorial republican society was challenged at its inception and demonstrated a vigorous response. In September 1795 both the new Constitution and the Two-Thirds Law were submitted to referendum. The Constitution got over 95 per cent approval, albeit on a meagre turnout of just over a million, but the Two-Thirds Law was only voted on by around 315,000, of whom over a third rejected it. This obvious anti-royalist ploy was scorned in many areas, and rejected by nineteen *départements* and forty-seven of the Paris sections. Many royalists had believed that a full set of legislative elections would bring them to power, and forces from the more conservative districts of west-central Paris were persuaded to rise in opposition to the new law on 5 October 1795 (13 vendémiaire IV). This rising was defeated by troops under the orders of the young general Bonaparte, brought in by Barras, who had met and promoted him at the siege of Toulon in 1793. 'Vendémiaire' was the stimulus for a change of direction in policy. Measures against popular radicalism, and against Terrorist attitudes, had been continuing. In August clubs and popular societies had been banned, in late September freedom of worship had been allowed, and two days after the Vendémiaire rising the Law of Suspects was formally repealed. However, several weeks later, on 25 October (3 brumaire IV), a new law banned all *émigrés* and their relatives from public office, along with those who expressed seditious views in electoral meetings, and re-applied all the anti-priest legislation of 1792–3. A list of republican national festivals and a scheme for republican education were announced the same day, and the following day *émigrés* were excluded from a general amnesty of political prisoners to mark the final closure of the Convention (document 34).

None of this prevented the one-third of the new Councils that was allowed to be elected showing a strong royalist element, and for the whole of its existence the Directory would find itself swinging between royalists and unrepentant Jacobins. Almost immediately after the anti-royalist measures of October 1795, a 'neo-Jacobin' movement began to show itself in Paris. A club was opened under the title of the 'Panthéon Club', and a newspaper, the *Tribune of the People*, was published by Gracchus Babeuf, a one-time feudal lawyer who had become a radical activist and proto-socialist thinker. By December (frimaire IV), Babeuf was in hiding to evade an arrest-warrant, and in late February 1796 (7 ventôse IV) the Panthéon Club and other similar societies were closed by order of the Directory. Babeuf went underground, and on 30 March (10 germinal IV) established an 'insurrectionary committee' to plan a *sans-culotte* rising.[6]

The agenda of Babeuf, like that of 'neo-Jacobin' opposition throughout the 1790s, was diffuse. At root was a belief that Jacobinism, Terror and the Constitution of 1793 embodied social justice, or more broadly the principles of the Revolution, whereas post-Thermidorian politics were 'counter-revolutionary'. Babeuf's conspiratorial efforts centred on a seizure of power at the centre, followed presumably by a reinstatement of Terrorists, and thus of Terror. What would happen after that was unclear. Amongst his plans were utopian schemes for collective landownership and exploitation, which earned him a later reputation as the 'first revolutionary communist', but his ideas of power focused on the central state. He and his associates made lists of potential sympathisers and activists who could be made part of an insurrectionary movement, but most observers agree that the plans had little substance in reality. Rumours reaching the Directory through their police apparatus painted the 'babouvists' as a grave threat, however, and in April advocating the *sans-culotte* goal of the 1793 Constitution became a capital offence (along with advocating a restoration, or the redistribution of land – a combination indicating the narrow middle way the Directory sought to follow). On 10 May 1796 (21 floréal IV) Babeuf was arrested, and his leading followers and associates were hunted down. The opportunity was also taken to expel suspect former members of the Convention, amnestied Terrorists and other 'unsafe' groups from Paris. The saga of Babeuf would continue for another year, as members of his group were eventually put on trial at Vendôme, and he and two others executed. Ironically, the executions came after the elections of 1797 had returned a further substantial royalist group, putting the Directory in danger from the right, and leading to a new swing in Directorial policy.

In carrying out this *politique de bascule* (seesaw politics), the rule of law and the respect due the Constitution received short shrift. Many of the political problems were of the Constitution's own making. The Directory stubbornly reverted to the laborious arrangements for elections begun in 1790, only briefly experimenting with any modifications. Such annual gatherings at once became arenas for factional politics, with a wide array of local and national posts up for grabs each year. The entrenched divisions between Jacobin and royalist networks in local society across France led to intense rivalry for all such posts, in the knowledge that victimisation by such authorities was a real threat. The electorate could not be persuaded to follow the centrist path of moderate republican stabilisation envisioned in the Constitution, and electoral assemblies became subject to splits, secessions and violence.[7]

By September 1797 the Directors would be driven to a *coup d'état* (18 fructidor V) against royalist elements in the legislature and administration; and in May 1798 the process was repeated as newly elected leftist deputies were purged (22 floréal VI). The politics of these years have been said to show the 'failure of the liberal republic', but this 'failure' must be measured against the state of the country in the late 1790s.[8] Colin Lucas has suggested that the 'First Directory' (from 1795 to 1797) had initially attempted a rigorous policy of enforcing the rule of law, which was ignored, or actively resisted, in many parts of the country. His study of the Loire *département*, to the west of Lyon, shows that a politics of intemperate revenge, political feud and resort to illegality was entrenched after the Terror of the Year II and the

'White Terror' of the Year III. Not only did local cadres of administration continue to house men with violent pasts, but local justice refused, through fear or sympathy, to act against those who continued such violence. In this sense, Lucas argues, it was not the Directory, but the country, which 'failed' to establish the rule of law (document 35).[9]

The violence of 1793–4, and its inverted repetition in the Year III, had left France savagely divided, and also increasingly unwilling to act against that division – Jacobins and royalists alike might dream of re-establishing their version of order, but the bulk of the population was indifferent, hostile in effect to all authority, preoccupied with local vendettas and alienated from the very idea of national politics. This trend is visible even within the army itself, which had effectively become an entire new social stratum. Since the great recruitments of 1793, there had been no release of troops from the colours, and men faced the alternatives of desertion or resignation to the military life. Under the Jacobins, and especially the *sans-culotte* War Ministry of Bouchotte, great efforts had been made to fire the patriotism of the troops, and to encourage politicisation, military popular societies, and distrust of unpatriotic officers. The Robespierrist Terror had cracked down on this potential source of indiscipline, and the situation of the following years saw the army increasingly distanced from civilian life and politics. This did not mean that it reverted to a passive instrument of state. Rather the various armies on the different frontiers acquired their own collective identities, and came to rely on their own leaders for advancement, even as they increasingly turned to looting for their provisions.

By 1796–7, the revolutionary armies were effectively professional forces, albeit rarely paid and sometimes politically partisan: the Army of Italy was known for its Jacobin sympathies, that of the Rhin-et-Moselle for royalism. Within the Army of Italy itself, Bernadotte's division used 'Monsieur' as a form of address, and clashed with Masséna's, which favoured the more republican 'Citizen'. General Bonaparte led this Army in 1796–7 on a stunning campaign of victories and pillage through northern Italy. From May 1796 he paid his men in coin, the first time this had been possible in years, and this, the victories, and the loot, guaranteed their loyalty. It was a loyalty to him personally, an increasingly common phenomenon in the Directorial military.

Troops who had been accustomed to seeing generals changed almost monthly during the Terror, with civilian representatives watching their every move, were now led by men who themselves wielded political influence, and were almost unshakeable in their military posts.

Thus those troops who remained in the armies became almost a society apart, with different loyalties, different priorities, and different politics. The army was, for example, almost the only bastion of a Jacobinism with any claim on a popular following by the late 1790s. At the same time, for civilians, especially in the countryside, the army itself was a source of fear. If the troops at the colours were mostly resigned to their life, a significant minority continued to desert, and many more evaded the periodic attempts to round up more recruits to the colours. Such deserters and *insoumis* (those who refused to submit to requisition) would be a problem of public order into the Napoleonic period.[10]

Those who merely fled to the hills to avoid military authority might remain connected to their home communities, and indeed might only flee from them at the approach of the forces of order. Others, however, often found brigandage a more viable lifestyle than agriculture in the chaotic conditions of the times. Such groups could merge with some truly brutal robber gangs that had flourished in the Thermidorian disorder, or become the rank and file for organised counter-revolutionary networks. In the southeast especially, such networks, supplied through Switzerland, dated back in many cases to the disorders of 1790, and since the Year III had become one of the most powerful forces in the politics of the region.[11] In some ways, the conflict between such brigands (political and non-political) and the army replaced and reproduced the conflict between pro- and anti-Jacobin forces in 1792–4.

After the dissolution of all the various irregular and 'Terrorist' militias, and the effective submergence of the National Guard into the military, the army represented the only available force for order in the later 1790s. Military rule, or at least military force used to ensure civilian rule, would be prevalent from 1797, and arguably the army came to represent the centralised Republic in the face of all the local and particularist resistances it confronted.[12] These would provide the Directory with some of its most persistent problems in restoring public order, and in the end only effective military rule, and the use of arbitrary tribunals and large-scale executions, would bring large parts of France back under central control. Such measures were part of what has been called the transition to a 'security state', a reflection by the late 1790s of the abandonment of republican ideals of inclusive citizenship, or even a relatively pacific rule of law. Instead, restoration of order meant the determined application of force to large sections of the country, the beating down of political opposition, and the extermination of banditry. Only then could social peace and effective government be reconstructed.[13] It was in the pursuit of this agenda that the liberal framework of the Directory was swept away in a last *coup d'état* on 9 November 1799 (18 brumaire VIII), elevating the dashing general Napoleon Bonaparte as First Consul of a new regime. The hope that he would merely be a suitable figurehead for the government of political survivors who backed him did not long survive his forceful personality, however.

The 'Brumairian' agenda was of course a view from the 'top down'. Many inhabitants of France wanted nothing more than peace and order (and indeed had never wanted more). Unfortunately, their definitions of what these terms meant differed widely, and might cause the state as much difficulty as those who chose to react more violently to the wider situation. One area where this issue was particularly acute was the question of religion. While the conflict with the Catholic Church had been a central component of the descent to Terror, and alternatives to revealed religion had marked its most radical phases, the Revolution had never found a convincing replacement for the role that Catholicism played in the life of the majority. Robespierre's virtue offered little to those who relied on blessings for the success of their crops and continued to fear the fate of their souls. Throughout the Thermidorian and Directory periods, religious confrontation continued to plague the administrations. Olwen Hufton has noted how, in their incomprehension and rage at women's refusal to abandon the signs and practices of Catholicism, agents of central government were driven to dehumanise such women with animal or even vegetable imagery. Despite persecution, Catholicism had in fact flourished in the mid-1790s. Men and women fought and died for the faith in a way that only determined opposition made possible, and a new generation of martyrs was created.[14]

After the post-Thermidorian relaxation, the Directory gave a further boost to this movement after the Fructidor coup of 1797, reinstating hostile measures towards refractory priests, and over the next year attempting to elevate the *décadi*, the tenth day of the republican 'week', over Sunday as a day of rest. By mid-1798, a bounty of 100 *livres* was on offer for the capture of refractory priests. The pope had become a French prisoner in February 1798, and would die in August 1799, a further 'martyrdom'. While attacking mainstream Catholicism, the Directory attempted to boost the fortunes of the constitutional, as opposed to refractory, Church, which from 1797 shared the regime's spiritual allegiance with the insipid cult of 'Theophilanthropy'. Neither of these made much inroad into the belief-systems of the peasantry. In the end, only conciliation of Catholicism under the Consular regime in 1801 would remove the tension between the French state and the souls of most of the French.

Revolutionary liberty, even if it gave the peasants more land and fewer taxes, continued to mean little to them if they could not follow their faith. When republican politics alternated between factional victory and *coup d'état*, and the only other arm of the Republic that reached out into society was the army which stole its sons, we can observe how far the Republic had moved from any meaningful connection with its citizens. Neither local autonomy nor national unity, the two great driving-forces of the decade, any longer served to link Republic and people. As a regime which claimed to rule in the people's name, there is no doubt that the Directory was as morally bankrupt by 1799 as the monarchy had been in 1789.

Notes

1 M. Lyons, *France Under the Directory*, Cambridge, 1975, pp. 8–9. This and D. Woronoff, *The Thermidorean Regime and the Directory*, Cambridge, 1984, are still the most recent general histories of the post-1794 period, and are drawn on for much of what follows. More detailed coverage of many relevant topics can be found in G. Lewis and C. Lucas (eds), *Beyond the Terror: Essays in French Regional and Social History, 1794–1815*, Cambridge, 1983.

2 B. Baczko *Ending the Terror: The French Revolution after*

Robespierre, Cambridge, 1994, esp. pp. 36–46, details much of this.

3 See *ibid.*, pp. 136ff.

4 See O. H. Hufton, *Women and the Limits of Citizenship in the French Revolution*, Toronto, 1992, pp. 42–9.

5 A social analysis of participants in these risings, and the later royalist Vendémiaire *coup* attempt, can be found in G. Rudé, *The Crowd in the French Revolution*, Oxford, 1972 (orig. pub. 1959), pp. 142–77. Like much scholarship of that generation, however, Rudé has little to say on the gender dimension.

6 On Babeuf, see R. B. Rose, *Gracchus Babeuf: The First Revolutionary Communist*, London, 1978; on the wider 'neo-Jacobin' movement, see I. Woloch, *Jacobin Legacy: The Democratic Movement under the Directory*, Princeton, 1970.

7 See I .Woloch, *The New Regime: Transformations of the French Civic Order, 1789–1820s*, New York, 1994, pp. 95–108; and also C. Lucas, 'The Rules of the Game in Local Politics under the Directory', *French Historical Studies*, 16, 1989, pp. 345–71.

8 L. Hunt, D. Lansky and P. Hanson, 'The Failure of the Liberal Republic in France, 1795–1799: The Road to Brumaire', *Journal of Modern History*, 51, 1979, pp. 734–59.

9 C. Lucas, 'The First Directory and the Rule of Law', *French Historical Studies*, 10, 1977, pp. 231–60.

10 The best general history of this phenomenon is A. Forrest, *Conscripts and Deserters: The Army and French Society during the Revolution and Empire*, Oxford, 1989. See also the broader text by the same author: *Soldiers of the French Revolution*, Durham, NC, 1990.

11 There is a classic study of one criminal gang in R. C. Cobb, *Reactions to the French Revolution*, Oxford, 1972, pp. 181–211. For the counter-revolutionaries, see G. Lewis, 'Political Brigandage and Popular Disaffection in the South-East of France, 1795–1804', in Lewis and Lucas, *Beyond the Terror*, pp. 195–231.

12 For a regional case study, see J. D. Devlin, 'The Army, Politics and Public Order in Directorial Provence, 1795–1800', *Historical Journal*, 32, 1989, pp. 87–106.

13 See H. G. Brown, 'From Organic Society to Security State: The War on Brigandage in France, 1797–1802', *Journal of Modern History*, 69, 1997, pp. 661–95.

14 See Hufton, *Women and the Limits of Citizenship*, pp. 89–130, 168–74.

Conclusion

As the 1790s drew towards a close, the Republic seemed almost to recapitulate in rapid succession the crises it had undergone in 1793–4. Their armies driven out of Italy by uprisings and enemy forces, threatened by a British force landed in Holland, the Directory and the Councils were at loggerheads in the summer of 1799. As in 1793, new demands for conscripts, this time enshrined in the Jourdan Law of 5 September 1798 (19 fructidor VI), provoked rural uprisings, and counter-revolutionary networks pounced on these to further stimulate revolt. On 18 June (30 prairial VII) the Directory itself was purged of two members under pressure from the Councils. In July a neo-Jacobin club began to meet in Paris, while local authorities were authorised to make hostages of *émigrés'* family-members, and an oath of hatred of royalty was decreed. On 1 August press freedom was permitted. Two weeks later the neo-Jacobin Manège Club was closed by the police, and on 2 September (16 fructidor VII) new laws against both left-wing and right-wing publications were imposed. Late August saw the defeat of internal risings, while September and October were marked by external victories. No longer, however, could these prevent a search for a more decisive solution to the endemic political instability, and it was out of the frantic conspiratorial manoeuvring of October and November that Bonaparte emerged as First Consul. From this figurehead position he rapidly out-manoeuvred those who had elevated him, to become effective master of France, and mounted the throne of his newly fashioned Empire in 1804.[1]

161

It will be evident by now that much of this political activity had long ceased to have any meaning to most French citizens, except where it imposed burdens of payment or service on them. After the promises, and the distinct gains, of its early years, the Revolution and its politics from Thermidor onwards appeared to do increasingly little to affect the lives of many. Richard Cobb, who famously entitled a chapter 'The Irrelevance of the Revolution', would go further, and say that there were many for whom the Revolution never did anything.[2] Cobb documented the continuing parade of the grimmer side of life that the Revolution was powerless to interrupt: drunken violence, rape, murder, beggary, prostitution, illicit childbirth and infanticide, the unremitting grind that was the life of the poorest, if anything made worse by the overall uncertainty of the times.

At first glance, it is indeed hard to locate much to cheer in the effects of the French Revolution on the members of its society. The economy was already in crisis when the political events of the late 1780s took hold, trade across France's borders slackened even before the isolation imposed by war from 1792–3, and employment in luxury production collapsed with the flight of the wealthy *émigrés*. Many of the rich simply moved their funds out of the country as conditions worsened. The state, prior to 1793, was in no position to assist the poor. On ideological grounds, the apparatus of Church charity was broken up, while little was envisaged to replace it. The majority of taxpayers were not contributing, so even if the state had wanted to support the poor, it lacked the resources. When this became more of a priority under the Republic, the solution found was to print more paper money, thus undermining the whole structure of the economy.

For those in the countryside, there was the chance to obtain lands from the sale of *biens nationaux*, but in many regions this was problematic, due to the excessive size and cost of the plots offered for sale, or conflicts with local desires to retain customary forms of agriculture. The consolidation of a new landowning class by the late 1790s marked the failure of this programme to introduce a radical break with past patterns. In the west and south-east of France, the Revolution left scars that would not heal for many years, as persecution and reprisal left communities at odds and individuals prone to assault and assassination. Even had the Jacobin projects of 1793–4 been more successful, it is doubtful whether they would have met with much popular sympathy – urban workers and rural producers alike would have been compelled to labour for fixed prices, their social and cultural lives regulated in the name of unity and virtue, and those who became the turncoats of Thermidor would doubtless have continued to enrich themselves at others' expense. As things were, the country was given up to a generation of military dictatorship, rigid authoritarian policing, and a harvest of death as the sons of France marched across all Europe from Lisbon to Moscow.

However, in conclusion, we must strike a different note. The anecdotal history of Cobb is able to expose a world of horrors in the revolutionary France of the 1790s, and a more systematic approach may show things as being little better, but Cobb's point is often that things were as bad before 1789. A recent revival of pioneering demographic work from the 1960s and 1970s suggests that the Revolution was actually a fundamental social transformation, and that the lives of the majority benefited from the changes in quite concrete ways.[3] Like any population-statistics from the pre-industrial age, these are reconstructions to fill holes and speculations to cover gaps in the evidence. Nevertheless, they have been tested against several other models since the 1970s, and have emerged largely triumphant.

What they suggest is that the lives of the French population were dramatically improved by the Revolution, so that within two decades, the life-expectancy at birth of the average person had risen by a third, from under thirty to almost forty. There was a sudden and unprecedented decline in the rate of deaths amongst the French population, unmatched by any other European country. Prior to the Revolution, less than half of French children survived to age fifteen; within a generation this had risen to almost two-thirds. Those surviving to age forty went up from slightly over a third to around a half. Nothing in the history of disease or climate suffices to explain these changes, and they suggest that we must again take seriously the positive social effects of the Revolution's changes. The unquestionable gains for the peasantry of the early Revolution – the destruction of feudal dues and tithes, the liberation of lands for purchase or rent through *biens nationaux*, the ability to retain a greater share of crops and income for consumption and productive use – all these had indeed left the vast bulk of the population better-off in the most concrete sense: they lived longer after the Revolution.

It has often rightly been pointed out that in terms of basic social structure, nothing so much resembled late eighteenth-century France as early nineteenth-century France, but this was no longer a structure that could be taken for granted. The 1820s, 1830s and 1840s saw a country where the land was still the dominant productive sector, supporting the bulk of the population, and where landownership was the key to political participation, in a society based on the rule of local propertied elites, the *notables*. This was the product of the Napoleonic period of stabilisation, which had ultimately reintegrated many of the *émigré* elites. However, the legal basis of this structure always remained fragile, and attempts to turn the clock back to the legal and social order of the 1700s, largely by *émigré* hardliners who had returned only in 1814–15, failed decisively in the 1820s. Political radicalism continued to flourish, alongside a slower but possibly more fundamental process whereby the peasantry bought up land at the expense of their 'betters'. The social changes of the Revolution, although temporarily submerged, continued to assert themselves, quietly in the countryside, more violently in the great cities, and especially Paris, where making revolutions became a speciality of the century.[4]

It would be a much longer time before the political desires that had been apparent in the optimistic 1789 Declaration of Rights would finally have real meaning for all members of society. Utopian goals were never realised, and indeed in 1871 those who shared the more radical heritage of the Revolution were massacred by the middle classes, who had secured from 1789 an entry into politics that they continued to consolidate over the next century. Nevertheless, that the French today, and all Europeans, live as free citizens in states that guarantee their rights, is the result of a process that began with those aspirations.

The French Revolution, for all the agony of its labour, was a birth of freedom. This was recognised as its heritage throughout the nineteenth century, both in a French republican and revolutionary tradition, and in a Europe-wide radical-democratic movement that had its first climax in the widespread revolutions of 1848.[5] For a long part of the twentieth century, it was possible to suppress the significance of this in the shadow of Soviet communism, the roots of which had grown after 1848 in a European socialist movement that often consciously drew on the heritage of Revolution. However, exactly 200 years after the French found the courage to seize their liberty, the peoples of central and eastern Europe showed the world that sometimes it is still necessary, in the words of the revolutionary oath of the 1790s, to live free, or die.[6]

Just as the history of the 1790s showed that a revolutionary 'moment' is not the end of a struggle, but the beginning, so the 1990s have again illustrated the perils and pitfalls of social and political reconstruction. Events in Bosnia, Slovakia, Chechnya, Moldova and elsewhere have shown that the currents of chauvinistic nationalism which also spring from the wells of the late eighteenth century are still flowing deep and dark.[7] Nonetheless, the revolutionary cry of 'Liberty, Equality, Fraternity', coined when each of those words was a radical challenge to the existing order of the world, remains meaningful today. It echoes in the words of the United Nations Universal Declaration of Human Rights, that 'All human beings are born free and equal in dignity and rights. They are endowed with reason and conscience and should act towards one another in a spirit of brotherhood.'

These are the words of the French revolutionaries, adapted to the twentieth century. Since they were agreed in 1948, it must be admitted that the progress of the world to their fulfilment has been as hesitant, and frequently as bloody, as the course of the 1790s. When such ideas first entered politics, they did so imperfectly, stained by prejudice and the dread of reprisal. The study of history, however, should teach us not to repudiate those early efforts, but to put them in their appropriate context. The French Revolution was in many respects a tragic period of history, for France and for Europe. This was not, however, because of its aims, but because of its enemies.

Whether or not one agrees with historians such as François Furet that Jacobinism was the essence of the Revolution, it is clear that Jacobinism emerged, and became Terror, because the Revolution, from its earliest days, faced those who would destroy it in its entirety. The choice of which side to prefer is, of course, for the individual to make. A historian like Simon Schama can make the Old Regime seem a glowing example of an advanced liberal culture.[8] It was also, as we have seen, a society of stark poverty, oppressive taxation of the poor, arbitrary justice, censorship and social prejudice. To judge the Revolution it is essential always to keep in mind the society that preceded it. To judge it against the ideal of a free liberal society is to forget that, without the Revolution, that ideal might not exist.[9]

Notes

1 For a review of the period of the later 1790s as a prelude to Napoleon's rise, and the stages by which he ascended to supreme hereditary power, see the brief but informative text by M. Crook, *Napoleon Comes to Power: Democracy and Dictatorship in Revolutionary France, 1795–1804*, Cardiff, 1998.

2 R. C. Cobb, *Reactions to the French Revolution*, Oxford, 1972, pp. 163–9, and the overall section '*La Vie en Marge*: Living on the Fringe of the Revolution', pp. 128–80.

3 P. G. Spagnoli, 'The Unique Decline of Mortality in Revolutionary France', *Journal of Family History*, 22, 1997, pp. 425–61.

4 Three texts which offer contrasting but complementary approaches to the longer-term history of this period are: C. Charle, *A Social History of France in the Nineteenth Century*, Oxford, 1991, P. McPhee, *A Social History of France, 1780–1880*, London, 1992, and R. Tombs, *France 1814–1914*, Harlow, 1996.

5 On the French tradition, see P. M. Pilbeam, *Republicanism in Nineteenth-Century France, 1814–1871*, London, 1995. For the 1848 movement, see J. Sperber, *The European Revolutions, 1848–51*, Cambridge, 1995. M. Broers, *Europe After Napoleon*, Manchester, 1996, discusses systematically the various political ideologies of the early nineteenth century, which are all linked, by affinity or opposition, to the revolutionary tradition.

6 For an eyewitness history of these revolutions, see T. Garton Ash, *We the People: The Revolution of '89*, Cambridge, 1990.

7 For a discussion of the emergence of nationalism, see E. J. Hobsbawm, *Nations and Nationalism since 1780: Programme, Myth, Reality*, 2nd edn, Cambridge, 1992.

8 S. Schama, *Citizens: A Chronicle of the French Revolution*, New York, 1989. On Furet, see Introduction.

9 For a somewhat similar, though not identical, assertion, see R. Darnton, 'What was Revolutionary about the French Revolution?', *New York Review of Books*, 19 January 1989, reprinted in P. M. Jones (ed.), *The French Revolution in Social and Political Perspective*, London, 1996, pp. 18–29.

Selected documents

A work of this size can offer only a small selection of the vast range of documentary evidence produced by the actors of the Revolution. Documents have been chosen to reflect on the conjunction between political and social attitudes and actions that lies beneath the surface of many great revolutionary acts and conflicts. As such, it does not reproduce any of the 'great' revolutionary texts, which are easily accessible in a variety of existing translations. The texts offered here are the author's translations from the collection of French-language texts published as *French Revolution Documents*, vol. 1, ed. J. M. Roberts and R. C. Cobb, Oxford, 1966, vol. 2, ed. J. M. Roberts and J. Hardman, Oxford, 1973. A selection of larger translated collections is listed in the bibliography.

Document 1

The *cahiers de doléances* offer such a wide range of views and expressions that there is no way briefly to offer a truly representative selection. However, one can indicate something of the range of more radical demands that made their appearance in them, demonstrating the extent to which parish assemblies were prepared to ask for fundamental change. Below is a 'composite' *cahier* of demands that succeeds in covering most of the social and political issues of 1789. The parishes are located by their *départements*, although of course these did not exist in 1789. Note that each of the parishes here had other, in some cases many other, demands as well:

From Longnes (Seine-et-Oise) (the rather poor grammar reflects that of the original):

> We request His Majesty to annul all the *gabelles* and that salt should become freely traded.
>
> We desire that His Majesty grant us, if it please him, to annul all the taxes established on all that is necessary for the sustenance of man and otherwise, of whatever nature it may be.
>
> We desire that His Majesty grant us that the *taille, capitation* and other taxes that we pay for the upkeep of the State be established on all lands such as châteaux, houses, ploughland, pastures, woods, coppices, wastes, vines, heaths, ponds and rivers and all other objects.
>
> We wish to have made known the abuses which occur in the opening of some useless road like that of some seigneur to communicate with his château.
>
> We request His Majesty to accord us the power to destroy the too-numerous game which cause considerable losses in the countryside, which are rabbits and escaped pigeons.

From Saint-Vincent-Rive d'Olt (Lot):

> There is a hospital established in the town of Luzech; our community pays towards this hospital, and yet our poor do not receive any aid from it. We would desire that our poor should find shelter in the general hospital of Cahors, and we would contribute to the expenses of this hospital with the funds that we pay to that in Luzech.
>
> The lands of nobles and the Church, should they not be submitted to taxation? Why protect them from it? Why subject the lands of poor people exclusively to it, and why thrust thus upon the Third all the burden of taxation?
>
> The militia to which the cultivator is subjected is a servitude entirely contrary to the constitutional laws of the state [this refers to the lottery for service in local armed forces].
>
> We request that, in each parish, the police should be exercised and administered each year in rotation by two of the principal inhabitants.
>
> Our community has so many charges to which it is subjected by a dozen seigneurs who have these rights recognised as easily as one changes a shirt.

168

From Lignères-la-Doucelle (Orne):

The inhabitants request that there exist in the kingdom only two taxes, one by the name of territorial [i.e. land] tax and the other under the name of industry.

That the *bureaux des finances, chambres des comptes* and *cours des aides* be suppressed. [Privileged corporations and courts involved in taxation.]

That the *élections*, salt-warehouses, duties on goods and other exceptional jurisdictions be suppressed.

That salt be sold freely.

That all seigneurs, gentlemen and other privileged persons ... of whatever kind ... pay taxes at the same rate as the commoner.

That seigneurial dues be declared redeemable ...

That milling privileges be ended, and each be free to grind his grain where it suits him.

That the *corvées* due to seigneurs be abolished ...

That all seigneurial jurisdictions be abolished, or at least that they be grouped together into districts, in which each seigneur may name an officer for a limited time, in the absence of which the king will provide one.

That the children of commoners living nobly be admitted to military service on the same basis as the nobility.

That the king does not grant hereditary nobility to just anyone, but only to those who have merited it.

That no nobility be granted by payments nor otherwise than by arms or service rendered to the state.

That no churchman may possess more than one office; that those who enjoy several be held to choose [one] within a fixed time.

That religious houses with fewer than twelve inhabitants be suppressed.

Document 2

The momentous events of May to July 1789 produced many reactions. Below is an early example of attitudes amongst the revolutionary elite to the activities of the people, and a very early intervention by one who would go on to far greater things:

Excerpts from a draft proclamation proposed by the noble *monarchien* Lally-Tollendal in the National Assembly, 20 July 1789:

The National Assembly considering that ... in perfect agreement between the chief and his representatives, and after the reunion of all the orders, the Assembly moves to occupy itself without respite with the great work of the constitution ...

That new troubles which may arise cannot but be contrary to this ... the National Assembly ... invites all the French to peace, to the love of order, to the respect for law, to the confidence which they must have in their representatives, to loyalty to the sovereign. Declares that whosoever would infringe these duties shall be regarded as a bad citizen ...

Declares finally, awaiting the organisation that may be fixed for municipalities, that it authorises them to form bourgeois militias, in recommending them to give the most severe attention to this formation, and to admit only those incapable of harming the *patrie* and capable of defending it.

A report of a response by the then-unknown Robespierre, 20 July 1789, in which the shadow of future attitudes is visible:

M. de Robert-Pierre, deputy from Artois, analyses the project of M. de Lally's proclamation, and analyses it with force. 'What has then come, he cries, from that riot in Paris? Public liberty, a little blood spilt, a few heads cut off no doubt, but guilty heads. Yes, Messieurs, the proclamation of M. Lally-Tollendal is misplaced, it seeks to sound the alarm. To declare in advance that men are guilty, that they are rebels, is an injustice. What might be, or rather what would be the motive for the Assembly to adopt this projected proclamation? Is it the riot in the capital? Well then Messieurs, it is to that riot that the Nation owes its liberty. What so pressing would thus engage the Assembly to deliberate in this moment?... And who says that there would not be new attempts? [he appears to refer here to the 'aristocratic plot' which sparked the July rising] and if we declare to be rebels the citizens who armed themselves for our salvation, who shall repel such attempts?'

Document 3

Popular anger and agitation over the food supply were a widespread phenomenon in the summer of 1789, confronting both 'revolutionary' and Old Regime institutions, as this report from the mayor of Dunkirk to the local *intendant* makes clear:

25 July: As tempers begin to rise and there have been threats, to loot the grain warehouses, and some houses, and even to burn

some, [and reports] that 300 men should assemble last night to that effect, we took the decision to raise a bourgeois guard; all merchants and honest persons of this town came yesterday, around noon, to the town hall to register. Arrangements were made in the afternoon, and patrols began at nine in the evening. The number of persons of goodwill grows considerably: we hope to find a sufficient number of them to oppose the ill-intentioned persons, of which the number is large, in relation with foreigners. We shall increase this bourgeois guard this morning, to 300 men, for today's market, where there would have been trouble if we had not taken this precaution ... [he reports also the import of extra grain to the market, and a lowering of the official prices, with provision to compensate bakers for losses] ... But tempers are very heated. The [tricolour] cockade, taken up two days ago ... has been the occasion and the cause of all the tumult which reigns presently; heads are heated in the bars; seditious outbursts, drunkenness, the cost of bread have excited this fermentation. Joined to this are events in neighbouring towns, all stirred up by a dozen bad characters who publicly make seditious statements ...

The market is finished, Sir: it is four o'clock. We brought there 200 measures of wheat; the white was sold at 30 livres, the red at 24. There was much noise, many people gathered. To avoid a revolt, I took the action of reducing the prices, which had been set at 34 and 26 livres. They wanted to force the farmers to sell their wheat at the same price, but I succeeded in arranging everything. Everyone has left, and I hope that we shall have peace until next Saturday. There remain some threats to the grain merchants, but, as the people is satisfied to have had wheat at a good price, we must hope that the police we are exercising will bring back tranquillity ...

Document 4

By late July, the countryside was well and truly roused against the 'feudal regime', as this complaint, written later in August, indicates. Note that 'foreign' and 'stranger' are the same word in French, and in a rural setting especially, had very much the same meaning:

On 29 July, a party of foreign brigands united with my vassals and those of Vrigni, the neighbouring parish to mine, came, numbering some two hundred, to my château at Sassy, parish of Saint-Christophe, near Argentan, and, after breaking the locks on the cupboards that held my titles, they took most of them, with the

171

registers, and carried them off or burned them in the woods neighbouring my château. These wretches had had the alarm sounded
in the neighbouring parishes in order to gather in a larger number.
I am even more unhappy at this loss, as I have never forced my
vassals to feel the odious weight of antique feudalism, from which
I was delighted that they could be redeemed in the present circumstances; but who may set out and ever prove the wrong they have
done to my properties? I appeal to your prudence for the National
Assembly to set out some method to return to me what I have lost,
above all the use of a common, useful to my parishioners as well as
my property, of which they have burned the titles.

I shall not take any action against those that I know amongst
these brigands, who, not content with burning my paper, have
killed all my pigeons. But I await justice from the spirit of equity
which rules you, and which gives me the greatest confidence.

Comte de Germiny.

Document 5

Suspicion of the dangerous popular activities in town and country continued, even if some of the root causes were apparently
tackled in the Night of 4 August. The decree which emanated
from that event was published on 11 August, but the Assembly
had passed a rather different motion the day before:

10 August 1789
The National Assembly, considering that the enemies of the nation,
having lost hope of preventing, by the violence of despotism, public regeneration and the establishment of liberty, appear to have
conceived the criminal project of arriving at the same goal by way
of disorder and anarchy; that amongst other means they have, at
the same time, and almost the same day, spread false alarms in the
different provinces of the realm, and in announcing incursions
and brigandages which did not exist, they have given rise to
excesses and crimes which attack equally goods and persons, and
which, troubling the universal order of society, merit the most
severe punishments ...

Considering that, in the general effervescence, the most sacred
properties, and even the harvests, sole hope of a people in these
times of dearth, have not been respected ...

Orders and decrees:
That all the municipalities of the kingdom, in towns as well as
the countryside, shall watch over the maintenance of public tran-

quillity, and that, upon their request, the national militias, as well as the *maréchaussées* [mounted police], shall be assisted by troops ...

That all seditious gatherings, in town or country, even under the pretext of hunting, shall be immediately dispersed by the national militias, *maréchaussées* and troops, upon request of municipalities;

That in [all municipalities] there shall be prepared a list of vagrants, those without occupation or profession, and without settled domicile, who shall be disarmed, and that the national militias, the *maréchaussées* and troops shall watch especially over their conduct;

[That militias and troops shall swear an oath to nation, king and law;]

That officers shall swear, at the head of their troops, in the presence of municipal officers, to remain faithful to nation, king and law, and never to employ those under their orders against the citizens, if it is not at the request of civil or municipal officers, such requests shall always be read to the assembled troops;

That the priests of town and country shall read the present decree to the parishioners gathered in the church, and they shall employ the influence of their ministry, to re-establish peace and public tranquillity ...

Document 6

The fundamental cause of the events which led to 1789 was of course the financial crisis of the monarchy, and at the beginning of November the Assembly, by now sitting in Paris, turned its attention to settling this issue. The notion of appropriating the property of the Church won out over other issues in debate, and this property was voted 'at the disposal of the nation' on 2 November. Here the marquis de Ferrières, a moderate and perhaps slightly cynical noble, gives his view of how this came about:

[The notion was first raised by the marquis de Lacoste] This attack on the property of the clergy excited some murmurs, but the [general] debate being taken up again ... it was not spoken of ... However, this idea, cast artfully into the nation, germinated in their minds ...

The Bishop of Autun [Talleyrand] said that it was necessary to strengthen the credit of the nation, that the best means was to pronounce in a positive manner concerning the state's creditors; that it would be supremely unjust to place on state bonds the lightest taxation [another view proposed at the time]; that this would be an attack on public faith; that a partial reduction in bond payments, under the name of taxation, was as culpable in principle as a total suppression ...

Mirabeau ... supported the motion of the Bishop ... Chapelier assured us that the question had been settled [against such a tax] by the decrees of 17 July and 13 June. All the capitalists and speculators of the Assembly (and there were many) rose up in tumult, cried that the realm was lost, if one waited a single instant to recognise the great principles demonstrated so triumphantly by the Bishop of Autun: they left no time for reflection. The Assembly, humiliated by Necker's reproaches, terrified by the capitalists' threats, adopted the decree, and sacrificed, by a culpable weakness, the provinces to Paris, the owners of property to the capitalists and speculators of Paris.

Document 7

Rural unrest continued into the new year, along with a more determined outlook of defiance on the part of many communities, as this seigneur's letter from Lorraine to the National Assembly indicates:

28 March 1790
Monsieur President,
I have the honour to inform you that the inhabitants of the village of Royaumeix, near Toul, of which I was formerly in part the seigneur, believe firmly that the intention of the National Assembly is that they need not pay any rent or seigneurial due, even those owing for 1789, and that they are permitted to shoot, at all times and everywhere, all types of pigeons belonging to former seigneurs.

I complain, M. President, that all the inhabitants of Royaumeix refuse to pay me what they owe in seigneurial dues for the year 1789; that in truth, a single inhabitant took it upon himself, in the month of January last, to shoot dead, in front of the eyes of my sisters and nephews, in the village, most of my pigeons; that the same man, a few days ago, abandoned himself to the same activity, and he says he has this right from MM the National Assembly and the king: this man belongs to the municipality ...

Comte de Brancion, marshal of the king's armies.

Document 8

Rather more serious rural unrest continued in the south, as this petition shows:

5 July 1790

After asking you, M President, for the conservation of the bread of my children, I come to ask you for tranquillity, security and justice for myself.

It is publicly notorious that on Sunday 20 June, the mayor of Garravet, after the parish mass, cried out before the church door that he had received a decree of the National Assembly which forbade the community to pay any dues and authorised them to seize the communal lands;

That, on the night of Saturday 27 June, the peasants of Garravet assembled at the sound of the drum, some of the municipality with them, and went through the village and hamlets to force those who were not part of their plot to follow them on pain of their lives. They went to two of my farms and cut crops which they fed to their beasts the next day; from there they came into my garden, beating down the fences, yelling furiously that they should burn the château, which they did not do as I was absent.

Since this event, several of them have had it said to me that they want to buy gunpowder to blow up my house; that I am forbidden to appear by day or night in Garravet; my men are forbidden to gather my harvest or to thresh in the usual places; the priest is forbidden to see me or allow me to stay with him; all are forbidden to pay me any dues or to grind their grain at my mill, on pain of death. I have been warned to watch out for myself, not to go out at night, that ... I shall be attacked by day or night if I do not renounce all of my rights ...

[On 3 July, the mayor admitted he had acted excessively, and he and the priest tried to calm the situation] The priest read all the decrees of the Assembly after the mass, and asked for calm until the Assembly should send a decree specifically to Garravet. They replied, in a majority, that they did not need such authority, that they were the masters; in consequence, they have put their beasts in all my fields, and I do not doubt that they will end with some disastrous blow.

... I beg you, thus, M President, to obtain swiftly the most precise orders to halt this insurrection, which may have fatal consequences, for myself and for the neighbourhood ...

Sailhas.

Document 9

By early 1791, the Civil Constitution of the Clergy was provoking unrest across the country. Here Legendre, an Assembly deputy from Brittany, writes to his constituents after hearing news from the region:

18 February 1791
We have just received the terrible details of the insurrection of the countryside around Vannes, excited to revolt by a seditious and fanatical clergy. The effective aid given by the town of Lorient, and which that town offers to redouble if need be, will succeed, we must hope, in preventing the spread of the evil; and the measures decreed by the National Assembly to remove the factious bishops from Lower Brittany, to send conciliatory commissioners to Vannes with imposing forces, will safeguard our country from the dangerous effects of the contagion ...

We learn with pain that M Dubuisson, our curate, has preached, from the throne of peace and truth, lies and the principles of fanaticism. If this licence cannot be contained in a city such as Brest, what must one not fear from the countryside! In relation to this, it was important undoubtedly to repress the offence, to send the guilty man before the vengeance of the law, if the crime is aggravated. However, we cannot exhort you too much, MM, to exercise much indulgence towards priests who are led astray at the moment. Intolerance can only embitter passions ...

Document 10

Alongside the concerns over the clergy, there arose in the spring of 1791 disputes in the urban labour-market. The old guilds were abolished in March, and workers set out to test their bargaining-power in the new system, at the same time as employers strove to keep a lid on demands and maximise their profits. This situation would lead in June to the Le Chapelier Law, which banned all workers' organisations, and remained effective for nearly a century. Before this, however, the municipality of Paris had already taken its own actions, as this order shows:

4 May 1791
The *Corps municipal* ...
Informed that its representations to workers of various professions have not produced the effect that one had the right to expect and

that acts of violence committed in various workshops continue to alarm citizens, to drive rich proprietors from Paris and to trouble the public peace ...

Declares null, unconstitutional and unenforceable the decrees made by the workers of various professions to forbid each other and to forbid any other workers the right to work at other wages than those set by the said decrees;

Forbids all workers to make in the future any such decrees;

Declares in addition, that the rate for workers' labour must be fixed by individual bargain between them and those who employ them; and that, the strengths and talents of individuals being necessarily different, workers and those who employ them cannot be subjected to any price-control or restraint;

Declares finally, that all workers who gather to mistreat individuals working in shops or workshops, to put them out through violence and to prevent them continuing their work are and must be regarded as perturbers of the public peace;

In consequence, enjoins the police commissioners to go at the first request, with sufficient force, in any place where such disorders should be committed by gatherings of workers, to arrest and make prisoners of the guilty and to send without delay details of the arrests to the public prosecutor ...

Document 11

The later months of 1791 saw a rising tide of rural unrest at the Revolution's religious settlement. Non-juror priests and anticlerical local authorities were frequently at loggerheads, and rural populations sometimes sided violently with the former, as this account indicates:

From the *département* administrators of the Maine-et-Loire to the National Assembly, 6 November 1791:

[We] ... send you an extraordinary despatch to tell you of the troubles which disturb the *département*. They are such that, if you do not take prompt measures, evils will result with incalculable effects. Assemblies of 3 to 4,000 armed men form at several points in our *département* and give themselves over to all the excesses of the delirium of superstition and fanaticism. Pilgrimages to a chapel of the Virgin, noctural processions led by seditious priests have been the pretext and prelude for these gatherings. It was easy to disperse pilgrims who carried only rosary-beads; but today their priests have intoxicated them with sacred fury, today they preach out loud that the administrators, municipal officers and oath-taking priests are enemies of religion; today the men are armed with muskets, pitchforks and pikes; today combat has taken place between them and the National Guard, it is no longer time to say: these are religious quarrels, they must simply be scorned.

Throughout the *département*, constitutional priests are outraged, assaulted even at the foot of the altar. The doors of churches closed by decree of the National Assembly are broken down with axes ... The tax-rolls are not completed in the countryside, because most municipal officers, insulted and threatened at work, have abandoned them. Three district *chefs-lieux* are effectively besieged; they are in danger of night-attacks, of being pillaged and burnt by these brigands.

The fermentation is at its height, and if you in your wisdom do not take guard, the explosion will be terrible, and the seditious priests, however contemptible they may be, might end by leading us to counter-revolution via civil war. It is not the interest of religion which animates them ... This is but the veil which these perverse men use to overturn the Constitution.

... Whatever troubles disturb us, whatever dangers surround us, we swear to you that we will execute the law, remain faithful to our posts, and die here rather than abandon them.

Document 12

The food supply was again of critical concern by the winter of 1791–2, as this letter from Bergues, in the Nord *département*, to its administrators, indicates:

13 February 1792
The large quantity of grain which passes daily through this town exposes us every day to the birth of most dangerous uprisings amongst our inhabitants, whose disquiet cannot be calmed; a convoy of grain, escorted by dragoons, was passing through this town on the 7th, when the people blocked its passage in a crowd, and demolished the parapets of a bridge to block the canal. We only succeeded with infinite difficulty in dispersing the gathering that had formed, by use of the public force, and it was easy to see that the National Guard, and the regular troops, only did this with the greatest repugnance; despite the large number of workers we employed from 9 a.m., it was midnight before the blockage was cleared and the convoy was able to pass. They had already

attempted to demolish the other bridges, which made us fear a repetition of the same scene, and our fears are all the more deserved as we are not assured of the aid of the public force, when it concerns protecting the transport of grain. We cannot conceal, Messieurs, that the enormous quantity of grain, always heading for Dunkirk ... is enough to alarm us, especially as we have every reason to fear finding ourselves in dearth before the next harvest, above all if exports continue, the farmers having already sold three-quarters of their grain. We beg you, therefore, to take our observations into account, and to put an end to this hoarding [*accaparement*]; this is the only way to calm our disquiet and that of the people, and to maintain tranquillity in our town and its environs.

Document 13

The persistent urban–rural tension is again exposed in this unofficial circular of 5 March 1792 from the Limours area (Seine-et-Oise), which contemplates direct action against rural municipalities over food supplies:

Brothers and friends, we invite you to find yourselves tomorrow at Briis at 9 a.m. to assemble all to make searches for grain to conduct this to market because we have orders deposited in the archives on 26 April 1789 which ordain that grain shall be exposed [for sale] at the markets and not elsewhere, and it is said by this decree that the municipalities will watch out that no grains are removed by night. As they do not wish to watch out for this, it is thus down to the National Guards to watch out, since they say that they have no orders. We have found them [the orders] on file Sunday the 4th of this month. From the [National Guard] major of Vaugrigneuse. Signed: Etienne Girard.

Document 14

By the summer of 1792, with a disastrous military campaign under way, political tensions in the capital reached new heights, as shown in the denunciatory letter from the *département* administrators of Paris to the minister of the interior:

12 June 1792
It is at the heart of our *département*, Monsieur, it is almost under our eyes, that the frightful poisons that are spread throughout all the

kingdom are at work with every imaginable art. We should be failing as citizens, unworthy magistrates of the people, if we had the
pusillanimity to remain silent on the fact that there exists at the
heart of the capital we are charged to survey, a *public pulpit of
defamation*, where citizens of every age and sex, admitted without
distinction to attend this criminal preaching, may drink daily of
that which contains the most impure calumny, the most contagious
licence. This establishment on *the former Jacobin site*, rue St Honoré,
takes the name of *society*, but far from having the character of a
private society, to the contrary it has all those of a public spectacle:
vast ranks of benches open to spectators; opening times fixed and
on display to the people for every session, and a printed journal
publishes the speeches made there. In surveying some issues of
this journal, notably those of the four or five recent sessions, one
finds the king, the courts, the administrators, the chiefs of our
armies, all those who bear some authority in France, there deliber-
ately reviled and calumnied.

... We cannot conceal, Monsieur, that such an establishment, a
scandal the like of which is offered by no other country or time,
perverts public morality with the most frightful rapidity. In invit-
ing us to spread instruction on citizenship and peace, do you not
remind us that our first duty is to preserve the people from all
immoral preaching and all criminal provocation?... As much as the
courageous exercise of civic denunciation gives energy to a free
government, so do cowardly and absurd calumnies contribute to
destroying all its mechanisms, and above all that of confidence
which should be the strongest of all. The effects that we fear manifest themselves all too clearly already. Everywhere we find the
spirit, tone and even the language of this pernicious school. Unjust
suspicions, vague mistrust, calumnies drawn from this source, cir-
culate in the squares, the marketplaces, in gatherings of citizens,
even in the workplace; there they are repeated by simple and
innocent mouths who spread them with all the more assurance, as
their intentions are pure ...

Document 15

The consequences of 'jacobinical' campaigns were manifest on 20
June 1792, when a crowd made vigorous demands of the king
after invading the Tuileries. In the wake of this, addresses
reached Paris from across the kingdom, many, like this one from
the active citizens of Rouen, less than sympathetic to such activity. It was reported to the National Assembly on 29 June:

Legislators. The *patrie* is in danger. Scoundrels plot its end: it is against them that we raise our voices ...

We wished for a Constitution which fixed the duties and the rights of the people and of the monarch: prejudices had to be uprooted, habits destroyed, abuses wiped out. A revolution was necessary, and the French made it. But now that the Constitution is established, that its care has been confided to the faith of the legislative body as to the attachment of all citizens, it needs only, to maintain it, courage and wisdom.

Proud of this, we have sworn to maintain it: legislators, you have sworn like us. We hold to our oaths, you hold also to yours ...

It should no longer be permitted to distract your attention from the true causes of our troubles with chimerical plots or vain declamations, of which the lightest scrutiny suffices to destroy their merit! Were they real, these plots, they would not deserve fear: you have, to destroy them, the courage and patriotism of all the French.

The true conspirators are those who, working without rest on a multitude easy to mislead, push them to crime, in intoxicating them with mistrust.

The true conspirators are those who disparage the sovereignty of the legislative body, by making it the echo of their private passions.

The true conspirators are those who recognise in France 44,000 sovereigns [i.e. each of the communes]; who talk of the *republic* in a state constituted as *monarchic* by the uniform wish of all the nation; who demand *appeal to the people*, in a representative government, where an appeal to the people, forbidden by the Constitution, would be nothing else but the proclamation of civil war.

The true conspirators are those who, by their actions, by their writing and speeches, strive to weaken the respect and trust that one owes to the king and the constituted authorities.

The true conspirators are those who preach indiscipline, revolt, and distrust of their generals to the troops, who cover our colonies with blood and ruins ...

Legislators, we say it firmly, the divisions which until now have reigned between you and the executive power afflict all good Frenchmen: they must end, if you do not want the *patrie* to perish in the division of the most fatal anarchy ... Impose an eternal silence on these agitators who, even within the sanctuary of legislation, dare to deify revolt and murder ... Punish the authors of the crimes committed, the 20th of this month, at the Tuileries. It is a public crime; it is an attack on the rights of the French people, who do not wish to receive their laws from some brigands in the capital: we demand vengeance for it from you ...

Document 16

A few days later, in a petition of 1 July 1792 to the National Assembly from the Bonne-Nouvelle section of Paris, we can see the language in use on the other side of the growing political divide amongst revolutionaries:

> We have asked you to dismiss the headquarters staff of the Parisian National Guard: it is this aristocratic corporation which is one of the sources of our troubles and divisions. Abusing the superiority and centrality of their forces, these traitors seem to have formed the project of directing public opinion to their will. All citizens being National Guards, they exercise their influence and their power upon all citizens. This institution is a modern feudality which will inevitably cause the Revolution to fail. If you do not oppose yourselves to the progress of this power, the civil magistrature will soon lose all its strength; and the people, enlightened by sad experience, will be forced to seize its liberty once more, to seat it upon better-calculated bases.
>
> This headquarters is a kind of aristocratic reserve-corps which, making a means of intrigue out of hierarchy, circulates by order the poisons of its opinions, to provoke against the wisest of your decrees the so-called suspensive veto. Where then is France, if the result of your deliberations, of your thoughts, if the national wish must fail against these culpable efforts at intrigue? We demand from you the suppression of this military directory.

Document 17

By the end of the month, the stakes were considerably higher. Here the Mauconseil section of Paris addresses the citizens of the capital on 31 July:

> The holiest duty, the law most cherished,
> Is to forget the law to save the *patrie*.

Citizens of all sections,
The National Assembly deliberates; but the enemy is approaching, and soon Louis XVI will give up our cities to the bloodied fetters of the despots of Europe.

> Citizens, arise, and come with us to demand from the Senate, if it thinks itself capable or not of saving the *patrie*; and, without leaving the chamber, let us obtain at last the right to forget the law to save the *patrie*.

The citizens of Mauconseil section have conceived the noble design of retaking their rights, of making liberty triumph or of burying ourselves under its ruins, and without doubt this generous example will be imitated in all the sections of the Empire [i.e. France].

That Paris should be again the astonishment of the universe and the horror of despotism.

Already for too long a contemptible tyrant has toyed with our destinies; we must not wait, to punish him, until his victory is assured; citizens, arise, and recall that a tyrant never forgives ...

Let us all unite to proclaim the dethronement of this cruel king. Let us say with one voice: *Louis XVI is no longer King of the French*.

Opinion alone gives strength to kings; well! Citizens, let us use opinion to dethrone him; for opinion makes and unmakes kings.

Louis XVI is given up to the most degrading reprobation, all parts of the Empire reject him indignantly, but none of them has expressed its opinion sufficiently.

The Mauconseil section declare therefore to all parts of the sovereign, that in presenting the general wish, *it no longer recognises Louis XVI as King of the French*, that it abjures the vow it made to be faithful to him, as an abuse of its good faith.

Perjury is a virtue, when one has promised a crime.

Citizens, imitate our example, then tyranny crumbles and France is saved for ever.

Document 18

The fall of the monarchy, of course, was not the end of the Revolution's troubles, and in the west especially disorders continued. Here is a letter from the *département* administrators of the Deux-Sèvres which was read to the National Assembly:

Niort, 25 August 1792, Year IV of Liberty.
The *département* council has told you, by the last post, of the deplorable events in the district of Châtillon. New information tells us that the gathering continues, that the chief of the brigands, far from dispersing them, leads them every day into new combats and new withdrawals. The council however has taken powerful measures, and there are at this moment three thousand National Guards in this area to establish tranquillity. We inform you with the greatest pain that six patriots have already been the victims of this band of scoundrels, but there have been at least forty of them killed.

We had hoped that these assemblies would cease as soon as the public force arrived: our hopes were misplaced, which gives us very great disquiet. Having disposed of all the armed force at our disposal, the *départements* of the Vendée, the Loire-Inférieure and the Maine-et-Loire have given us in these circumstances unequivocal proof of fraternity and good neighbourliness in sending us aid; and without these *départements* these unfortunate areas would today be the prey of revolts ...

We cannot conceal from you, Messieurs, that a severe and prompt example is needed. Already several of these brigands have been arrested, and the *département* council requests from you a decree, that the criminal court of Niort may judge this affair without appeal. This is the only way to bring back peace to this unfortunate land; and we hope that you will not refuse this request.

Document 19

Once the new National Convention met, it was not long before political tensions broke out into acrimony. Here on 29 October 1792, the Girondin Louvet condemns the September Massacres, and then accuses Robespierre, who was on the provisional municipality at the time, of plotting a takeover:

Louvet de Couvrai: The supposed friends of the people have wanted to cast onto the people of Paris the horrors with which the first week of September were soiled; they have done them a mortal outrage; they have unworthily calumnied them. I know them, the people of Paris, because I was born, and have lived, in their midst; they are brave, but, like brave men, they are good; they are impatient, but generous; they feel an insult strongly, but after the victory they are magnanimous.

I do not mean to speak of this or that part that are led astray, but of the immense majority, when it is left in its natural happy state. (*Applause.*)

They know how to fight, the people of Paris; they don't know how to murder. (*New applause.*) It is true that we saw them all on 10 August before the Tuileries; it is false that they were seen on 2 September before the prisons. (*Repeated applause.*) Inside them, how many killers were there? Two hundred, not that many, perhaps; and outside, how many spectators could one count, drawn by a truly incomprehensible curiosity? Twice as many, at most.

Interruption from the extreme left.

Louvet: Well, you deny it? That one should question virtue! The fact I put forward, I have from Pétion [mayor of Paris], he told it to me. (*Applause.*)

[The speech continues, eventually pointing the finger at Robespierre as leader of a plot. After considerable disorder, in which Robespierre is refused leave to rebut the accusation, Louvet resumes his speech, naming various other measures he holds Robespierre responsible for.] It is thus that already this despot approached the proposed goal: to humiliate before the powers of the municipality, of which he was the real chief, national authority, awaiting the moment he could wipe it out: yes, wipe it out; for at the same time, by that famous committee of surveillance of the city, the plotters covered France with that letter in which all the communes were invited to murder individuals ... and which is more, to assassinate liberty, because it concerned nothing less than obtaining a coalition of all municipalities together, and their union with Paris, which would thus be the centre of communal representation, and overturning from top to bottom the form of your government. That was assuredly the system of their plot, that you see them even now continuing ...

Robespierre, I accuse you of having for a long time calumnied the purest and best patriots; I accuse you of it, because I think that the honour of good citizens and of the representatives of the people does not belong to you!

I accuse you of having calumnied the same men with even more fury during the first days of September, that is, when calumnies were proscriptions!

I accuse you of having, as far as you could, scorned, persecuted and reviled the national representation, and of causing it to be scorned, persecuted and reviled!

I accuse you of having put yourself forward as an object of idolatry, of allowing it to be said before you that you were the only virtuous man in France, the only one who could save the *patrie*, and twenty times of having given to understand this yourself!

I accuse you of having tyrannised the electoral assembly of Paris by all the means of intrigue and horror!

I accuse you of having evidently aimed at supreme power; which is demonstrated by the facts that I have noted, and by all your conduct, which speaks for itself to accuse you!

I request that examination of your conduct be sent before a committee ...

Document 20

The views expressed above did not prevail, though tensions continued through the epoch of the king's trial. Shortly thereafter, food riots again erupted in Paris, and here Marat glosses such events with his own brand of totalising critique, in the *Journal of the French Republic*, 25 February 1793:

> It is incontestable that the capitalists, the speculators, the monopolists, the luxury-merchants, the instruments of chicanery, the old judges, the ex-nobles, etc., are all, more or less, instruments of the Old Regime, who miss the abuses that they profited from to enrich themselves from the public spoils. How then could they join in good faith in the establishment of the reign of liberty and equality? With the impossibility of changing their hearts, in view of the failure of the methods employed to date to recall them to their duty, and despairing of seeing the legislators take great measures to force them to it, I see that only the total destruction of this cursed breed can bring tranquillity to the state, that they will not cease to work [against it] so long as they are standing. Today they redouble their zeal to desolate the people through the exorbitant rise in prices of goods of the first necessity and the fear of famine.
>
> Awaiting the moment when the nation, weary of this revolting disorder, takes to itself the task of purging the earth of this criminal race ... one should not find it strange that the people in each town, pushed to despair, should make their own justice. In every area where the rights of the people are not empty titles confined pompously in a simple declaration, the pillage of a few shops, at the doors of which one hangs the hoarders, would soon put an end to these corrupt abuses, which reduce five million men to despair, and which have let thousands die in indigence ...

Document 21

Through the spring of 1793, as the internal and external situation worsened, the Convention tried to impose order from the centre. The representatives sent out in the spring often worsened tensions, nowhere more so than in Marseille; this petition of protest bearing 25,000 signatures was read to the Convention on 25 May 1793:

> Representatives, the head of the despot has fallen beneath the blade of the laws; the ambitious, the traitors, the lesser tyrants must

suffer the same fate. The Marseillais, in rising up again, have given them their first blows ... [This refers to their moderate uprising against the Jacobins of Marseille, and the commissioners they complain about.]

Your commissioners, upon arrival at Marseille, surrounded themselves solely with the factious and the disorganisers; should one be astonished that, led astray by such guides, they have been nothing but apostles of discord and anarchy?... In every section they have tried to erect a wall of separation, which, in dividing the citizens, could produce nothing but the fomentation of hatred and the igniting of civil war.

They allowed Pâris, president of the *département*, who accompanied them on this visit, to preach in their presence a crusade against property.

Marseille owes only to the wisdom of its citizens, to their respect for the authorities, to their mistrust of perfidious suggestions which have too often duped them, the fact of having stifled the seed of discord that the incendiary discourse of your commissioners was tending to produce ... A great number of patriots, victims of personal animosities, had been mixed in with suspect citizens and arbitrarily disarmed; by an even more inconceivable abuse, they had been allowed to rearm themselves through payment of a levy as unjust as it was vexatious. [The commissioners did nothing about this, while sending away the local National Guard, and importing troops from outside the area] ... If this substitution of forces from one *département* to another did not hide perfidious intentions, at the least it is an evident proof of the most complete incapacity, and of a pointless and unheard-of prodigality with the finances of the Republic.

Representatives, the commissioners who come from you with unlimited powers must be responsible for all their actions, and the Marseillais make no distinction between traitors and unfaithful mandatories ...

Document 22

After the events of 31 May – 2 June 1793 and the triumph of the Jacobin 'Mountain', radical calls for further action did not diminish. Here is an account of a Cordeliers Club session in which the voice of the *enragés* made itself heard:

22 June 1793
A reading was made from the *Evening Journal*; upon noting the

headline which spoke of a motion to sound the alarm, the reader halted and cried: Yes, yes, we must sound the alarm; but it must be swiftly for the blow, I swear, on my honour, we will do for the intriguers.

The day's main business was the remedies for the dangers we face. Jacques Roux complained bitterly that the Commune had passed over the motion he had made to punish speculators with death. If that article was not in the Constitution, he said, we could say to the Mountain; You have done nothing for the sans-culottes, because it is not for the rich that they fight, it is for liberty; if the bloodsuckers of these good people can still drink their blood drop by drop in the shadow of the law, liberty is like *a beautiful woman who has lost an eye.* I invite the Cordeliers Club to present this petition themselves tomorrow to the Convention and to have this principle consecrated, before giving thanks to the Holy Mountain; that all the people surround the Convention, and cry to it with one voice: We adore liberty, but we do not want to die of hunger, suppress speculation and we have nothing more to ask.

Jacques Roux's proposition is adopted and twelve commissioners named to present the petition [amongst them is one Duret], but the latter refuses the mission, saying angrily: I am indignant that we speak of petitions, when we must arm ourselves with cannons and knives ... Let us rise up and if we made nothing but clear water on 31 May, let this new insurrection be written in the annals of history in letters of blood; we need a tenth of August, the heads of the scoundrels must roll. (Very long and noisy applause.) ...

Varlet [another *enragé* spokesman] took the stand; he spoke with fire: I have known the people for four years, I am in the groups; the sans-culottes of Paris, Lyon, Marseille and Bordeaux are the same; *they alone compose the people*; we must thus establish a line of demarcation between the shopkeeper, the aristocrat and the artisan; the first two classes must be disarmed; the people of Paris, in the name of all the *départements* must tomorrow give a mandate to the Convention; within twenty-four hours, they must decree that all nobles shall be turned out of places that belong only to sans-culottes; tomorrow the people must triumph, tomorrow we must finish our work ...

Document 23

The *enragés* were not the only forces on the extreme left, and Hébert's *Père Duchesne* took a slightly different line on the crises of the summer, writing in no. 269 of that journal, around the beginning of August 1793:

[Hébert describes the plans of the counter-revolutionaries to undermine the armies and seize Paris.] There, f—, there's the vile blow that's being prepared, what must we do to prevent it? What must we do, f—? First we must put all the suspects away, chase all the nobles and intriguers out of our armies; then we must renew the Convention, and this time only fill it with real republicans; we must, before anything else, organise an executive power, and not unite all powers in the same hands. The Counter-revolution will be made before a month is up, if we leave the Committee of Public Safety organised as it is now. The ministers are no more than clerks without responsibility, because they are obliged to walk like blind men, and obey the Committee's orders like slaves. I know, f—, that it's composed, for the majority, of excellent citizens, but there is more than one black sheep in the flock; besides, the Committee will be renewed, and in the place of Robespierre [etc.] I foresee some villains inserting themselves who covet the fifty million that the Convention allows to the Committee; watch out for pillage and counter-revolution, f—.

Document 24

By the autumn, the Revolution was emerging from its greatest crisis, and the Terror was building in all its dimensions. One area less frequently remarked-on than some is the problem of linguistic conformity, in a land where the majority did not have 'standard' French as their first language. Here, the representative Jullien reports to Robespierre from Lorient, 25 October 1793:

Brittany is encrusted with aristocracy. Jullien requests the despatch by Bouchotte [war minister] of bulletins and good newspapers for the soldiers; the countryside is infected with priests; fanaticism reigns there, and federalism, or rather royalism, in the towns. He proposes to the Committee [of Public Safety]:

1. To require the renewed administrations of Ille-et-Vilaine, Finistère, Morbihan, Loire-Inférieure to have translated into low Breton and circulated in the countryside the new laws, bulletins and republican writings;

2. To invite the popular societies to detach a member who possesses the country idiom to develop the public spirit there and to elaborate for the people the benefits of the Revolution;

3. To have established in the canton *chefs-lieux* masters of the

189

French language in order than the coming generation should not
be separated from the other citizens of the republic by a difference
of language which would lead to a difference of opinions and sentiments. Language must be one, as is the Republic.

Document 25

A few days earlier, on 12 October, the Committee of Public Safety
had written to the representatives at Lyon, recently fallen to the
army of the Republic. On this day the Convention had decreed
that Lyon was to be destroyed and renamed 'Ville-Affranchie'
(Freed-town). In the autumn and winter of 1793, hundreds were
executed, and many buildings demolished in pursuit of this
order:

> The National Convention, citizen colleagues, views with pleasure
> your entry into Lyon; but its joy could not be complete when it saw
> that you have yielded to the first impulses of sentimentality with
> too little thought of policy. You appear to have abandoned your-
> selves to a people who flatter their conquerors, and the manner in
> which you speak of so great a number of traitors, of their escape,
> that one would believe to be militarily protected, of the punish-
> ment of too small a number and the departure of almost all, must
> alarm patriots, who are indignant to see so many scoundrels
> escape through a breach and carry themselves off to the Lozère
> and principally to Toulon. We therefore do not congratulate you
> on your success, before you have done all that you must for the
> *patrie*. Republics are demanding; there is no national recognition
> except for those who wholly merit it. We send you the decree that
> the Convention has passed this morning on the Committee's
> report. It has proportioned the vigour of its measures to your first
> account ...

Document 26

From September 1793 onwards, dealing with the Terror and its
consequences became a way of life. Here Hébert, author of the
Père Duchesne, acts in his official capacity as a deputy municipal
prosecutor, revealing the social and sexual prejudices of official
'sans-culotterie':

From the *Journal de Paris*, reporting a municipal session:

> 'I saw this morning at the police [offices], a crowd of pretty women besiege the offices, to request releases [of prisoners] ... they possess the art of captivating men. One will repulse the wife of a good sans-culotte, because she is not elegantly dressed and does not have pretty eyes; while a cunning coquette, accustomed to deceiving the deceivers themselves, will be admitted ... I require in consequence the posting at all the doors of police offices a prohibition on entry for the pretty petitioners [*les jolies solliciteuses*]' – The Council ordered that 'all pretty intriguers' would have no access to the police offices.

Document 27

The puritanism of the revolutionaries is well documented in this municipal decree of 2 October 1793:

> The municipal prosecutor having exposed the great principles of the revolution and of liberty, which can only be supported by public morality; having made felt the indispensable necessity to oppose the rapid and frightful progress of libertinage.
>
> The General Council, struck by the principles developed ...
>
> Orders: 1. That it is forbidden to all girls or women of ill-repute [*mauvaise vie*, 'bad life'] to stand in the streets, promenades, or public squares and to incite there libertinage or debauchery, under pain of arrest and trial as corrupters of morals and disturbers of public order;
>
> 2. It is forbidden for any booksellers, print or picture-sellers to display indecent items, shocking to modesty, under pain of confiscation and destruction of the said items;
>
> 3. Police commissioners are ordered to make frequent visits to areas infected with libertinage, under pain of being removed from their posts ...
>
> 4. Patrols will arrest all girls and women of ill-repute that they shall find inciting libertinage ...
>
> The General Council calls to its aid for the execution and maintenance of this decree, republicans who are austere and friends of morality, the fathers and mothers of families, all constituted authorities, and the teachers of youth, as all being specially charged with conserving the morals of young citizens, upon which rest the hopes of the *patrie*; it invites old men, as ministers of morality, to keep watch that morals should not be outraged in their presence ...

Document 28

By December 1793, with the Girondin/Federalist threat fading into the past, the Montagnards and their allies in the Parisian sectional movement began to turn on each other. Here, the Hébertists in the War Ministry and Paris *armée révolutionnaire* are attacked in the Convention on 17 December (27 frimaire II). Fabre d'Eglantine began the process, after which others stood up to condemn them:

> Bourdon de l'Oise: Goupilleau and I thought it necessary to suspend Rossignol [a *sans-culotte* general]: we were using only the powers delegated to us. Vincent denounced me to the Cordeliers Club, and succeeded in extorting from them a petition demanding my head ...
>
> Lebon: I declare that, at the end of a meal I attended, along with Vincent, I heard him say: 'We shall force the Convention to organise the government according to the Constitution, we are sick of being the valets of the Committee of Public Safety' ...
>
> Couthon: Do not doubt it, all these ultra-revolutionary measures taken by the men denounced to you tend only to halt the revolutionary movement in order to organise counter-revolution or some private movement, thanks to which they could seize power. And as these dangerous men have agents even within the Committees, I invite my colleagues, committee-members, to make a list of all the clerks and agents therein, to take careful note of who they have been, and what they have merited, and this should be read to the Convention. The time has come, and the Jacobins shall give a great example of this: the time has come when this podium must become the place of censorship and purification. All those salaried by the republic must be known to you, and recognised as worthy of the public trust ... [The arrest of three leading figures was decreed.]

Document 29

Through the winter and spring of 1794, the radical republican movement tore itself into its component factions, and one by one these were annihilated or forced into silence. A response from 'street-level' is visible in this anonymous placard recorded on 6 March 1794 (16 ventôse II):

Sans-culotte it is time beat the drum sound the tocsin arm yourself and be quick, for you see that they are pushing you to your last breath, if you want to believe me it's better to die defending your Glory for the *patrie* that dying in a famine, where all the Representatives want to plunge you, don't trust them it is time, civil war is being prepared, turn the tables on all the scoundrels who say they govern the republic, they are all conspirators and all merchants of Paris I denounce them, some of those who will read my few words written, which are the pure truth will say that I am a conspirator because I speak the truth.

Document 30

Throughout the Year III royalist and anti-Jacobin mobs were active in the south-east, often with the collusion of the authorities. Here a National Guard volunteer grenadier testifies in germinal IV (March 1796) about events he had witnessed the previous June in Marseille:

[He had been on duty in a guardroom.] They were ordered to take up arms, and accompany the Representatives Chambon, Isnard and Cadroy. It was then eight or nine p.m.

Arriving at the Fort Jean gate, they found it closed. The sentry inside refused to open, despite the Representatives' repeated orders; ... the grenadiers broke down the gate; they entered and advanced to the drawbridge, which was raised. The commander appeared, and at first refused to lower it, but after repeated orders and threats from the Representatives, it was lowered, and [they] entered.

They found two bourgeois [i.e. National Guard] sentries inside. The Representatives and grenadiers halted by the canteen. The square was full of killers [*égorgeurs*, 'throat-cutters'], who were engaged in massacre. Cadroy addressed them: 'What's this noise? Can you not do what you're doing in silence? Stop firing off pistols. What are these cannon? It makes too much noise, and alarms the town.' Cadroy went into the canteen, and coming out, said to the killers: '*Enfants du Soleil* ['Children of the Sun', the name of a royalist murder-gang], I am at your head; I will die with you, if we must. But haven't you had enough time now? Stop. That's enough of it.' The killers surrounded him, shouting, and then he said: 'I am going, do your work.'

Cadroy removed some assassins from the hands of the grenadiers who had seized them. The declarant saw murders and assassinations committed in his presence.

The killers engaged the declarant and his comrades to eat and drink, and proposed to them that they should loot the bodies. These brigands, they said, have assignats and jewels ...

Document 31

The later 1790s were marked by the re-emergence of social distinctions and continued division, albeit with the boot of state power on the other foot from 1792–4. Here a caricature from July 1795 describes the *jeunesse dorée* as if their sartorial and behavioural affectations were the symptoms of a disease:

> ... The pathiognomonic signs of this degeneration are first a total failure of the optic nerve, which obliges the sufferer to constantly use eye-glasses, the necessity of which grows with the proximity of objects; and a cooling of the natural warmth which is difficult to overcome, at least with a very tightly-buttoned coat, and a cravat folded six times into which the chin disappears, and which threatens to mask them up to the nose. At the present time the legs appear to have resisted this cold. At least one notes that the foot is almost uncovered, and that the coat, which affects a quadri-lateral form, descends scarcely to the knee. Beyond the foreshortened stature, and the slender form, and the short sight of individuals, another proof of the weakening is the use of a short stick weighted with lead, of equal size at each end, which appears to me to perform the function of a counterweight such as that used by tight-rope-walkers ...
>
> I am far from thinking this malady incurable, and I like to recall that this same youth, whose infirmity causes me civic disquiet, knew, upon occasion, how to seize a sabre, handle a musket with as much vigour as skill, and gave voice to male sounds, animated song, war-cries and victory-shouts ...

Document 32

The Thermidorian regime ended the regulation of prices, the General Maximum, at the end of 1794. Here the Committee of Public Safety requests information on prices from district national agents, and illustrates both the thinking and the apprehensions of the Thermidorians on this issue:

8 February 1795 (20 pluviôse III):

The government has not concealed from itself the fact that suppression of the Maximum law and the freedom given to commerce and industry would occasion a rather strong rise in the price of provisions, wages, and in general of various objects of consumption. Nothing was more natural than this reaction against an overstrong compression that had to be ended. But, as it is necessary for the government to have always in mind the movements operating in the variations of prices up and down, we charge you to note for us on the attached table the current usual prices of the objects mentioned there, and those that they commonly commanded before the Maximum law. We are not asking for a rigorous appraisal, but only a reasonable approximation, this will suffice to fulfil our wishes in producing this table, which we have not judged it appropriate to make more complete, in order to avoid any idea of returning to general arrangements on this issue ...

Document 33

Within Paris, a careful watch was kept over the population, as it had been throughout the eighteenth century. Police reports from the period are highly coloured by political conformism, but they do indicate the level of alarm visible amongst the population, and outline the solutions sought:

18 February 1795 (30 pluviôse III):

Public spirit. Groups and cafés: The various cafés were less-frequented yesterday than usual. In the groups [gathered in public places], while relatively few, due to the rigour of the cold, they murmured greatly against the Subsistence Commission, that they accuse of being the cause of the rise in prices of all provisions; they are astonished that the constituted authorities do nothing to remedy the discredit of the assignats, notably in the *départements* where farmers refuse to sell their grain, except for coins or an excessive price in assignats.

In other groups, workers complain of the lack of coal arriving and fear, after such a long and harsh winter, being plunged into the extremity of poverty; they hope that the Convention will open its eyes to the calamity.

It is reported that the sectional assemblies have been very stormy ... that they only just succeeded in restoring calm, and that at the Butte-des-Moulins a fairly long list was read out of former Jacobins, since 1793, and others who were all termed dilapidators, terrorists and men of blood ...

20 May 1795 (1 prairial III):

Public spirit: The events of yesterday, very well-known, leave memories too painful to recount them. Those who threaten us to-day follow on from this; they give us the saddest forebodings. It appears, according to the reports we have before us, that heads are still heated, and, from the details we have managed to gather, we have reason to believe that the shortage of subsistence has been the pretext, unfortunately too plausible, which the agitators have used to lead credulous citizens astray, but that the cause of the popular movement, organised long ago, comes from the faction of the old ringleaders, who caused the people today to demand, along with bread, the re-establishment of the Commune, the Constitution of 1793, the release of all the Montagnard deputies and all the members of the old revolutionary committees. The [police] inspectors have noted, in almost all sections, that the proclamation yesterday evening of the law against these movements excited the greatest discontent and provoked seditious outcry and determined revolt against the Convention, notably against those representatives known for their principles of justice ...

Document 34

In October 1795, in the wake of the proclamation of the Constitution of the Year III, and the unsuccessful royalist Vendémiaire rising, the authorities attempted to pacify France with an amnesty. One can note, however, the contrast between the expansive mood of the opening declarations and the substance of measures which follow, more attuned to political realities. 'General peace' would not come until several years after Napoleon's rise, and measures such as this were by then long void:

Decree of 26 October 1795 (4 brumaire III):

1. Dating from the day of the declaration of general peace, the death-penalty shall be abolished throughout the French Republic.
2. The *Place de la Révolution* [in Paris] shall henceforth bear the name *Place de la Concorde* ['harmony'] ...
3. The Convention abolishes, from this day, all decrees of accusa-

tion or arrest, all arrest-warrants whether outstanding or not, all procedures, prosecutions and judgments concerning actions relative only to the Revolution. All detainees from these events shall be released at once, if there exist no charges against them relative to the conspiracy of 13 vendémiaire.

4. Crimes committed during the Revolution, and covered by the Penal Code, shall be punished by the appropriate sentence indicated therein.

5. In every mixed accusation, where it shall concern at the same time both acts relative to the Revolution and crimes under the Penal Code, investigation and judgment shall bear upon the latter only.

6. All those who shall be accused of theft from the public purse, embezzlement, extorsion of taxes with peculation on the part of those levying the charge, or any other such acts in the course of and due to the Revolution, may be prosecuted, either in the name of the nation, or by those individuals harmed; but the cases may only be judged as civil matters, with restitution of property as the sole penalty.

7. The Executive Directory may defer the publication of the present law in insurgent *départements*, or those that shall become insurgent, with the charge to report such acts to the legislative body, including the number of *départements* affected, and when it may be implemented, as soon as circumstances permit.

8. Formally excluded from amnesty are:
    1. Those sentenced in their absence for acts in the Vendémiaire conspiracy;
    2. Those against whom action has begun, or evidence been collected, for acts within the same conspiracy, or against whom such may be acquired shortly;
    3. Priests who have been deported, or who are subject to deportation;
    4. Fabricators of false assignats or false coinage;
    5. *Emigrés*, whether or not they have re-entered the territory of the Republic.

9. This law cancels none of the dispositions of the law of the third of this month [a sweeping measure against *émigrés*, their relatives, priests, and any 'seditious' persons, barring them from public office and confining their movements].

Document 35

The south-east of France was particularly troubled with factional conflict, and the following two letters from the national agent in the district of Aix show the level of activity of political factions, and the language of reaction used against any 'terrorist' manifestation:

31 October 1794 (10 brumaire III):

> The intriguers and men of blood and money still dominate the people through fear and thus prevent the explosion of proofs of their crimes and dilapidations. Their presence still inspires dread in proportion to the wrong they have done ... They spread themselves throughout the countryside and in the small communes to lead the people astray by calumnying the Convention ...
>
> One of them pushed villainy so far as to exhort the inhabitants of a commune not to deliver grain to Aix *because we are in counter-revolution*, which is how they describe the events of 24 vendémiaire which swept out the impure and immoral men from the administration ...
>
> Another spreads alarm about subsistence and threatens a commune with the sight of its grain taken away for Aix *where they are reduced to eating grass.*
>
> The representatives of the people have strongly ordered me to pursue these guilty men. The local magistrate chooses to do nothing and, in place of doing his duty, wishes to excuse them.
>
> The public spirit of morality, probity and justice will not be linked throughout the district to the pure love of the *patrie* until all the small communes have been purged.

11 April 1795 (22 germinal III):

> The position of the commune of Jouques renders the execution of arrest-warrants very difficult, due to the impossibility of quickly surrounding the commune and of guarding all the wooded areas close by.
>
> The terrorists, counting on the lie of the land to offer a retreat at the first sign of alarm, become only more audacious; they never sleep in the village; they are only there in daylight; they leave every night, and no one is brave enough to follow their tracks.
>
> Here are some details on their conduct given to me by the national agent in Jouques:
>
> The address sent by the Convention to all *départements* was torn

up almost as soon as it was posted.

On 13 nivôse, at 8 p.m., there was a great assembly at the tavern of one Bernard Fauché, composed of almost all the terrorists; it was said there that the Jacobins in Paris had won their case and that they had killed more than three thousand aristocrats.

They went out then, spread through the streets, yelling with all their strength: Long live the Mountain! Long live the Jacobins! Let us embrace! They must support us! We shall never perish! ...

Bibliographical essay

This essay aims to complement the information offered in the chapter endnotes, although many titles are repeated, as they are important or standard works. One of the advantages of studying the French Revolution for the English-speaker, as compared with other episodes of 'foreign' history, is that its popularity means that many works originally in French are rapidly produced in translation. I shall refer mainly to these here, noting only those works in French which are both significant and unavailable in English.

There is now a wide variety of books which seek to introduce the reader to the Revolution. Some are very brief texts, such as the combative Gwynne Lewis, *The French Revolution: Rethinking the Debate*, London, 1993. Two other such short books are T. C. W. Blanning, *The French Revolution: Class War or Culture Clash?*, Basingstoke, 1998, and Hugh Gough, *The Terror in the French Revolution*, Basingstoke, 1998. These both focus more on thematic and historiographical considerations than the present text. A second form of introduction is the 'reader' of selected pieces from historians' work. Peter Jones (ed.), *The French Revolution in Social and Political Perspective*, London, 1996, is a good recent example, and helpfully indexes contributions to earlier readers on the Revolution. This volume offers rather short edited pieces, whereas T. C. W. Blanning (ed.), *The Rise and Fall of the French Revolution*, Chicago, 1996, is made up of longer essays originally published in the *Journal of Modern History*. Somewhere between the two comes Gary Kates (ed.), *The French Revolution: Recent Debates and New*

Controversies, London, 1998.

Conventional narrative histories are of course designed for the beginning reader as well. For a plunge into the details of social conflict, D. M. G. Sutherland, *France 1789–1815: Revolution and Counter-revolution*, London, 1985, is still hard to beat, and has the advantage of carrying the story through the Napoleonic period. William Doyle, *The Oxford History of the French Revolution*, Oxford, 1989, is very readable, with a focus on politics and international affairs. Simon Schama, *Citizens: A Chronicle of the French Revolution*, New York, 1989, should not be overlooked, though I find its political assumptions dubious, and François Furet's recently translated *The French Revolution 1770–1814*, Oxford, 1996, is sweeping in scope, if also demanding some prior knowledge. A slightly older, but detailed, narrative can be found in a trilogy of works originally written in French: Michel Vovelle, *The Fall of the French Monarchy, 1787–1792*, Cambridge, 1984; Marc Bouloiseau, *The Jacobin Republic, 1792–1794*, Cambridge, 1983; and Denis Woronoff, *The Thermidorean Regime and the Directory, 1794–1799*, Cambridge, 1984.

Turning to more thematic considerations, and starting with the Old Regime, Peter Jones, *Reform and Revolution in France: The Politics of Transition, 1774–1791*, Cambridge, 1995, is an excellent discussion of the later years of the century. James B. Collins, *The State in Early Modern France*, Cambridge, 1995, takes a longer-term approach, and has a contrasting, but complementary, interpretation. On the intellectual currents running through late eighteenth-century France, an up-to-date survey is Dorinda Outram, *The Enlightenment*, Cambridge, 1995. This focuses on social contexts of ideas, whereas the classic Norman Hampson, *The Enlightenment*, London, 1968, concentrates on the ideas behind the upheavals. For the intrusion of new ideas into public life, see Sarah C. Maza, *Private Lives and Public Affairs: The Causes Célèbres of Prerevolutionary France*, Berkeley, 1993, and David A. Bell, *Lawyers and Citizens: The Making of a Political Elite in Old Regime France*, Oxford, 1994. Margaret C. Jacob, *Living the Enlightenment: Freemasonry and Politics in Eighteenth-Century Europe*, Oxford, 1991, offers a look at those who embraced change with more fervour than most. Roger Chartier, *The Cultural Origins of the French Revolution*, Durham, NC, 1991, reviews the possible relation between these currents and the Revolution.

Two approaches should also be noted which explore pre-revolutionary politics from 'below': Arlette Farge, *Subversive Words: Public Opinion in Eighteenth-Century France*, Cambridge, 1994, which is really only about Paris, but fascinating nonetheless; and Robert Darnton's works, which look at the spread of books, especially clandestine ones, from a variety of interesting angles. His early work is brought together in *The Literary Underground of the Old Regime*, Cambridge, MA, 1982, and his latest major work is *The Forbidden Best-sellers of Pre-revolutionary France*, London, 1996. A recent counterpoint to all of this, focusing on the robe nobility and emphasising their traditionalist approach to their lives and offices, is Richard M. Andrews, *Law, Magistracy and Crime in Old Regime Paris, 1735–1789*, vol. 1 *The System of Criminal Justice*, Cambridge, 1994.

Many aspects of Enlightenment thought and its consequences touch on debates about gender, and one history of the period which concentrates on this is Dena Goodman, *The Republic of Letters: A Cultural History of the French Enlightenment*, London, 1994. Joan Landes, *Women and the Public Sphere in the Age of the French Revolution*, Ithaca, 1988, puts gender at the heart of the whole period, though sometimes in rather polemical terms. Sarah Hanley, 'Engendering the State: Family Formation and State Building in Early Modern France', *French Historical Studies*, 16, 1989, pp. 4–27, introduces ideas about the long-term interaction of conscious gender-constructions in the Old Regime, while Lynn Hunt, *Politics, Culture and Class in the French Revolution*, Berkeley, 1984, carries these over into the Revolution. A different set of gendered concerns, reliant more on speculation about revolutionary psychology, are highlighted in Lynn Hunt, *The Family Romance of the French Revolution*, London, 1992. An alternative vision, tying gender together with issues of bodily behaviour, can be found in Dorinda Outram, *The Body and the French Revolution: Sex, Class and Political Culture*, New Haven, 1989. This approach has recently been broadened out by Antoine de Baecque, *The Body Politic: Corporeal Metaphor in Revolutionary France, 1770–1800*, Stanford, 1997, which is an excellent tour of revolutionary uses of images and ideas of the body to represent themselves and their enemies, both individually and collectively.

The more conventional origins of the Revolution, or at least the 'revisionist' version of them, are summarised in William Doyle,

Origins of the French Revolution, 2nd edn, Oxford, 1988. There is not yet a book-length 'counterblast' to this approach, though Gwynne Lewis (cited above) has a fair attempt. See also Colin Jones, 'Bourgeois Revolution Revivified: 1789 and Social Change', in Colin Lucas (ed.), *Rewriting the French Revolution*, Oxford, 1991. Sarah Maza has recently contributed to this debate: 'Luxury, Morality and Social Change: Why There Was no Middle-Class Consciousness in Prerevolutionary France', *Journal of Modern History*, 69, 1997, pp. 199–229, which despite its title is a genuine advance on the 'revisionist' position. Meanwhile, however, Keith M. Baker, *Inventing the French Revolution*, Cambridge, 1990, remains essential reading on high-level political thinking running into the Revolution.

It was Baker who introduced the term 'political culture' to wider debate on the Revolution, and masterminded the conferences which have produced a series of multi-author texts addressing this area. Not all the contributors share Baker's approach, and overall this collection is a valuable resource on a wide range of issues: *The French Revolution and the Creation of Modern Political Culture*, vol. 1, Keith M. Baker (ed.), *The Political Culture of the Old Regime*, Oxford, 1987; vol. 2, Colin Lucas (ed.), *The Political Culture of the French Revolution*, Oxford, 1988; vol. 3, François Furet and Mona Ozouf (eds), *The Transformation of Political Culture 1789–1848*, Oxford, 1989; vol. 4, Keith M. Baker (ed.), *The Terror*, Oxford, 1994. Under the inspiration of Furet, many French writers have also studied political culture, and the emergence and development of political concepts in the revolutionary era. Many of the texts in the above collection are French, and one of the most widely noted books in this area is Marcel Gauchet, *La Révolution des droits de l'homme*, Paris, 1989. Meanwhile, the standard work on the details of politics running up to the Revolution remains Jean Egret, *The French Pre-revolution 1787–8*, Chicago, 1977.

Elements of 'political culture' and of high and low cultural expressions (i.e. from opera to carnival) are also covered by Emmet Kennedy, *A Cultural History of the French Revolution*, New Haven, 1989. The output of the press, the primary cultural and political conduit of the revolutionary years, is discussed in Jeremy D. Popkin, *Revolutionary News: The Press in France, 1789–1799*, Durham, NC, 1990; Robert Darnton and Daniel Roche (eds), *Revolu-*

tion in Print: The Press in France, 1775–1800, Berkeley, 1989; and Hugh Gough, *The Newspaper Press in the French Revolution*, London, 1988. The enormous production of material objects portraying the Revolution and its symbols can be seen in the hundreds of illustrations gracing the *Chronicle of the French Revolution 1788–1799*, London, 1989, an otherwise rather odd tabloid-newspaper account of the Revolution. The 'material culture' of the Revolution is also treated by M. Vovelle (ed.), *Les images de la Révolution française*, Paris, 1988, and M. Vovelle, *La Révolution française: images et récit 1789–1799*, Paris, 1986.

A consideration not to be forgotten is the overwhelmingly rural nature of France in the 1790s. Peter Jones, *The Peasantry in the French Revolution*, Cambridge, 1988, is an able and indispensable summary of work on the subject published up to the 1980s. John Markoff, *The Abolition of Feudalism: Peasants, Lords and Legislators in the French Revolution*, University Park, PA, 1996, adds to this a ground-breaking study of rural demands in the *cahiers* of 1789, and of rural social and political demands over the next four years. The Russian historian Anatoli Ado carried out influential work many years ago which has only just become available in a French translation: *Paysans en Révolution: terre, pouvoir et jacquerie, 1789–1794*, Paris, 1996. A longer-term regional study of relations between state and peasantry can be found in Hilton Root, *Peasants and King in Burgundy: Agrarian Foundations of French Absolutism*, Berkeley, 1987. Another valuable case study is Steven G. Reinhardt, *Justice in the Sarladais, 1770–1790*, Baton Rouge, 1991.

On the other hand, it must also be acknowledged that the revolutionary political culture, as it emerged, was an intensely urban one. Leaving aside Paris, a wide range of monograph studies of urban society and politics are available for comparative reading: Alan Forrest, *Society and Politics in Revolutionary Bordeaux*, Oxford, 1975, and *The Revolution in Provincial France: Aquitaine 1789–1799*, Oxford, 1996; William Scott, *Terror and Repression in Revolutionary Marseilles*, London, 1973; Olwen H. Hufton, *Bayeux in the Late Eighteenth Century: A Social Study*, Oxford, 1967; William D. Edmonds, *Jacobinism and the Revolt of Lyon 1789–1793*, Oxford, 1990; Paul R. Hanson, *Provincial Politics in the French Revolution: Caen and Limoges, 1789–1794*, Baton Rouge, LA, 1989; Gail Bossenga, *The Politics of Privilege: Old Regime and Revolution in Lille*, Cambridge, 1991; Martin Lyons, *Revolution in Toulouse: An*

Essay on Provincial Terrorism, Bern, 1978; T. J. A. Le Goff, *Vannes and its Region: A Study of Town and Country in Eighteenth-Century France*, Oxford, 1981; Malcolm Crook, *Toulon in War and Revolution: From the Ancien Régime to the Restoration, 1750–1820*, Manchester, 1991. A valuable study of the south-east, possibly the region most convulsed by revolutionary violence, is Hubert C. Johnson, *The Midi in Revolution: A Study of Regional Political Diversity, 1789–1793*, Princeton, 1986.

The interface between town and country, and between agriculture and manufacture, was developing throughout the eighteenth century. Two interesting studies of this are Liana Vardi, *The Land and the Loom: Peasants and Profit in Northern France, 1680–1800*, Durham, NC, 1993, and Gwynne Lewis, *The Advent of Modern Capitalism in France, 1770–1840: The Contribution of Pierre-François Tubeuf*, Oxford, 1993.

Paris was a city and a culture apart, in the eighteenth century and the Revolution, despite its umbilical links to rural producers. Its culture, and the formation of its politics, have been much discussed. On the eighteenth century, the work of Arlette Farge previously cited can be augmented with her more general study, *Fragile Lives: Violence, Power and Solidarity in Eighteenth-Century Paris*, Cambridge, 1993, and her joint study with Jacques Revel, *The Rules of Rebellion: Child Abductions in Paris in 1750*, Cambridge, 1991, an excellent example of the use of an unusual case study to get below the surface of a culture. David Garrioch, *Neighbourhood and Community in Paris 1740–1790*, Cambridge, 1986, is a more systematic attempt to plot the outlines of community life. The study of Daniel Roche, *The People of Paris: An Essay in Popular Culture in the Eighteenth Century*, Leamington Spa, 1987, is good for details of 'material culture': what people owned, wore, used, etc., and what that says about them. Roche carries this approach further in *The Culture of Clothing: Dress and Fashion in the Ancien Régime*, Cambridge, 1994.

The control of the city is the subject of Alan Williams, *The Police of Paris, 1718–1789*, Baton Rouge, LA, 1979, and how that slipped away in 1789 is described in Jacques Godechot, *The Taking of the Bastille, July 14th 1789*, London, 1970. George Rudé, *The Crowd in the French Revolution*, Oxford, 1959, projects a relatively simple picture of the growing political involvement of the the common people (critiqued interestingly by Colin Lucas in vol. 2 of the

Baker collection above), and much writing on the subject of popular radicalism has been fairly uncritically approving: for example R. B. Rose, *The Making of the Sans-culottes: Democratic Ideas and Institutions in Paris, 1789–1792*, Manchester, 1983; and Morris Slavin, *The French Revolution in Miniature: Section Droits-de-l'Homme 1789–1795*, Princeton, 1984, and *The Making of an Insurrection: Parisian Sections and the Gironde*, Cambridge, MA, 1986. The classic study of the *sans-culotte* movement is Albert Soboul, *Les sans-culottes parisiens en l'an II: mouvement populaire et gouvernement révolutionnaire, 2 juin 1793 – 9 thermidor an II*, Paris, 1956. (The English translation, *The Parisian Sans-culottes and the French Revolution, 1793–4*, Oxford, 1964, is of the analytical/structural sections only, leaving out the massively detailed account of radical politics.) This approach has been specifically challenged by Richard M. Andrews, 'Social Structures, Political Elites and Ideology in Revolutionary Paris, 1792–4', *Journal of Social History*, 19, 1985–6, pp. 71–112. A collaborator of Soboul, Raymonde Monnier, has recently begun to move beyond this position: *L'espace public démocratique: essai sur l'opinion à Paris de la Révolution au Directoire*, Paris, 1994. A variety of works by Michael Sonenscher have offered a different view of the artisanal environment of the prototypical *sans-culotte*, of which the most comprehensive is *Work and Wages: Natural Law, Politics and the Eighteenth-Century French Trades*, Cambridge, 1989.

Turning to the politics of the Revolution, detailed study must now begin with a trio of recent books on the early revolutionary National Assembly: Harriet B. Applewhite, *Political Alignment in the French National Assembly, 1789–1791*, Baton Rouge, 1993; Michael P. Fitzsimmons, *The Remaking of France: The National Assembly and the Constitution of 1791*, Cambridge, 1994; and Timothy Tackett, *Becoming a Revolutionary: The Deputies of the French National Assembly and the Emergence of a Revolutionary Culture (1789–1790)*, Princeton, 1996. These can be followed with C. J. Mitchell, *The French Legislative Assembly of 1791*, London, 1988. On the National Convention, older 'standard' works still hold sway: Alison Patrick, *The Men of the First French Republic: Political Alignment in the National Convention of 1792*, Baltimore, 1972, or the even older Michael Sydenham, *The Girondins*, London, 1961.

Looking from the centre to the provinces, as well as the various city-studies already cited, Part 2 of Hunt, *Politics, Culture and Class* (see above) is a political sociology of revolutionary local administration, and Ted Margadant, *Urban Rivalries in the French Revolution*, Princeton, 1992, examines the effects of such rivalries on the organisation and conduct of the new revolutionary structures. These structures themselves are studied with an eye to the longer term by Isser Woloch, *The New Regime: Transformations of the French Civic Order, 1789–1820s*, New York, 1994. Malcolm Crook, *Elections in the French Revolution: An Apprenticeship in Democracy, 1789–1799*, Cambridge, 1996, examines the mechanisms of political participation first implemented in 1790, and their subsequent vicissitudes.

By the birth of the Republic in 1792, political clubs were as important as official bodies in the formation of policy, if not more so, and amongst these the Jacobins were paramount. Michael Kennedy has produced the so-far definitive study of the national Jacobin movement: *The Jacobin Clubs in the French Revolution: The First Years*, Princeton, 1992; *The Jacobin Clubs in the French Revolution: The Middle Years*, Princeton, 1988. More is presumably to come. On the wider Parisian club scene, the work of R. B. Rose cited above is all that is currently available in English. A classic text on the organisation and activities of the Cordeliers Club in 1791 is Albert Mathiez, *Le Club des Cordeliers pendant la Crise de Varennes et le Massacre du Champ de Mars*, Paris, 1910 (Reprint edn, Geneva, 1975), which includes many original documents.

Work on the period of the Terror includes vol. 4 of the Baker/ Lucas/Furet set, and the introductory book by Hugh Gough cited above. Much attention focuses on the personalities of the leading figures, and how they led France into civil war and their own destruction. Norman Hampson has written some excellent biographies: *The Life and Opinions of Maximilien Robespierre*, Oxford, 1974; *Danton*, Oxford, 1978; *Saint-Just*, Oxford, 1991. On Marat, there is a new biography in French: Olivier Coquard, *Jean-Paul Marat*, Paris, 1993. English readers have the standard study by Louis Gottschalk, *Jean-Paul Marat: A Study in Radicalism*, Chicago, 1967; or the newer Ian Germani, *Jean-Paul Marat: Hero and Anti-hero of the French Revolution*, Lampeter, 1992. Norman Hampson, *Will and Circumstance: Montesquieu, Rousseau and the French Revolution*, London, 1983, and Carol Blum, *Rousseau and the Republic of Virtue: The Language of Politics in the French Revolution*, Ithaca, NY, 1986, are both important studies of the philosophy underpinning much terrorist discourse.

On the period of purges in the spring of 1794, see Morris Slavin, *The Hébertistes to the Guillotine: Anatomy of a 'Conspiracy' in Revolutionary France*, Baton Rouge, 1994. Michel Brugière, *Gestionnaires et profiteurs de la Révolution*, Paris, 1986, looks at the men who did well out of the Revolution, complemented by Howard G. Brown, *War, Revolution and the Bureaucratic State: Politics and Army Administration in France, 1791–1799*, Oxford, 1995, which discusses the interface between politics, bureacracy and business, and the men who survived and prospered in Terror and Counter-terror. Bronislaw Baczko, *Ending the Terror: The French Revolution after Robespierre*, Cambridge, 1994, is an important study of attitudes and practices in the Thermidorian period.

On the later 1790s in general, there are the standard accounts: Martin Lyons, *France Under the Directory*, Cambridge, 1975; Denis Woronoff, *The Thermidorean Regime and the Directory*, Cambridge, 1984; along with the essays in G. Lewis and C. Lucas (eds), *Beyond the Terror: Essays in French Regional and Social History, 1794–1815*, Cambridge, 1983. These have recently been complemented by Malcolm Crook, *Napoleon Comes to Power: Democracy and Dictatorship in Revolutionary France, 1795–1804*, Cardiff, 1998. On the history of radicalism after 1794, see R. B. Rose, *Gracchus Babeuf: The First Revolutionary Communist*, London, 1978, and Isser Woloch, *Jacobin Legacy: The Democratic Movement under the Directory*, Princeton, 1970.

On the history of women and gender in the Revolution, as well as the works cited in relation to the Old Regime above, see Olwen H. Hufton, *Women and the Limits of Citizenship in the French Revolution*, Toronto, 1992, and Sarah Melzer (ed.), *Rebel Daughters: Women and the French Revolution*, Oxford, 1992. Dominique Godineau, *Citoyennes tricoteuses: les femmes du peuple à Paris pendant la Révolution*, Aix-en-Provence, 1988, is a rich study in French. For some personal accounts, see Marilyn Yalom, *Blood Sisters: The French Revolution in Women's Memory*, London, 1995. See also the documents and commentary in Darline G. Levy, Harriet B. Applewhite and Mary D. Johnson (eds), *Women in Revolutionary Paris, 1789–1795, Selected Documents*, London, 1979. For a comparative perspective, see Harriet B. Applewhite and Darline G. Levy (eds), *Women and Politics in the Age of the Democratic Revolution*, Ann Arbor, 1990, and Siân Reynolds (ed.), *Women, State and*

Revolution: Essays on Power and Gender in Europe since 1789, Brighton, 1986.

For reference purposes, the Revolution is exceptionally well-served by texts. Colin Jones, *The Longman Companion to the French Revolution*, London, 1988, is invaluable for chronology, maps and specific factual information. Samuel F. Scott and Barry Rothaus (eds), *Historical Dictionary of the French Revolution 1789–1799*, 2 vols, Westport, 1984, is a conventional 'encyclopaedia' of brief articles. François Furet and Mona Ozouf (eds), *A Critical Dictionary of the French Revolution*, London, 1989, contains fewer, longer articles, mostly in line with Furet's particular vision of the Revolution's significance. There are now some eight thematic volumes in the series *Atlas de la Révolution française*, edited overall by Serge Bonin and Claude Langlois, which have appeared steadily since 1987, and at least two more volumes are projected. Even those who do not read French should be able to decipher the many maps offered. Michel Vovelle, *La découverte de la politique: géopolitique de la Révolution française*, Paris, 1993, is also a heavily graphic-oriented presentation. Those who can read French will find a massive selection of original materials in the two-volume set of *French Revolution Documents*, vol. 1, J. M. Roberts and Richard Cobb (eds), Oxford, 1966, vol. 2, J. M. Roberts and John Hardman (eds), Oxford, 1973. For documents in English, as well as the collection on women cited above, see Keith M. Baker (ed.), *Readings in Western Civilisation 7: The Old Regime and the French Revolution*, Chicago 1987; John Hardman, *The French Revolution: The Fall of the Ancien Régime to the Thermidorian Reaction 1785–1795*, London, 1981; and the largest selection available, John H. Stewart, *A Documentary Survey of the French Revolution*, New York, 1951. Lynn Hunt (ed.), *The French Revolution and Human Rights*, Boston, 1996, is a brief documentary survey of revolutionaries' attitudes to what we would now call issues of race, class and gender.

Mention must also be made of the many essay-collections appearing around the 1989 Bicentennial. The major Baker/Lucas/Furet four-volume set is one example, but there were many other conferences and colloquia which produced interesting accounts of new and ongoing research and debate. In no particular order, the following all contain much worth reading, and often cover many of the themes discussed above: Bryant T. Ragan and Elizabeth A. Williams (eds), *Re-creating Authority in Revolutionary France*, New Brunswick, NJ, 1992; Alan Forrest and Peter Jones (eds), *Reshaping France: Town, Country and Region in the French Revolution*, Manchester, 1991; R. Waldinger, P. Dawson and Isser Woloch (eds), *The French Revolution and the Meaning of Citizenship*, Westport, 1993; Colin Lucas (ed.), *Rewriting the French Revolution*, Oxford, 1991; Ferenc Fehér (ed.), *The French Revolution and the Birth of Modernity*, Berkeley, 1990; Steven G. Reinhardt and Elisabeth A. Cawthon (eds), *Essays on the French Revolution: Paris and the Provinces*, College Station, TX, 1992; Sandy Petrey (ed.), *The French Revolution: Two Hundred Years of Rethinking*, Lubbock, TX, 1989; David G. Troyansky, Alfred Cismaru and Norwood Andrews, jr. (eds), *The French Revolution in Culture and Society*, Westport, 1991; Bernadette Fort (ed.), *Fictions of the French Revolution*, Evanston, 1991. A similar process was of course going on in France, and various volumes summarise the research output of the period: Michel Vovelle (ed.), *Paris et la Révolution: actes du colloque de Paris I, 14–16 avril 1989*, Paris, 1989; Antoine de Baecque and Michel Vovelle (eds), *Recherches sur la Révolution: un bilan des travaux scientifiques du Bicentenaire*, Paris, 1991; Michel Vovelle and Raymonde Monnier (eds), *Révolution et République: l'exception française*, Paris, 1994. For the view by an American observer of the immense cultural production and intellectual disputes of the French Bicentennial, see Steven L. Kaplan, *Farewell Revolution*, 2 vols, Ithaca, NY, 1995.

To conclude with a few works on the regime which supplanted the Revolution, Martin Lyons, *Napoleon Bonaparte and the Legacy of the French Revolution*, Basingstoke, 1994, is explicitly a discussion of continuities between the two periods. Jean Tulard, *Napoleon: The Myth of the Saviour*, London, 1984, examines the relationship between Napoleon and France, while Pieter Geyl, *Napoleon, For and Against*, London, 1949, is the classic study of reactions to Napoleon by historians and others in the 150 years after his rise.

Index